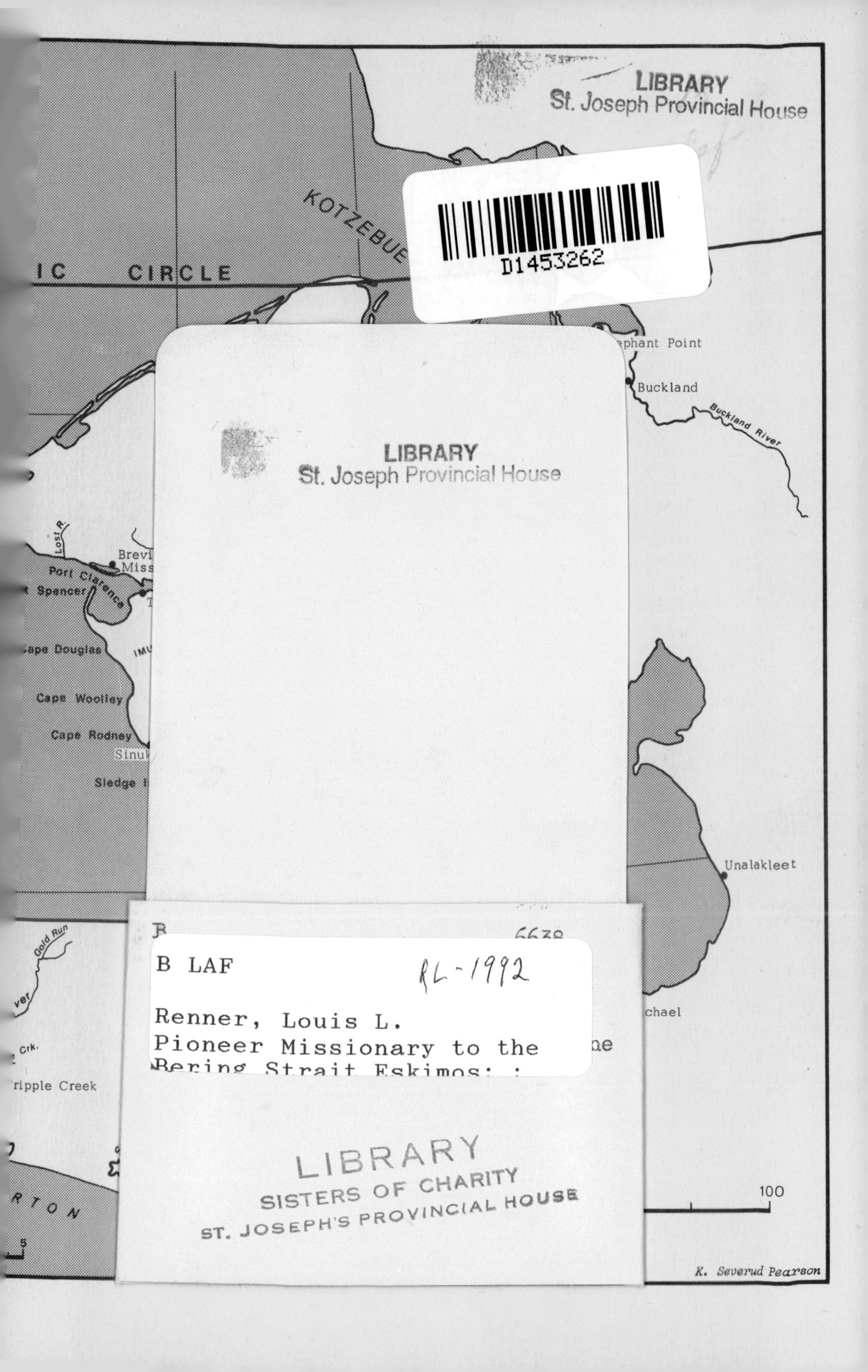
KOTZEBUE
IC CIRCLE
Elephant Point
Buckland
Buckland River
Lost R.
Port Clarence
Spencer
Cape Douglas
Cape Woolley
Cape Rodney
Sledge
Unalakleet
Gold Run
Cripple Creek
100
K. Severud Pearson

Pioneer Missionary

to the Bering Strait Eskimos:

Bellarmine Lafortune, S. J.

Father Bellarmine Lafortune, S. J., about 1934. *(Oregon Province Archives)*

Pioneer Missionary
to the Bering Strait Eskimos:
Bellarmine Lafortune, S.J.

By

Louis L. Renner, S. J.

B
Laf

In collaboration with

Dorothy Jean Ray

Published by

Binford & Mort

2536 S.E. Eleventh • Portland, Oregon 97202

for the

Alaska Historical Commission

Pioneer Missionary to the Bering Strait Eskimos:
Bellarmine Lafortune, S. J.

Printed in the United States of America

Library of Congress Catalog Card Number: 79-53362
ISBN: 0-8323-0343-7

First Edition 1979

Preface

Alaska's History and the Humanities

In December, 1977, at the invitation of the Alaska Humanities Forum, the Alaska Historical Commission submitted a proposal for the establishment of a joint publication program entitled, "Alaska's History and the Humanities."

Since its inception in 1972, the Forum's program has had as one of its goals that of relating the universality of the humanities to Alaska's setting, problems, and environment. As defined by the National Endowment, the term "humanities" includes, but is not limited to, the study of language, both modern and classical; linguistics; literature; history; jurisprudence; philosophy; archeology; comparative religion; ethics; the history, criticism, theory, and practice of the arts; those aspects of the social sciences which have linguistic content and employ humanistic methods; and the study and application of the humanities to the human environment with particular attention to the relevance of the humanities to the current conditions of national life. Another goal of the Forum has been to establish a sense of community among the diverse cultural, linguistic, geographic, ethnic, economic and social groups within the State and to demonstrate the relation of the humanities to improvement in our quality of life.

The goal of the Alaska Historical Commission, an agency of the State of Alaska, is to assure accurate, inclusive, and comprehensive data about the Great Land. Efforts at achieving this are four-fold: information retrieval and dissemination; education in historical methodology and interpretation; research; and publication. From May, 1973, when its office was first established through statute, the Commission envisioned research and publication directed at producing references, chronicles, and narratives. Initial emphasis has been on research tools and the development of an historical methodology series to encourage citizen participation in researching community history and biography.

Where possible, the Commission has joined both the private sector and other public institutions, foundations, and agencies in sponsoring research and publication. This volume is such a venture.

Professor Louis Renner was granted a sabbatical leave by the University of Alaska, Fairbanks, which he used to research the life and work of Bellarmine Lafortune. The manuscript was produced with the collaboration of Dorothy Jean Ray. Funding for publication was provided through the Gifts-in-Matching Program of the National Endowment For The Humanities administered by the Alaska Humanities Forum, a State-Based activity of the NEH. The Alaska Society of Jesus and the Alaska Historical Commission contributed equally to the Endowment's matched gift. Finally, the Alaska Historical Society acted as fiscal agent to Binford & Mort, Publishers.

It is anticipated that Renner's *Pioneer Missionary to the Bering Strait Eskimos: Bellarmine Lafortune, S. J.* will be the first in a series on the theme, *Alaska's History and the Humanities*. The dialogue which has been at the center of the Forum's concern since its Alaskan beginnings now has achieved new dimensions of time and space. The Commission trusts this series will advance the expansion, development, and better understanding of the Great Land's past.

Gary H. Holthaus
Executive Director
Alaska Humanities Forum

Robert A. Frederick
Executive Director
Alaska Historical Commission

Foreword

The seventy-five years that have passed since Father Bellarmine Lafortune, S. J., arrived in Nome, in 1903, have brought many changes to the entire Bering Strait area. The city of Nome has grown from a white man's gold-rush town to one whose population is largely Eskimo in the 1970s. The villages of Sinuk and Marys Igloo, which Lafortune knew so well, have been abandoned, and the mission at Pilgrim Hot Springs is deserted. The King Islanders have left their island to live permanently in Nome, where, on a flat, gravel-filled section of town, they have new, roomy houses with electric ranges, refrigerators, deep freezers, radios, and television sets.

The King Island children whom Lafortune baptized when he first arrived are now grandparents and great-grandparents. The youngest, baptized before his death in 1947, are themselves parents. Some have gone away to college, and some have made their marks in the outer world, far removed from their old occupations of hunting and longshoring, about which Lafortune wrote with such pride. There is no going back to the hardships and dangers of what was an almost traditional Eskimo way of life, especially for the King Islanders. Lafortune's descriptions of Bering Strait life between 1903 and 1947, therefore, are a golden legacy. The story of his own life is that of a man who lived up to every demand of his religious training and vows, but his missionary work encompassed more than his priestly duties, for he was a social worker and humanitarian with single-minded loyalty to the people he served.

Father Renner's narrative of Lafortune's life and work as a missionary is the first general account ever written about Lafortune and the Catholic Eskimo missions during the first forty years of the church in the Bering Strait area, and is unusual by virtue of being based almost entirely on manuscript sources—Jesuit house diaries, correspondence, and unpublished reports. This account, furthermore, provides details and facts about many episodes of Bering Strait history that have become somewhat hazy and legendary with the passage of time. Among them are the founding of the orphanages and missions at Marys Igloo and Pilgrim Hot Springs; the building of sleds by the Nome Eskimos for one of Vilhjalmur Stefansson's expeditions; the tragic death of Father Frederick Ruppert, S. J., near the Hot Springs; the establishment of the church on King Island; the visit of Father Bernard Hubbard, S. J. (the "Glacier Priest"), to King Island in 1937-38; the influenza epidemic of 1918 that killed hundreds of native persons; the founding of the Kotzebue mission; and the crash of the first Catholic missionary airplane, the "Marquette Missionary," in Alaska.

Lafortune considered himself to be a simple farm boy who had received a strong calling to spend his life in the work of God, but his writings, which lay bare his dreams and plans for the welfare of his beloved Eskimos; his deep love for the earth, as well as for the physical and spiritual components of a human being; his dislike of artifice; and the variety of his own talents are evidence, instead, of a complex man.

Much of the reconstruction of Bering Strait history pertinent to this account is from Lafortune's own writings. In that lies a paradox, for Lafortune did not consider himself to be a writer, yet even in his letters he wrote the kind of luminous passages that characterize interesting literature. He did not consider himself to be a poet, but many of his phrasings, both in English and in French, are poetry. He was uneasy about scientists, including archeologists and cultural anthropologists, yet his notes, written over a span of forty years, are the stuff of which ethnographies and ethnohistories are composed.

His intense appreciation for the natural environment around him was second only to that for its native inhabitants. His admiration for the "beautiful souls" among the people, as well as for the arctic landscape, is repeated throughout his letters and diaries. He once wrote that poets, had they tried to describe the awesome majesty of Alaska, "would have thrown their pens into the fire out of despair," and the painters "would have lost their minds." But believing, or pretending, that he was not a poet, or writer, or anthropologist, Lafortune kept a rational pen, providing us with an account of Eskimo culture change, and an intimate glimpse into what it was like to be a priest on an arctic frontier.

Dorothy Jean Ray

Contents

An Appreciation

The

ALASKA HISTORICAL COMMISSION

wishes to express its appreciation for this partnership of public and private effort. Publication was made possible through generous grants from the

ALASKA HUMANITIES FORUM

NATIONAL ENDOWMENT FOR THE HUMANITIES

ALASKA SOCIETY OF JESUS

THE STATE OF ALASKA

and with the support of

THE UNIVERSITY OF ALASKA, FAIRBANKS

and

THE ALASKA HISTORICAL SOCIETY

Acknowledgments

Surely few biographers can claim a better support team than the one I had. It is no less a pleasure, then, than it is a duty to acknowledge my deep indebtedness to the many members of that far-flung team.

My greatest debt of gratitude is owed to many archivists who faithfully and generously responded to my many requests: Sister Rita Bergamini, S. P., of the Sisters of Providence Archives in Seattle; Sister Jean Marie Wilkins, O. S. U., of the Ursuline Archives in Santa Rosa, California; the staff of the University of Alaska-Fairbanks Archives; Father Francis E. Mueller, S. J., of the Diocese of Fairbanks Archives; Father Clifford Carroll, S. J., and Father Wilfred P. Schoenberg, S. J., both of the Oregon Province Archives in Spokane.

To all these, for their constant friendliness and willingness to help, my sincerest thanks. But there is one more archivist to whom I am indebted in a unique way. Fully aware that I am risking offense to those just mentioned, I nevertheless feel compelled to single out for special commendation Père Joseph Cossette, S. J., of the Archives de la Compagnie de Jésus in Saint-Jérôme, Quebec, Canada. To him, a very special *merci* for providing me with those indispensable French sources, and much encouragement besides.

I am also especially grateful to Augusta Bernard Perry for sending me Lafortune letters addressed to her and to her parents, and for her personal informative letters to me; to John Lord for doing extensive research for me in the National Archives of the United States; and to Father John Morton, S. J., for copying many essential documents in the Toronto libraries.

For valuable information, my thanks to Eskimo friends in Nome: Ursula Ellanna and Barbara Kokuluk, with special thanks to Mike Saclamana. It was in his umiak that I was able to visit King Island. I wish to thank Father James E. Poole, S. J., for his hospitality while I was in Nome, and Jeanne Gabriel for gathering information for me in Nome and Teller.

I am grateful to Father Harold O. Small, S. J., who was able to obtain several important documents for me from the Archivum Romanum Societatis Iesu while he was in Rome. I am indebted to Frances Ross for eye-witness information concerning Lafortune and King Island. Dr. Michael E. Krauss and Larry Kaplan, both of the University of Alaska-Fairbanks, put their expertise in the Eskimo language at my disposal. To them my thanks. Thanks also to Father Joseph O'Connell, S. J., for information about French Canada, and to Father Edmund A. Anable, S. J., for his constant readiness to help. I am grateful to Emil Kowalczyk of the Bureau of Indian Affairs, Juneau office, for sending me records concerning the school on King Island.

For their reading of the manuscript and their invaluable suggestions, I thank very sincerely the following persons: Father George E. Carroll, S. J., Gisela Dykema, Dr. William R. Hunt, Dr. Michael E. Krauss, Patricia Roppel, and George W. Sundborg.

And lastly, but by no means least, warm thanks to Sheila Cox, for attending, always with a smile, to the task of typing the manuscript.

L. L. R.

Introduction

From the time I first heard about King Island, shortly after entering the Society of Jesus in 1944, my imagination was fired by the island and everything associated with it. I wanted very much to go there, but how was I to manage it? In 1946, I wrote to Father Bellarmine Lafortune, S. J., the pastor on King Island, and in 1948, to Thomas Cunningham, S. J., Lafortune's successor, proposing that I spend two years there learning the Eskimo language. Both Cunningham and the Most Reverend Francis D. Gleeson, S. J., D. D., bishop of Alaska at the time, thought that my proposal was a good one. In Rome, however, it was an idea whose time had not yet come.

For more than twenty years, therefore, King Island lay just below the horizon of my active interest. I had meanwhile gone on to complete my preparatory studies and to be ordained to the priesthood. After teaching high school in Fairbanks for two years, and serving as a campus minister at the University of Alaska at the same time, I was sent to Europe for advanced studies. In 1965, having finished my degree in philosophy from the University of Munich, I returned to the University of Alaska to teach German. King Island, the King Island people, and their first pastor and founder of their mission, Father Lafortune, seemed permanently out of my life until August 1972, when, for a week, I replaced the pastor at Nome. Here I met some of the King Islanders.

Of greater importance, however, I came across a photostatic copy of Lafortune's "History of the Mission of King Island," a 153-page handwritten account in diary form of every aspect of life on the island, which I read through several times. My old interest in King Island and Father Lafortune was rekindled by this singular chronicle, and I began further research. In the Oregon Province Archives in Spokane, Washington, I saw the original "History" and many of Lafortune's extant letters. These, along with numerous pictures of him and of King Island and its inhabitants, brought the unique, half-century-long King Island-Lafortune saga dramatically to life. To the extent that my teaching duties at the University of Alaska allowed during the next two years, I gradually amassed such a volume of documentation from various archives and libraries that I felt the time had come for me to undertake the writing of Lafortune's life and work in the Bering Strait area.

Lafortune had written about the island in his "History": "More than of any other country it can be said of this place that 'one has to see it to know it.' No amount of writing or talking or picture taking will ever give to people the real idea of this place." These two sentences kept haunting me. I felt it imperative to make a trip to the island to get some "real idea" of the place before I undertook to write about Lafortune; therefore, I visited the island in the spring of 1974.

For countless generations, King Island had been the permanent home of the King Island people, but about 1950, more and more families began to make Nome their year-round home. Nome offered job opportunities, better medical care, and a less arduous and hazardous way of life. By the summer of 1966, the island was completely abandoned, and the village has become a ghost village on a ghost island except for a few weeks, usually in late spring, when several boatloads of King Islanders visit the island to hunt walrus, gather greens and eggs, or simply visit their ancestral home again.

It is by no means easy for a white man to find a place in a native skinboat about to make the annual trip to the island. First of all, space is very limited because many of the natives themselves want to make the trip; and, secondly—and this is a more serious obstacle to overcome (or to be overlooked by the natives)—the white man is just that, a white man and not an Eskimo. The trip is regarded as an exclusively Eskimo affair and jealously kept as such. When it was learned, however, that I was planning to write Lafortune's life story and work, and hoped to see at first hand the very important setting of Lafortune's long apostolate to the Eskimos, space was found, and I was graciously welcomed along. In the ten enchanted days that I spent intensively exploring that extraordinary village and island, I soon learned what Lafortune meant when he said, "One has to see it to know it."

With my field work accomplished, and research in archives more or less completed, I still needed uninterrupted time to do the writing. After ten years at the University of Alaska, I was long since eligible for sabbatical leave, which was granted for the academic year, 1975-1976.

This account is based almost exclusively on original, unpublished documents. Often in the story that follows, these documents have been left to speak for themselves. Lafortune's own written legacy is extensive; hundreds of letters and hundreds of diary pages are still in existence. Many of his statements that I have used cannot be improved upon by paraphrasing or editing, and the direct quotations preserve a unique feeling of bygone days, bringing to life the unusual man who wrote them.

Throughout his life, Lafortune spoke and wrote English in a unique Franco-American idiom. Gallicisms abound in his writing. I have translated his French letters (and all other letters in French and Latin) into the contemporary English idiom, but have left, as written, his English documents—including his "History of the Mission of King Island"—with their charming Gallic flavor. Only a few changes have been made in punctuation, and some obviously misspelled words, written in haste, have been corrected. The temptation to scatter *sic* generously into quoted passages presented itself repeatedly, but was resisted successfully for the most part. Therefore, the arbitrary switching of tenses, the frequent deviations from common English usage, and some inconsistencies in spelling have been transcribed without alteration.

Not all the quotations are integral, though they may seem to be. Nonrelevant parts of quoted passages have often been left out. In some nonintegral quotations, where the quoted passage has not been distorted by omissions, ellipses marks (. . .) have not been used. Eskimo surnames and Eskimo words, spelled variously by Lafortune and his contemporaries, have, in many cases, been standardized, and geographical place-names are spelled according to modern map usage.

Published primary sources and original manuscript materials used in this work are found in the following archives: Archives de la Compagnie de Jésus—Province du Canada-français, Saint-Jérôme, P.Q., Canada; Archivum Romanum Societatis Iesu, Rome; The National Archives, National Archives and Records Service, Record Groups 26 and 75, Washington, D.C.; Oregon Province Archives of the Society of Jesus, Crosby Library, Gonzaga University, Spokane; Sisters of Providence Archives—Sacred Heart Province, Seattle; University of Alaska, Elmer E. Rasmuson Library and Archives; Ursuline Archives, Santa Rosa, California.

Louis L. Renner, S. J.

1 / Beginnings

For more than forty years, Bellarmine Lafortune, S. J., was the spiritual leader of the people who lived on King Island, one of the most rugged and inaccessible islands located anywhere in Eskimo territory. From 1904 until his death in 1947, there was not a summer (and there were not many winters) that Lafortune did not spend some time with them. His work, however, was not confined exclusively to the King Islanders. He also founded missions at Igloo, Pilgrim Hot Springs, and on Little Diomede Island, and exerted more influence over the Catholic Eskimos of Seward Peninsula than any other priest. The life of Father Lafortune parallels a large part of the history of the Catholic Church in the Bering Strait region, and at the time of his death the Church in northwest Alaska was only two years older than his tenure of service in the Alaskan mission field.

Lafortune has been called the Catholic Apostle of the Seward Peninsula and Bering Strait Eskimos, an honorific title that he repeatedly refused to accept. To Martin Lonneux, S. J., a fellow missionary in Alaska, he wrote in 1922, "You are wrong to call me the apostle of the Eskimos and I want that to be taken out of your history entirely. Father [Joseph M.] Cataldo is the one who started the work among the Eskimos here [in Nome in 1902]. In spite of his old age he tackled the language and became able to teach them the rudiments of religion. The first Catholic Eskimos were instructed and baptized by him."[1]

There were no Catholic Eskimos on the Seward Peninsula or anywhere north of it before 1902, although several priests had visited Nome soon after the gold strike of 1898, and in 1901 Aloysius Jacquet, S. J., had become the first permanently assigned priest.[2] Lafortune arrived in Nome on 16 July 1903[3] when he was thirty-three years old. His stay was to have been only temporary, Nome being a stopping place on the route to Holy Cross, 600 miles up the Yukon River, where he was assigned.

Lafortune was born in the small French-Canadian town of Saint-Roch-de-l'Achigan, about forty miles north of Montreal, on 11 December 1869. He was baptized the next day,[4] and named after the Italian Jesuit Cardinal, Saint Robert Bellarmine. He was one of eleven children—seven boys and four girls—born to Joel Tellier-Lafortune, a farmer, and his wife, Perpétue Beaudry. A big family on a small farm meant poverty and hard work, but these circumstances, combined with an atmosphere of straight and narrow Christian orthodoxy, only served to strengthen young Bellarmine's native vigor of body and spirit, which characterized him to the end of his long life. His early years on the farm developed a hardiness and resourcefulness, which enabled him to cope with the many hardships and disappointments that he encountered during the more than four decades of his life in Alaska. He always had excellent health, and his muscular and well-knit body (five feet four inches tall) was officially described as "*robuste*" during his early training.

In 1882, at considerable financial sacrifice, Bellarmine's parents placed him in the Jesuit Collège de l'Assomption, where he learned with "good success and awards."[5] On 30 July 1890, at the age of twenty, he entered the Jesuit novitiate at Sault-au-Récollet near Montreal, where he began his thirteen-year period of training as a Jesuit. In keeping with the French-Canadian attitude of those times, the training was rigid, conservative, and voluntaristic, but his intellectual life was not neglected; and in keeping with the broader French tradition, his training encouraged individual initiative and personal responsibility.

During the two-year novitiate, Lafortune was thoroughly schooled in the Spirituality of Saint Ignatius of Loyola, the founder of the Jesuit Order. Rooted in Sacred Scripture, the Ignatian Spirituality teaches the Jesuit to commit his entire person to the Lord Jesus, and to serve Him by serving his fellow men, "loving Him in them, and them all in Him." The Jesuit is to be a "contemplative in action" and is to manifest his love for God and neighbor more in deeds of love and service than in words. He is challenged "to find God in all things," in the distracting, vexing occupations of the workaday world as well as in solitude and prayer. Called to apostolic activity, the Jesuit is to consider himself an instrument in the Divine Master's hands, but while always attributing a primary importance to God's grace and assistance, he must also value natural gifts and use them skillfully. The Jesuit is always motivated and guided by the motto of his Order: *omnia ad majorem Dei gloriam* (A.M.D.G.), "all to the greater glory of God."

After his novitiate, Lafortune spent a year studying the humanities in Montreal, and then three more in the study of philosophy and the sciences. In 1896, he was assigned to teach physics and chemistry at the Collège de Saint-Boniface in Winnipeg for two years. He was so successful that he was sent to Paris, in 1898, for a year's advanced study in mathematics. This has led some of his admirers to say that he held a doctorate in physics (some say in mathematics) from the Sorbonne, but there is no evidence in the official documents to support such a claim. On the contrary, records indicate that he did not earn this advanced degree.[6] After his year in Paris, Lafortune spent three years in theological training, and on 27 July 1902 was ordained to the priesthood.

Lafortune was not a brilliant man. During his early training, he ranked below the class average, but in the later years he rose to near the top of his class as a result of determination and dedication to his work. He was not only an indefatigable student, but a man with a great sense of duty and of fraternal charity, according to his classmates. The farmer in him was by no means dead, and he took pride and satisfaction in raising flowers for the hallways and the altars in the houses where he studied.

Immediately after his ordination, Lafortune made his tertianship at Poughkeepsie, New York. (A "tertianship" is a ten-month period —following the many years of academic studies—during which the young Jesuit is renewed spiritually. Long hours are devoted to prayer and meditation, as well as to the Constitutions and spirit of the Society of Jesus and the implications of living in it the rest of one's life.)

From Poughkeepsie he wrote a niece, "Where will I be sent? That I don't know yet, but I am just about certain that it will be to Alaska. In any case, I don't much care where."[7] This letter is the first indication that he was so much as even thinking about going to Alaska, although it is very likely that he had thought about it for some time, and had discussed the possibility with his religious Superiors. He probably had even volunteered for the Alaska mission. If even routine religious vocations—if there are such—are regarded as mysterious phenomena, then a spiritual calling to Alaska at the turn of the century can be regarded as nothing less than a vocation within a vocation. Lafortune's call to Alaska apparently came from within his own spiritual depths, where it matured gradually during the long years of his Jesuit training.

When Lafortune took leave of his family and his native Quebec in the late spring of 1903, it was a final leave-taking. He never saw any of his relatives or his native land again. (He became a U.S. citizen on 11 September 1918.)

By the time the Jesuits arrived in Nome, a number of other religious denominations had already established missions in various parts of western Alaska. The Jesuits themselves had gone to the upper Yukon River in 1886, and had founded Holy Cross on the lower Yukon in 1888. They had been in Saint Michael, the ocean port for the Yukon, since 1898.

In 1885, Moravian missionaries founded Bethel at the site of an Eskimo village called Mumtrekhlagamiut on the Kuskokwim River. The Mission Covenant of Sweden (now called the Evangelical Covenant Church of America) had set up a mission at Unalakleet in 1887, and one at Golovin in 1893. In 1890, the United States Bureau of Education established "contract schools" in conjunction with three separate Protestant groups in northern Alaska: the Congregational Church at Cape Prince of Wales, the Episcopal Church at Point Hope, and the Presbyterian at Point Barrow. In 1900, a Lutheran mission began at the old Teller Reindeer Station, later named Brevig Mission.[8]

Before gold was discovered on Anvil Creek in 1898, the beach on which the town of Nome sprang up was used by the Eskimos only at different parts of the year for fishing and seal-hunting camps. (The nearest permanent Eskimo village, with a population of about 80, was at Cape Nome, ten miles to the east.) Two years later, the bleak, treeless site at Nome had a population of 30,000 stampeders who had come from all over the world and from all walks of life: adventurers, prostitutes, and gamblers; but also skilled prospectors, engineers, lawyers, and missionaries.

The mission field among so-called "uncivilized" peoples had always been inviting to a certain kind of missionary, but the discovery of gold at Nome drew a much greater variety of religious temperaments and outlooks. Little did Lafortune dream, when he was studying higher mathematics in Paris at the very time that gold was discovered, that this would be the scene of almost all of his apostolic labors.[9]

Miners from the Klondike gold fields in Canadian territory had rushed overland to the new gold-rush camp of Anvil City (Nome's first name) during the winter of 1898-99 before the news of the strike had reached the "Outside." In August 1899, the first Jesuit to visit Nome, Jean Baptiste René, S. J., the Prefect Apostolic of Alaska, saw a sizable town already changing from a tent camp to a permanent metropolis. René stayed only a short time, but the people pleaded with him to send priests, and Sisters to open a hospital, and he promised to do what he could.

A second priest, Joseph Tréca, S. J., visited Nome briefly from Saint Michael a month later in September, and again in February 1900. He also set out from Saint Michael for Nome a year later, but he and a native boy who was helping him with the dogteam had to end their trip at Unalakleet after both were frostbitten in a strong, freezing wind.

On 4 July 1901, the forty-one-year-old Aloysius Jacquet, S. J., officially established the Nome parish. In August, Jacquet bought a piece of land and immediately began building a church and a house for priests. By 17 September, Jacquet and his new assistant, John Van der Pol, S. J., were able to sleep in the house.[10] In less than two months a church, 43 feet by 64 feet, and a two-story rectory stood on "a piece of land some 50 steps by 20 steps of a man of average size."[11] St. Joseph's Church, as it was named, was the westernmost Catholic church in North America, and was topped by a steeple that dominated the skyline of Nome.

This was no ordinary steeple. It was crowned with a golden cross of electric lights that seemed to hang by an invisible thread in the dark arctic sky. This "white man's star," as the Eskimos called it, measured six feet by eight feet, and was visible from a distance of more than twenty miles. It was illuminated each evening at the town's expense to serve as a beacon to many a weary miner or musher groping his way through the winter darkness or a blizzard.[12]

The speedy erection of the parish house and the church was dearly paid for, however. Van der Pol wrote in the Nome parish diary for 7 October that "Fr. Jacquet is feeling unwell," and a month later, "Rev. Fr. Jacquet was declared insane by the civil authorities . . . .The committal made a misfortune of what threatened to be a

Nome, about three months after Lafortune's arrival. The view is from the "sandspit," looking east. The present town is situated to the far east (top) of this photograph. *(Historical Photograph Collection, University of Alaska Archives)*

Holy Cross Hospital, with St. Joseph's Church in the background, about 1917. *(Photograph by Moldt. Oregon Province Archives)*

scandal and a disgrace. . . .God be thanked: the most painful 3 weeks of our life are over.''

On 8 October, Jacquet's physician, Dr. Francis L. Anton, had written to Leopold Van Gorp, S. J., the Superior of Holy Cross mission, about Jacquet's condition, and after complimenting Jacquet on ''a fine parochial house, and a church (almost completed) which is an ornament to the city,'' he said, ''But during the last two weeks he has been in a veritable fury of nervous excitement. This is destroying very largely the general respect and love which his business ability and his first intercourse with the public had established for him. . . .I fear that his mind is beginning to give way under the pressure of work and worry, and his natural nervousness and excitability.''

At that time, and for many years thereafter, the commitment of a person considered to be insane was decided by the courts on the basis of medical evidence and testimony of doctors and other witnesses. On 6 November 1901, after a hearing in the United States District Court, Judge James Wickersham judged Jacquet to be insane, and ordered him to ''be confined in some proper place for treatment and safekeeping.''[13] The ''proper place'' in Nome, with constant medical attention and three guards, would have cost one thousand dollars a month, which the fledgling parish could ill-afford.[14]

This sum, added to the embarrassment that his continued presence in Nome would have caused Van der Pol and his parishioners, moved Van der Pol to petition the court to have Jacquet sent to the Holy Cross mission, where he thought there were adequate accommodations for his treatment at no expense to the government. His petition was granted, and Frank H. Richards, the United States marshal, obtained the services of Dr. Samuel J. Call and two dogteams and two drivers to make the 600-mile trip without compensation.[15]

They left Nome on 22 November and reached Holy Cross on 18 December, rested two days, and returned to Nome on 14 January. But the entire 1200-mile journey was all in vain. The staff at Holy Cross, knowing nothing of Jacquet's condition until he arrived, found Nome's solution to the problem wholly unacceptable since they lacked the resources necessary to provide the kind of care Jacquet needed. Van der Pol, who was new to Alaska, had mistakenly assumed that Holy Cross had adequate facilities and personnel. Within five days, John G. Stanley, the deputy marshal at Holy Cross, sent Jacquet to Saint Michael. (From there he returned to Montreal, where he died in 1922.)

When word reached Nome concerning this turn of events, a series of strongly worded letters was exchanged between Nome and Holy Cross. To his deputy at Holy Cross, Richards expressed surprise "that any one could be as heartless and cold blooded as Father Van Gorp seems to have been in his treatment of Father Jacquet."[16] Richards considered Jacquet's transfer to Saint Michael to be a direct violation of the Court's decision, and called for the arrest of Stanley and Van Gorp. He reserved his harshest words for Van Gorp, who, he said, "alone is responsible for this outrage, and the people of this portion of Alaska will not soon forget what seems to them his inexcusable cruelty and heartlessness." Van Gorp denied the charges in a letter, and pleaded for an understanding of the actual conditions at Holy Cross.[17]

The *Nome Nugget* devoted space to the controversy and to the establishment of the parish, and it was apparent that the work of the Jesuits in Nome was off to a good start as far as buildings were concerned, but off to a bad one in regard to the Jesuit image because of the Jacquet affair. When Jacquet left Alaska after the spring breakup in 1902, the Nome parish was so burdened with debts and scandal, and the priests were the objects of such bitterness and antagonisms that only by time and the great efforts of the pastors were the troubles resolved.

In mid-November, while Jacquet was still in Nome, Rogatien Camille, S. J., arrived from Saint Michael to assist Van der Pol, but on 14 July 1902, Edward J. Devine, S. J., arrived from Canada to replace Camille, who had returned to Saint Michael. Devine, who was an able writer, contributed a series of informative articles—his "Alaskan Letters"—to *The Canadian Messenger of the Sacred Heart*. In his third "Letter" he wrote his first impressions of Nome:

"From the sea, the town looked quite respectable. Houses, cabins, tents, large and small, extended for a couple or three miles along the beach. The large commercial warehouses, recognized by their lofty lightering-derricks, stood prominently in the foreground; then the hotels and stores and other buildings; then, towering high above everything else, the Catholic church spire tipped with a golden cross. The spire gave such a civilized and homelike tone to this scene in the North-land, that my first impressions of Nome were favorable. Here was surely not a mining-camp, hardly three years old, but a good-sized city. And it was a startling experience, when one stepped ashore at last, to find oneself on a street planked from side to side, and lined with wholesale and retail stores, hotels, banks, and official buildings; to hear newsboys crying out the daily papers; to see telephone and electric light wires strung overhead; and one started to think that all the place needed now were the trolley-cars and a university.''[18]

On 1 August 1902, Joseph M. Cataldo, S. J., arrived from Nulato to replace Van der Pol, who had been called to Seattle. Cataldo inadvertently was to help dispel the cloud of ill will and bitterness that still hung over the Nome Jesuits and their work from the Jacquet affair. This occurred in connection with the celebration in Nome of his golden jubilee as a Jesuit, on 23 December. He had left ''the vine-clad hills and orange groves of Sicily'' (in the words of the Nome city attorney, Mark Sullivan, the main speaker for the occasion) at fifteen years of age to begin his life in the Society of Jesus. (Cataldo spent another twenty-seven years as a priest, until his death in Pendleton, Oregon, in 1928 at the age of ninety-two.) Before he came to Nome he had spent most of his time with various Indian tribes of northwestern America, especially the Nez Percé. He was General Superior of the Rocky Mountain mission for several decades, and in that capacity was instrumental in starting the Alaska mission when he sent Pascal Tosi, S. J., and Aloysius Robaut, S. J., to the Yukon River with Archbishop Charles John Seghers in 1886.

The jubilee celebration was well attended—almost too well in the opinion of some endowed with hypersensitive noses. Devine wrote in the Nome diary: ''During the address the Eskimos—fifty-six of them—were crowded around us. The inseparable, unsuperable, insupportable, unmistakable and unhappily not incommunicable odor of seal oil, fish and __________ *[sic]* permeated the room and made us long for the vine-clad hills and orange groves of Sicily. Bro. [Bartholomew] Chiaudano burned incense and sugar which made things bearable.''

Good will was also increased among the Nome people with the establishment of the Holy Cross hospital before the year was out. Four Sisters of Providence had arrived from Montreal on 19 June to renovate a building conveniently located in the center of town near the old post office.

The spring breakup of the Bering Sea was unusually late in 1903, so it was well into June before the first steamer was able to penetrate its ice fields and anchor in the Nome roadstead. Yet within a week, four thousand miners and 35,000 tons of freight had landed on the beach.

Lafortune arrived—along with Van der Pol—on 16 July, without fanfare or other notice because he was not expected to remain in Nome.

Lafortune wrote, "Rev. Fr. Cataldo seeing the number of Eskimos who were around here without pastor, stopped me and obtained from the Superiors the permission of keeping me here. That permission was granted to him and so it happened that I stayed here. From that time on I had the charge of the Eskimos." Cataldo postponed his trip to Spokane for two weeks to teach Lafortune what he knew of the Nome Eskimo dialect.[19]

Devine had moved to the mining camp called Council City, eighty-two miles northeast of Nome, where he was building a church and enjoying the spruce timber country after the monotonous, treeless tundra that surrounds Nome.

Nome of 1903 was beginning to take on an air of respectability. No longer did the president of the Chamber of Commerce have to threaten, as he had four years earlier, "[to] hang the first man who unnecessarily spills human blood if we have to go to Council City to get the tree to hang him on."[20] The days when both God and Washington were far away seemed to be gone, and a lawless element, which had imbued the town with both dash and dread, seemed more or less under control. Robbery at gunpoint was no longer a daily occurrence. Quite a few false-fronted saloons—of more than a hundred several years before—still operated along Front Street, and gamblers could still part a man from a hard season's earnings with a flick of a card or the toss of the dice. Prostitutes were still active, though now discreetly confined to a row of little green houses "behind the fence."

Several million dollars worth of gold was still being taken out of the Nome area each season, but the unscrupulous claim jumpers of only several years before were no longer illegally staking their neighbors' claims since the courts had imposed heavy penalties. In the five years since its birth as a frontier mining camp, Nome had become a more or less stable civic community with organized law enforcement.

Lafortune's first autumn in Nome was mainly taken up by the routine duties of an assistant parish priest. He wrote in the Nome diary for 25 October that "the navigation closes," a simple-sounding phrase, but for many of the 3,185 persons who had remained behind it meant loneliness and isolation because the mining community was on its own, virtually without a link to the outside world for eight months. They could not expect the first mail of the winter (first-class matter only) before the middle of January because it took three months by dogteam on a cross-country trail from Dawson in Canada, down the frozen Yukon River, and then along the coast to Nome.

On 31 October, Van der Pol and Lafortune organized a new parish club, the Miners' Home Club, which welcomed non-Catholics as well as Catholics, with equal privileges for all. Housed in the parochial residence, the members had the use of two large halls and the library from seven o'clock until eleven o'clock in the evening. The club was a reading club, which provided "innocent games for the instruction or amusement of the members," and occasional lectures. Politics were taboo. Club members collected money to buy books and to pay the coal and light bills.[21] Such a club had been in Jacquet's plans, and his spacious building had later made it possible for what he had envisioned: "Rooms. . .kept heated at all times and fitted up with piano, books, games, etc., with a view of keeping young men away from saloons."[22] By 14 January 1904, there were 310 members, and Lafortune recorded in the Nome diary that the "Nomeites begin to speak highly of the club."

At that time, the Miners' Home Club was but one of many clubs in Nome. In 1902, the Alaskan Academy of Sciences had been organized for the purpose of collecting geographical, geological, botanical, and ethnological data of Alaska. The women formed the Kegoayah Kozga (Eskimo for "Aurora Club"), which met once a week to listen to readings of papers on various topics: literature, art, and women's rights and duties. These, and other clubs—the Arctic Brotherhood, the Polar Union, the Pioneers of Alaska—helped to shorten the long winter nights. They not only provided recreation, but also contributed money to worthy causes. The proceeds of several entertainments sponsored by the clubs helped to buy coal for St. Joseph's Church, and to decorate the interior. One evening's entertainment in 1903 brought in nearly a thousand dollars for the benefit of Holy Cross hospital.

In those early days of Nome, there was an almost continuous round of banquets, entertainments, and fancy-dress balls during the winter. Not to be outdone, the Ladies Tabernacle Society of St. Joseph's Church put on a Catholic ball at the Golden Gate Hotel to close out the year 1903. It was called a great success, except that too many of the participants slept through the New Year's Day mass the next morning—if they came at all.

In December 1903, Lafortune was called upon to preach to the Sisters of Providence their annual retreat. They were so well satisfied that they called on Lafortune to preach to them almost every retreat that they made during their sixteen years in Nome. In the middle of January 1904, several clubs held a benefit masquerade ball for the Holy Cross hospital. To the young Lafortune, "that does not look very neat."[23] During the autumn of that year the Sisters opened the first parochial school (with Sisters Odile and Michael as teachers) in Nome, and although Lafortune was not deeply involved in this undertaking, it—along with the hospital already in operation—made minor, but nevertheless nuisance demands on his time, which he had already carefully budgeted.

While some of Lafortune's regular pastoral duties during his first winter in Alaska were mainly concerned with teaching catechism to white children in order to prepare them for their first holy communion,[24] he had already begun evangelizing the Eskimos, although he lamented that he had so "very little time to consecrate to that work."[25] He catechized and baptized his first converts while trying to learn their language without books of any kind. (The language in question here is *Iñupiaq*, the language spoken north of Unalakleet on Norton Sound, across all of northern Alaska and Canada, as well as in Greenland. It is one language with different dialects.) They came to him for instructions and baptism into the Catholic faith in small but steady numbers, and by the end of his first year in Nome he had about 40 converts.[26] His evangelizing was hindered, however, by his inability to speak the many dialects of the various Eskimo groups who came to Nome, and by the fact that, according to his severe and hasty judgment, "the great majority of them" had been "corrupted to the bones" by drunkenness and debauchery. He also felt that his progress was considerably slowed up by his having to "struggle against the influence of other religions."[27]

At the end of 1904, the debts incurred by Jacquet were still a burden to his successors. In late 1904, Lafortune lamented, "It is a little over 3 years that this event occurred and we still feel the after effects thereof. One of the worst is the enormous debt that we are obliged to pay in spite of the protestations of our parishioners. Fr. Jacquet, before his condemnation, unable to manage his business properly, spent in prodigalities the money gathered to build the church. . . .His presence was a disaster and for the Society and for the parish."[28]

In order to help pay off the debt, Lafortune and his fellow priests often went to various mining camps scattered across the vast tundra behind Nome to collect money or "some [gold] dust." Yet the primary purpose of the visits was to bring the mass and the sacraments to the miners. From the very beginning of their stay in Nome, the priests had gone out to the mining camps as far away as Council, Gold Run, and Teller, and they unanimously agreed that the miners, no matter what their religion, received them charitably and with friendliness.[29] The Providence Sisters also found the miners generous when they made occasional excursions to the creeks and the camps to beg money for the support of their hospital.

Among the tens of thousands of miners who came from over a dozen different countries and from every imaginable background, there was a fairly large percentage that admitted to being Catholic. The Catholicity of the majority, however, did not bear close inspection, and for many of them, religion was of little importance. Few attended church, and fewer still received the sacraments regularly, but when it came to dying, most of them, recalling the religion of their childhood, eagerly welcomed the priest to their bedsides. Perhaps they could be excused by the hard work and the long hours that they had to endure during the short summer season of gold mining in the subarctic.

2 / The Nome Parish and the Mission to the Eskimos Expand

Father Lafortune exercised a ministry over a large area of the Bering Strait without even leaving Nome. This was made possible by the fact that Eskimos from many villages came to Nome in the summer to trade, and occasionally some stayed for the winter. They came from Wales, Teller, Sinuk, Marys Igloo, and from the islands—Sledge Island, King Island, and the Diomedes—in their large umiaks, or skinboats, by the first week in July after they had finished their spring hunting and the pack ice had left. Before Nome was founded they had gone to other places for trading and fishing during the summer, but Nome's new trading possibilities proved to be a great magnet.

The various groups camped in different places. The King Islanders, who came in flotillas of eight to twelve boats, which carried a total of a hundred or more persons, pitched their camp east of Nome. The Diomeders and others camped on the "Sandspit," west of town. In those days it did not take them long to set up housekeeping by pitching a tent or turning over a skinboat so they could be ready for the Fourth of July festivities, to which their own traditional athletic contests, kayak and umiak races, and dances added color and excitement.

The Eskimos traded native goods among themselves, and sold their old artifacts, fur goods, and ivory carvings to the white man. The island people, especially, were masterful ivory carvers, and their carvings were eagerly bought by the early Nomeites and tourists already among them.[1] At the end of summer the Eskimos took home provisions and white man's food bought with cash from selling their native products or from wages earned as longshoremen or laborers on mining

The notation on the back of this photograph of the early 1900s is: "Camp of the natives of King Island when they are in Nome." *(Oregon Province Archives)*

Eskimos sitting under an overturned umiak, which was the usual temporary shelter when traveling in the early 1900s. *(From a postcard, Lomen Brothers photograph. Oregon Province Archives)*

Eskimo Church, Nome, in 1917. *(Oregon Province Archives)*

Interior of Eskimo Church, Nome, 1917. *(Oregon Province Archives)*

crews, but as time went on they took back something less tangible—a new religion.

Lafortune, viewing his mission to the Eskimo as an all-inclusive one, sought out all of them during their annual summer visits to Nome with hopes of bringing them into the Catholic fold. Some were already Christians; others—among them the King Islanders and Diomeders—were still "pagans." These are the ones who received his special attention, and Lafortune was the first to bring many of them "the Christianity."

By 1905 and 1906, the Nome parish diary shows that many Eskimos were coming to Lafortune for instructions and baptism, not only from Nome and the immediate vicinity, but also from distant villages. The systematic teaching of catechism led to converts, and these, in turn, drew others to the Church. This meant still more catechizing—and more converts. This endless circle made considerable demands on Lafortune's time, but it was also most gratifying to him.

The Eskimos usually went to Lafortune for their instructions, but he also visited them regularly in their own homes, especially when they were sick. He often made the calls on foot (once, in July 1906, he and Father John B. Carroll, S. J., walked to Cripple Creek, a round-trip distance of twenty-six miles, to see a sick woman), but when the distance was too great or the case too urgent, he hired a dogteam and driver to take him. He also visited the white people in Nome and the miners scattered across the tundra and along the creeks in mining camps, sometimes turning these errands into pleasant outings when the trail and the weather were good.

During the summer of 1905, Lafortune's dream of an Eskimo mission gradually took shape, and on 18 August he wrote in the Nome diary that Van der Pol had bought machines for a workshop, and vestments, candlesticks, and the like for the chapel of the Holy Angels mission. On 5 September, Carroll wrote in the diary that the foundation boards of the chapel and the workshop (24 by 40 feet, and both designed by Van der Pol) were laid by four carpenters, who were helped by Van der Pol, Lafortune, Brother Chiaudano, and two Eskimos.

On 13 September, a big fire on Front Street interrupted progress on the new building, but ten days later the building was completed. On 2 October (the feast of the Holy Guardian Angels) the workshop of the new Eskimo building was opened to the natives. The opening was celebrated with games, the singing of hymns (translated into Eskimo by Lafortune), and a short instruction in Eskimo. On 8 October, Joseph R. Crimont, S. J., Prefect Apostolic of Alaska since March 1904, assisted by Lafortune, dedicated the new building in the presence of about fifty Eskimos, and celebrated the first mass in it.

The population of Nome was slowly declining by this time. Why was a special chapel for the Eskimos needed? According to Augusta Bernard Perry, who was a resident of Nome at that time, "When he [Lafortune] took over the natives, and got them attending mass, the smell of seal oil was so great that parishioners objected, and then he built the little chapel in back of St. Joseph's just for the Eskimos."[2] Although some of the white parishioners doubtless did complain about the smell of seal oil, their complaints cannot be regarded as the sole, or even the principal, reason for the building of the Eskimo chapel. During the early 1900s the maintenance of separate churches for minority groups was still a common practice, and there were, furthermore, advantages to having a special combination chapel-workshop building exclusively for the natives. The building served many useful purposes, including that of providing a spacious working area in the workshop, which was adequately heated and lighted the year round. There they could carve ivory, make and repair hunting equipment, and build boats and sleds. Within a short time, a cottage industry of building and repairing sleds of all kinds was thriving.[3]

A memorable day in the lives of the small community of Nome Jesuits was 3 August 1906, when Father Lafortune was appointed Superior. This was good news for all but Lafortune himself, who found this new office a burden rather than an honor. While this new responsibility did not consume a great deal of his time, it did gnaw away time already too short for all that he felt needed to be done among the Eskimos. This same day brought Joseph Bernard, S. J., a young, newly ordained priest from Burgundy, to help Lafortune in his mission work. During the following decade, Bernard became well-known as a missionary to the Seward Peninsula Eskimos and as a photographer of Eskimo life.[4]

In this year also, the Holy Cross hospital was relocated in a large, new building next to the parish rectory. Though it rendered good service for more than a dozen years, it was already somewhat too large and too late for the fading mining community.

By 1906, Lafortune was well established among the Eskimos, and could speak their language. They seemed to love him, and had begun calling him *Ataatazuuraq*, "the little Father." By the end of that year several hundred Eskimos were members of the extended Nome parish, not a very impressive number, but considering the short time involved, and the small number of "convertible" Eskimos in the area, the priests felt encouraged.[5] They were far from complacent, however, because they were up against a big obstacle in convert-making: the "protestant sects and preachers," who "were in the field first" and sowed "the weeds of heresy."[6]

Lafortune, never one to mince words, expressed himself forcefully on this subject. "If it was not for the baneful action of the trado-preachers [preachers more interested in trading] who spread the poison of their doctrine wheresoever they put their feet, all the Eskimos would readily become Catholics. They are religiously inclined. The country is inundated with those preachers. All the sects are represented, even the Mormons. Wheresoever there is a chance of making money, you see some schemer who makes himself preacher. It is never question of showing one's credentials, of course. The natives are deceived by their apparent honesty. They are the ravenous wolves disguised as sheep."[7]

Such harsh and biased words are repeated throughout many of his writings. They make dismal and depressing reading, but no religious historiography of early Alaska would be complete without mentioning them. They can be partly understood when read within the context of the prejudices of pre-ecumenical days when Reformation and Counter Reformation bilateral bigotry, interdenominational strife, and decidedly unchristianlike name-calling were still the fashion. No doubt there were pseudo-ministers, "trado-preachers," and charlatans who knew how to reconcile the service of God with the service of Mammon, but to condemn generally the great majority of non-Catholic ministers was certainly an injustice to many sincere men of God.

On 13 November 1906, Lafortune "took his last vows," meaning that he was now considered to be a "formed Jesuit"; that he pronounced for the last time the three simple vows of a Religious—poverty, chastity, and obedience; and henceforth, he and the Society of Jesus bound themselves one to the other inseparably and forever.

Lafortune's missionary plans were expanded when he dispensed with hired dogteams and drivers and bought a dogteam of his own for

$200 on 31 January 1907.[8] How could Lafortune resolve a seeming conflict between this apparent luxury and his vow of poverty?

St. Ignatius of Loyola, under the heading, "Principle and Foundation," in his *Spiritual Exercises*, enunciates his famous *tantum-quantum* principle: "All other things on the face of the earth are created for man to help him fulfil the end for which he is created. From this it follows that man is to use these things to the extent that they will help him to attain his end. Likewise, he must rid himself of them insofar as they prevent him from attaining it." The whole of Lafortune's personal spiritual and apostolic life was based on the principles contained in the *Spiritual Exercises*. Accordingly, his use of dogs was governed by the *tantum* ("to the extent that")-*quantum* ("insofar as") axiom. Buying and maintaining an adequate dogteam in Nome was an expensive undertaking in 1907, but in the light of the *tantum-quantum* principle, Lafortune, who scrupulously observed his vow of poverty, saw no conflict between his vow and having a dogteam. On the contrary, his vow and the *tantum-quantum* principle rather demanded that he have one, for the dogteam was necessary for the evangelization of the Eskimos entrusted to his spiritual care. A team of his own meant independence and mobility to leave, at a moment's notice, on a sick call or other important errands.

Lafortune thus became a "musher" in his own right, and by all reports he was an excellent one. John A. Concannon, S. J., recounting some of Lafortune's trips over the southern half of the Seward Peninsula, said, "It was journeys such as this—year after year, in all kinds of weather—that earned for him the title 'The Toughest Musher in the North.' How often have I heard him called that—and always with a note of admiration in the voice of the speaker."[9]

Lafortune was a serious musher who did not tolerate any nonsense from the dogs that he himself raised. Yet he loved them, fed them well, protected them from the winds, and was inordinately proud of them. To Lonneux he wrote, "I wish the dog feed would cost me nothing. I would have a string of trail-burners that would put everybody to flight," and at another time he said, "My dogs seemed to be made of steel."[10] He knew the pleasure that dog mushing afforded, but he was also aware of the dangers of the trail, and once wrote that "one takes his life into his hands when he sets out on a trip" in the dead of winter.[11]

Although he realized that few winters passed without one or more mushers dying on the trails, he mushed endless miles, winter after winter, for a quarter of a century, without hesitation and with courage that sometimes bordered on recklessness. To some persons, he appeared to be endowed with an uncanny, almost sixth, sense for survival, and no matter how overwhelming the odds against him seemed, he came through all his trips unharmed, except for an occasional twisted ankle or a patch of frostbite.

He was a capable musher largely because of the kind of man he was: determined, practical, disciplined, and physically tough. He was resourceful and planned his trips carefully, anticipating all of the hazards that could befall him on the trail. And, above all, he had common sense and good judgment about even the most "elementary things. . .how to gauge the strength of your dogs and your own. . .how to camp and when and where."[12] (The first Jesuit to lose his life on the winter trail was Brother Ulric Paquin, S. J., who, new to Alaska, froze to death when he was overtaken by a blinding snowstorm on the trail between Stebbins and Saint Michael on 27 January 1911.)

On 13 March 1907, Lafortune left for a trip "to the North" and returned on the 27th, "having had a very hard trip for himself and dogs, and having witnessed much poverty and misery among the natives along the coast."[13] Lafortune had encountered one of the blinding blizzards that can come up suddenly on the trail, blinding the driver and eradicating all signs of the trail. Father Joseph Bernard, who was in Nome at that time, wrote that Lafortune had to struggle against the storm for a night and half a day, not knowing where he was or where his dogs were leading him, but fortunately he had a good lead dog that led him and the team safely to shelter.[14]

Shelter in the North usually meant either the roadhouses that had been built after the gold rush at more or less regular intervals along the trails, or the "poor hovels" of the natives. Given a choice, a musher would in any event find himself in a dwelling that was overcrowded and underventilated. A roadhouse had beds or bunks, and Lafortune considered it a matter of fruitless conjecture to decide when the bed clothes were last changed. A guest in an Eskimo house used his own sleeping bag or blankets, or hides provided by his Eskimo hosts. Yet, both the roadhouses and igloos were always welcome oases to the travel-weary musher.

Lafortune, however, often avoided the roadhouses, preferring to sleep in a snowbank along the way, because "it costs too much to pass the night in those miserable inns."[15] That was probably more of an alibi than the real reason, since he had learned that the noisy, boisterous hostels were not conducive to meditation, prayer, and sleep.

The hardships of the winter trail gave the white men an indication of the weather conditions the Eskimos had to contend with all their lives. The Eskimos had learned the signs of danger and were cautious, whereas a white man might have been foolhardy. Lafortune has left a graphic description of a January blizzard that he had encountered on one of his trips to Cape Prince of Wales (probably in 1920): "At about 30 miles from here, at the mouth of the Sinrok [Sinuk] River, lived a few Catholic Eskimos and quite a settlement of Lutherans and Methodists. On account of the disposition of the mountains, Sinrok seems to be a nest of storms. Two days before my arrival there, two white men had been frozen to death and partly eaten up by their dogs at about 2 miles from the village. When I reached the place, there was not a speck in the skies and a very gentle breeze was blowing from the northwest. I anticipated an easy day for the morrow. After taking a bite with the natives, I fed my dogs and I noticed that the old man and his boy got busy after my sled. They were lashing it on a kind of rack with strong rawhide ropes and they secured everything on the sled. I told them not to go to all that trouble, for I intended to start early the next day. 'Don't think of going tomorrow,' said the old man. 'You are here for at least three days. You will learn what Sinrok is.' I looked at him. He was serious.

"Well, the old man was right. Of all the storms I have seen in this country this one was way the worst. No human being could live in that storm. The Eskimos are not wont to be very tender for their dogs. Well, that time I saw all the natives digging holes in the snowbanks to protect their canines. For three days the hurricane never stopped a minute. Tired to be in that small igloo, I tried to go out a few times. I had pretty good fears. The old man recommended me very strongly not to go out of reach of the door. 'If that wind catches you, we will never see you anymore,' he said. He had a pile of wood outside at about 20 feet from the house. He did not dare go to it. The 3rd day, to make fire, he used the floor of his storm door that was made out of small logs. If the storm had kept on, he had made up his mind that we would rather be without fire than to go for his wood. You may imagine how I did thank Almighty God not to be caught in that thing. I would surely have perished and all my dogs."[16]

Lafortune's fond wishes of being a missionary only to the Eskimos took a big step toward realization when John Forhan, S. J., arrived on 28 September 1908 to assume the role of pastor of the Nome parish as well as the role of Superior of the local Jesuit community. Lafortune, who had little taste for the office of Superior, was therefore free to devote his whole time and energies to all of the Eskimos of Seward Peninsula.

Lafortune spent more time on the trail with his dogteam after January 1909 than during any of the previous years. When he was not in the Eskimo workshop or in the Holy Angels chapel with the Eskimos, he visited the various Eskimo encampments and villages located on the Bering Sea coast. Reading about several trips which he took along the coast, in only a few weeks' time, gives an idea of his dedication to his mission work. On 14 January 1909, Lafortune went to Port Safety, about twenty miles from Nome, where he found the Eskimos to be "hard up. No seals, no tomcod,"[17] and on the eighteenth he mushed to Cripple Creek despite very cold weather. On 8 February, he set out for Cape Douglas, about sixty miles west of Nome, and stopped at Sinuk on the way.

Because the weather was good it took him less than six hours to get to Sinuk, where he had a congregation of five—all in one family—who were faithful and devout despite their living in a Protestant stronghold. Others of the village even came to hear him preach, although the Sinuk schoolteacher was also the minister.

Before his conversion to Christianity, Lafortune's host had cut off his wife's nose during a drunken fight, and in remorse had taken the same knife and hacked off half of his own nose. He proudly told Lafortune that he had not touched a drop of "spirit of the devil" since his conversion.

Lafortune reached Cape Douglas, thirty-five miles north of Sinuk, the next day after only a five-hour trip. He was warmly received by his one Catholic family, and welcomed into their dwelling. Seals—whole and dismembered—covered the entire floor, but by careful rearrangement of seals and household goods, room was made for his mass kit and "bed," a wolf skin. After sharing the supper of his hosts, he gave an instruction, and the next morning, while the family prepared their confessions, he improvised an altar. Before Lafortune left, the head of the family gratefully gave him a 200-pound seal, reassuring him that his dogs were strong enough to haul it all the way back to Nome.[18]

In the Nome diary, Father Forhan marveled at Lafortune's dedication to duty: "Just think of a priest being obliged to make a journey of 30 miles, to visit one family at Sinrock, and another of 60 miles, to see a few persons at Cape Douglas. Seven Eskimos in all!"[19]

Forhan was a man who counted everything exactly, but a mere seven Eskimos did not impress him at all. During his six years in Nome he counted exactly the number of people at masses and meetings, the number of people ministered to, the number of people he visited, and every penny that came in and out of the Church. But he was not necessarily miserly or stingy—just thrifty in a declining parish in a declining mining frontier with heavy financial burdens.

Although both Lafortune and Forhan were Canadians, they were quite different. Lafortune could live and cope with human frailty and fallibility, and thought nothing of tramping off across the tundra on a forty-mile hike to visit a single sick Eskimo, let alone seven Eskimos on an even longer trip. Forhan, on the other hand, seemed virtually incapable of tolerating anything or anybody not genuine 24-carat Holy Roman Catholic. He was disinclined to seek out the straying sheep of Nome, and saw an anti-Catholic force in everything non-Catholic. He constantly strove to separate and isolate his parishioners from all other groups and organizations in Nome. Despite bitter protests from club members, Forhan disbanded the Miners' Home Club, and replaced it with the Catholic Library Club because he said that the M. H. C. was "in nowise Catholic; in fact, the majority of its members are protestants, infidels, or free-thinkers," although he admitted that it kept a number of men out of the saloons and gambling halls.[20]

Although Lafortune, one of the founders of the club, opposed Forhan's decision, he went along with it—as he did with many decisions made by Forhan, who was his Superior. Lafortune did not complain publicly about the man with whom he worked, and appeared to get along well with him. After Forhan had been there a year, Lafortune, in his official capacity as consultor, wrote to his Father Provincial, saying that he did not know yet what to think of Forhan: "I am afraid that he might be too brusque, too impatient with the class of sinners we have up this way. . . .His preaching and conversations are, in my opinion, too scathing. The women of the congregation have had little assistance. . . .The Father does not hide enough his profound hatred of everything that is protestant or renegade.''[21]

Probably fearing that his harsh judgment would cause Forhan to be relieved of his duties, and that he would be left alone in Nome, Lafortune added the hopeful note that in time Forhan would probably become popular; but four years later he admitted that ''Rev. Fr. Forhan is hated by many on account of his excessive severity.''[22]

For four years Forhan kept the Nome diary, and because of its nature as a semipublic document, the severity of his statements was softened by a semisardonic, semiserious character, sometimes with a bit of humor. But despite the wit, the well-turned phrases, and interesting observations about the mores of a declining gold-mining town, it is scarcely what one would expect from a man invested with his office.

Forhan was not a good choice for Nome. He reacted negatively to just about everything: the climate, the town, the people, and even his Catholic community. He kept up a stream of letters-to-the-editor to the Nome press, especially if the papers printed articles contrary to official Church teaching or to his own private views. If none of the papers printed his letters, he read them from the altar, and though much of this verbal jousting may have been entertaining, it did more to alienate people than to win them over. Scarcely anyone escaped his scorn—all non-Catholic clubs (especially the Free Masons), whiskey-drinkers, and women. He believed that ''all human beings of the female persuasion should be suppressed,'' and that ''women are a necessary evil.'' The nuns were not excluded, and he described the Sister Superior as ''a thundercloud in petticoats.''[23]

He was equally hard on his own parishioners, many of whom, he said, were ''indifferent, non-practical or apostate Catholics. . .a queer congregation. . . .One more hopelessly corrupt and unmanageable it would be difficult to find.'' He said that the ''backsliders'' were legion, ''so many renegades as you could shake a stick at,'' and when two miners, ''neither [of whom] ever put his foot inside the church,'' died in their cabin from asphyxiation, he recorded, without a hint of compassion, ''Nome has two renegades less.''[24]

''Nome,'' he said, ''is not a locality in which the exercise of the ministry gives any very great consolation,'' and on 8 September 1914, he rendered his greatest service to Nome and to himself when he sailed south on the *Victoria*, never to return.[25]

Father Joseph Bernard, S. J. *(Oregon Province Archives)*

Father Lafortune with his dogteam, Nome, February 1907. *(Oregon Province Archives)*

Father Hubert A. Post, S. J., and St. Joseph's Church, Nome, about 1917. *(Oregon Province Archives)*

Forhan was relieved as pastor of St. Joseph's Church by Hubert A. Post, S. J., who arrived on 25 September 1914.[26]

In 1907, the mission had been placed under the Province of Canada (from 1886 to 1907 all of the Alaska mission had been under the care of the Turin Province of the Society of Jesus), and in August 1908, two visitors from his native land arrived, Edouard Lecompte, S. J., the Father Provincial, and his assistant, Albert Bellemare, S. J. Lafortune noted that "Rev. Fr. Provincial has made a great endeavor to organize the mission."[27] On 17 May 1912, northern Alaska was again transferred, to the California Province of the Society of Jesus. On 2 June, Joseph Carrière, S. J., the Father Provincial of Canada at that time, wrote to the Provincial of the California Province, James A. Rockliff, S. J., regarding the mechanics of effecting the transfer. Carrière said that "some Fathers are very likely to insist on staying up in Alaska, and might be allowed to stay, i.e., FF. Jetté, Lafortune, Forhan (the three most useful of our men, I think)." By 22 September, news of the transfer reached Lafortune, who wrote to Bellemare, "Behold, the mission of Alaska has passed into other hands. We may yet wind up belonging to Japan."[28] (The Alaska mission was transferred again—in 1932—to the Oregon Province.)

On 30 September, Carrière wrote to Rockliff regarding Lafortune: "Rev. Fr. Lafortune is a man of rare merit, the best and most efficient missioner at present in Alaska, and the most fitted to replace Rev. Father [John L.] Lucchesi as *Superior Regionalis*. All this is on the authority of Rev. Fr. Lecompte, my predecessor. Seeing this, I feel I am making a sacrifice for the Alaskan mission's sake in renouncing all claims on him." On 11 October, Carrière informed Rockliff that "with regard to Fr. Lafortune, it is fair that he be requested to choose his Province himself, as all other Canadians will." Lafortune, however, left the decision up to his Superiors.[29] In order that he might stay on in Alaska without legal complications, they transferred him to the California Province.

3 / The Mission at Marys Igloo

Marys Igloo was the first Eskimo village in the Bering Strait area to have a permanent Catholic missionary. During the gold rush a town grew up on the banks of the Kuzitrin River near the house, or igloo, of a woman whom the miners called Mary. She had often given lost and lonely prospectors food and friendship, and before long ''Mary's Igloo'' at the head of navigable waters of the Kuzitrin became a mining camp. As soon as the miners settled there, Eskimos from the vicinity of the Imuruk Basin (many of whose ancestors had lived in Kauwerak, an old village nearby) also began to settle in Marys Igloo. When the mining boom collapsed a few years later, the Eskimos remained.[1]

During December 1906, Lafortune wrote a long letter to his ecclesiastical Superior, the Prefect Apostolic, Crimont, for his ''opinion concerning the things to be done next spring,'' for Lafortune was actively conceiving new ideas and proposing new plans for his missionary endeavors. His Superior welcomed his views, which he explained: ''The Eskimo question becomes more and more important here. Next summer, Fr. Bernard will know enough of the language to be able to take my place here [Nome] and I could go and open a new mission. The only places yet open to us now are Mary's Igloo, which is at about 80 miles north of Nome and where we have some 20 Catholic Eskimos; King's Island [*sic*], which is at about 100 [35] miles off shore; Diamedes Islands [*sic*], one of which is in the Russian Territory and the other in the American. It is hard enough to know in which of these 3 places we could do more good. I am inclined to think that Mary's Igloo is the best place. I think we could make a good camp of it. We could probably have a good many of the coast Eskimos winter there, for the wood gets rarer on the coast and there is a good deal of it at the Igloo.

Moreover, there is no or hardly any winter fishing along the coast, whilst in Mary's Igloo there is a great deal of it. . . .

"King's Island is sometimes a hard country to live in. . . .Even its naturals desert it now and then. There are not more than 90 natives there [119 in the 1910 census report] and the coast Eskimos would certainly never make up their mind to go and live there, not even for one winter. We have some Catholics on that island and they want by all means to have a missionary. I am ready to go.

"Diamedes Islands, according to the sayings of their inhabitants, are a real paradise. They have all what they want and more. But thanks to the whalers, who sell whiskey to those natives, they are very corrupted. They kill one another in their orgies, therefore a good many of them run away not to be killed. A good number of our Nome Catholic Eskimos are coming from that country, and they say that if we would go up there they would all return to their country.

"Finally, our congregation [is] increasing rapidly enough. The chapel that you have blessed 2 years ago is too small. We will be obliged to enlarge it, which means an expense of at least $1000, for to enlarge the chapel we have to take in the workshop. Therefore we will have to build another shop at least as large as the one we have now. . . .I expect from your Reverence some light as to what is to be done."[2]

Lafortune had firmly believed from the beginning that the pastor of the natives and of the whites should not be one and the same person. He wrote to Crimont again in 1907, restating his views, and rather complaining that he could not take the necessary trips to the Eskimo communities as long as he had the responsibility also of the Nome parish. "I cannot do any of those things [trips to King Island, Marys Igloo, and other places] for I would have been absent from the parish nearly all summer."[3]

He had gone to Marys Igloo for the first time in 1906. There he had visited the roadhouse of the Bruce Lloyd family, and had said mass for them and a few Eskimos whom he had previously baptized in Nome. Convinced that Marys Igloo should have a chapel, Lafortune bought the roadhouse in 1907 and spent two months converting it into a chapel and quarters for a priest, but as yet no priest remained there permanently.[4]

By 1907, there were thirty-five Catholics in Marys Igloo. In all, approximately 250 Eskimos had been converted to the Catholic faith in

Catholic Eskimos of Marys Igloo, June 1915. *(Photograph by Father Joseph Bernard. Dorothy Jean Ray collection)*

The first church at Marys Igloo, April 1907. A man, Ullak, is behind the sled. The part on the right (16 by 20 feet) was the church and meeting room; the one on the left (14 by 16 feet) was used as living quarters. *(Copied from a French postcard, photograph by Father Bernard. Dorothy Jean Ray collection)*

The second church at Marys Igloo. *(Copied from a French postcard, photograph by Bernard. Dorothy Jean Ray collection)*

the Bering Strait area: sixty on King Island, twelve in Wales, and a few in small groups all along the coast from Wales to Port Safety.[5]

In 1908, Lafortune unfolded some elaborate plans for Marys Igloo, and wrote to Crimont on 27 March: "Here are our needs for Mary's Igloo, if we want to start something really serious and permanent. Our idea is to build there a church and an orphanage. That would mean two Sisters, a Brother (carpenter) and a Father attached permanently to that place. . . .To that orphanage would be admitted also all the boys and girls who want to learn a trade; and by a trade I mean for the boys carpentry and some blacksmithing, for the girls housekeeping and sewing (no fancy work). We do not want at all to make white people out of the natives; we see too much the wrong of it every day. . . .Therefore we want them to remain Eskimos and to make of them good, honest, self-supporting Eskimos. The people here appreciate our work, just because we have taken that standing and because they see that there is no bluff about our work."[6]

He also suggested that a house large enough to accommodate the staff and twenty children would have to be one hundred fifty feet by twenty feet. He proposed that the outside walls be built of willows and a thick coating of sod, and the inside walls, floor, and roof made of rough boards covered with burlap, linoleum, and roofing paper. He estimated that, by economizing, the building and its furnishings would cost three thousand dollars.

Lafortune envisioned Marys Igloo as a native center because it seemed to him that the coastal Eskimos were suffering at that time from a shortage of wood and game. He concluded his letter to Crimont: "The only thing is to organize the natives and for that we have to be with them winter and summer. Here in Nome it is hard to organize the natives because we cannot be with them in summer. We cannot make a fishing camp because we are obliged to stay here for the strangers who flock here every year."

Lafortune's attitude toward helping the Eskimos was opposite to the one which he thought the schools were espousing—that is, he wanted to isolate them from what he considered to be degenerate whites and a deterioration of their environment. Throughout his long missionary career he clung to his original plans of establishing "centers," and "organizing the natives" into self-enclosed, self-sufficient social, economic, and religious communities. He was opposed to "civilizing" or "domesticating" them, as he thought the schools were doing.

Father Bernard was chosen to be the priest at Marys Igloo. He arrived in September 1908, and remained until 1915, with only a year taken out, from July 1909 to 1910, which he spent in Europe receiving his final year of Jesuit training. Lafortune then included this village, which had fifty-one Catholics by then, in his rounds.[7]

Bernard had been at Marys Igloo for eight years when he left Alaska rather suddenly, on 16 June 1915, to answer the call of the *tricolore* of his native France.[8] During his years at Marys Igloo he had learned the Eskimo language; had taken a large number of photographs; and had acquired an admiration for all things Eskimo and Alaskan, which had not diminished by the end of the war. He wanted to return to Alaska, but was not permitted to do so, despite his many impassioned pleas. The refusal was probably because of the casual way he had handled funds, as well as the fact that he had not obtained permission to leave Marys Igloo from John B. Sifton, S. J., the General Superior of the Alaska mission, who, as a former German citizen (by name of John B. Sifferlen), may have resented Bernard's abrupt departure to fight against his former homeland. For almost forty years, Bernard, living somewhat in the past, wrote articles about the Eskimos for French missionary magazines and sent devotional literature to the Eskimos of the Igloo-Teller area.[9]

Shortly after Bernard's departure for France, a rumor was spread in the Marys Igloo area by the white schoolteacher, Edwin Hunnicutt, to the effect that Bernard had been chased out of the country by his Jesuit Superiors because of some "misconduct."[10] According to Lafortune, the rumor "spread like wild fire; and, among the whites as well as among the Eskimos, among Catholics as well as among protestants, the rumor gained in maliciousness and falsity in direct proportion as it spread." Lafortune, who had left Nome, on 21 September 1915, to replace Bernard at Marys Igloo, found the situation "very painful," especially when a Protestant Eskimo, John Otok [Octuck], "who pretended to be a missionary," did everything in his power to prevent the people from attending Catholic services. According to Lafortune, in order to prepare himself for his anti-Catholic crusade, the Eskimo minister had read "about twenty evil books" sent to him by a Nome missionary until "the poison of hatred against the Church penetrated to the very depths of his soul."[11]

Lafortune's missionary work at Marys Igloo became easier within a few months when the Eskimo minister, his wife, and baby drowned in two feet of water on New Year's day, 1916. Protestant Eskimos started to attend Lafortune's services, and more than a dozen were admitted into the Catholic Church.

At Marys Igloo, Lafortune was stationed alone for the first time since his arrival in Alaska. He had almost more duties than he could handle: the ministry, housekeeping, woodcutting, water carrying, and dog keeping. "If the good Lord had not given me a constitution of steel," he wrote, "I could not hold out for two weeks."[12]

During the year he remained at Marys Igloo he continued to make his dogteam trips to see his converts scattered over the vast Seward Peninsula all the way from Cape Prince of Wales to Council, saying mass, giving instructions, and filling baptismal, marriage, and burial registers.

4 / Lafortune's Practical Projects

Lafortune was a practical man who was constantly experimenting, inventing, and improvising, and trying new ways of improving the living conditions of those around him. He helped the Eskimos build sleds, boats, and even make fishing nets.[1] He manufactured soap from seal oil. He made many coffins. He built a folding bed, which lifted up and fit into the wall. This was a practical space-saving device in a room built small to conserve heat. And he invented a way of burning crude oil in the parish house stove without leaving ash or dirt, cutting the fuel bill in half. He tried bookbinding. The Nome diary for 14 May 1909 notes that "Fr. Lafortune bound several copies of 'Truth' into quite a respectable volume."[2]

In 1916, Lafortune and his fellow priests obtained an old printing press and began to print the catechism in Eskimo. Later, they branched out into prayer and hymn booklets, also in Eskimo. Lafortune thus became an author, publisher, and printer.

He even learned to knit so that he could show the Eskimos how to do it, and he taught some of the women how to make flowers with dyed ptarmigan feathers. "He was so proud of the first bouquets they made," said one of his former parishioners.[3]

Lafortune also had to help with jacking up and releveling the church and parish buildings every year after the spring thaw. Many of the buildings of Nome are built on permafrost, the part of the ground that remains permanently frozen unless disturbed by removing the insulating vegetation. When disturbed, the ground becomes unstable, and the buildings are likely to sag a bit more each succeeding year.

Construction problems in the North interested him, and he had several occasions to write about the Eskimo houses, which have often been extolled as being warm and desirable dwellings. One of his descriptions conveys wonderfully what the old houses must have been like; at least we know what he thought of them:

"Many were their ways of building their houses. Along the beach they used driftwood. They built low log houses and covered them entirely with soil. The window was in the roof. Having no such thing as glass, they had recourse to the intestine of the seals or the sea lion. When that intestine is cut open and dried and stretched, it is transparent and makes a pretty good window. In front of their houses they have always a tunnel, at the outer end of which is their storehouse. That tunnel is a horrible affair, never more than four feet high and four feet wide and sometimes twenty feet long. You have to crawl in that thing till you reach the door of the house. Once there, the trouble is not over. The door proper is nothing else but a hole just large enough to pass your shoulders. If the floor of the tunnel happens to be level with the floor of the house, you enter in the house on your four. To go out you have to go backwards like a crawfish. If, on the contrary, the floor of the tunnel is below the floor of the house, then to enter the house you emerge from under the floor through a hole made in the floor. To go out is a job. The reason for all that is to keep the heat in the house. When once out of the tunnel, you are not altogether outside yet. You are only in the storehouse. It is a place as large as the house, in which they put their meat, their bags, their snowshoes and so on. Before the snow falls, they go out of that storeroom through a door level with the ground; but after the first storm, that door is very often obstructed and instead of shoveling out the snow, the inhabitants make an opening in the roof of the storeroom and for the whole winter use a ladder to go out. A trap door covers the entrance. The wind blows out the snow from that trap door. Now the uninitiated has to be very careful when going down that ladder, for it is greasy. Moreover, the fellows of the ladder are not equally apart, and, finally, it is pretty dark in that hole. Such are the hovels in which a good many Eskimos live even nowadays."[4]

One of Lafortune's dreams was to own his own boat, something he had thought about almost as soon as he arrived in 1903. He broached the subject a few years later to the Prefect Apostolic. "Another coronation of our work here," he wrote, "would be a schooner that would permit to the natives to go and hunt their seals and walrus and whales, etc. etc. Now the wood alone of a schooner would cost at least $500.''[5] His own boat would make him independent and self-sufficient on water as well as on land; he already had his dogteam when the *Immaculate of Nome* was launched on 6 June 1907. The *Immaculate* was a two-masted schooner, thirty-four feet long, flat-bottomed with a centerboard, and with a little pilothouse that looked as if it would be swept overboard by the first heavy sea.[6] Lafortune expected that both he and the Eskimos would use the boat. The Eskimos needed it for hunting seals and walrus that migrated far out on the moving ice floes of Bering Strait in the spring, and for trading, fishing, and gathering driftwood during the summer. He hoped to use it on his missionary trips to the villages on the coast and on the islands.

Although the *Immaculate* was used for some years, it did not prove to be the kind of boat that Lafortune and his Nome Eskimos needed because the cargo capacity was too small. In 1908, he therefore supervised the building of a new schooner, forty feet long, eleven feet wide, and five feet deep, which was to cost $700. Some men came from a hundred and eighty miles away to help build it. He again expected that the Eskimos would use it for walrus hunting, but the boat was never finished because he was told by experienced boatbuilders that it would be too fragile for the ice, so the unfinished boat was dismantled and the wood sold at a slight profit.[7]

In the spring of 1913, Lafortune was busy building a third boat—this time a gasoline launch. This boat was also a joint venture for the mutual benefit of Lafortune and the Eskimos, for hunting expeditions and missionary trips. Just before he began to build it, he wrote to his niece, Sister Marie-Flavius, that he needed it to visit his ''Catholics who are perched on the islands of the Bering Sea,'' and to help the Eskimos hunt seals, walrus, and sea lions, but the thought of it was ''already enough to make me seasick. I don't really know how I will take it all. The odor of the gasoline, of the Eskimos, of the sea mammals, added to the lurching of the boat are going to make my heart jump right over my head. Happily, it is all for the good Lord. I would never do that for the love of man [alone] or of money.''[8]

The keel of the *Immaculate II* was laid in 1912, and a year later, on 27 May 1913, she had her first test when Lafortune, A. Frantzen, John Korhan, and three Eskimos attempted to go to King Island and Little Diomede. Lafortune's first trip to the islands was accompanied by bad luck almost from the start, mainly because of a light-duty, twelve-H.P. motor that Lafortune had bought to economize. They had been on their way only five or six hours when they had to dismantle the engine. Finding that one of the piston rods was blocked, they cleaned it and went on. But when they were only twenty miles from King Island, they encountered the ice field without a lead (open water) in it anywhere. Therefore, they gave up going to King Island and headed toward Cape York, hoping to get to Little Diomede from there, but as soon as they emerged from the ice field, the sea became rough, and the engine stopped. They worked on it all night, and after finding the trouble next morning, went on to Cape York and Wales, where Lafortune said mass for some Eskimos. They then headed for Little Diomede. Upon reaching a lead in the ice, however, they found themselves surrounded by walrus, and became so excited they lost their bearings. In the fog they wandered to Siberia, Big Diomede Island, and finally, to Little Diomede, but fearing the ice, hurried back to Cape Prince of Wales. There, the engine gave out altogether, and under a makeshift sail the crippled *Immaculate* returned to Nome.[9]

Eskimos starting out to hunt seals in the floating ice in the *Immaculate*, Nome, 1914. *(Oregon Province Archives)*

Lafortune knew that he would have to replace the engine, and appealed to the readers of the *Messager Canadien* for contributions. They responded generously, and Lafortune renamed the boat *Le Messager.*[10] The boat ran various errands of mercy, such as visits to the sick, hauling sick to the hospital, taking food to the hungry, and lightering stranded King Islanders and their possessions to the revenue cutter *Bear* so they could go home, as was their custom at the end of summer.

One of Lafortune's favorite projects was the workshop, which became the success that he had hoped it would be. By 1913, it was a lively place as described by Michael O'Malley, S. J., who was Lafortune's assistant from September 1912 to August 1913: "Fr. Lafortune lived for the Eskimos: was their pastor, doctor, adviser, supervisor and provider of part of their work. They made better and more attractive sleds than did the white men. . . .The Eskimos made sleds and carved designs on walrus tusks in the workshop that was an extension of their chapel. Every evening, winter and summer, the Eskimos, men, women and children, gathered in the workshop for conversation and recreation. The men talked more than the women. The children played in the center. From time to time Fr. Lafortune, always smiling, would appear, opening the folding door and calling a group into the chapel for instruction in religion, in Eskimo, sending a group out into the workshop. . . .On Sundays about one hundred men, women and children would attend mass in the chapel and sing with gusto. The Eskimos sang in English, Latin and Eskimo, and were eager to sing and ready to learn the hymns. A few could play the organ well enough. There was always an air of friendliness, piety and subdued hilarity in the place."[11]

By 1914, the Catholic Eskimo community of Nome had grown so large that a larger chapel was considered necessary, so the partition between the chapel and the shop in the Eskimo building was removed to make one large chapel, and a new workshop was built.

In 1913, the Eskimo workshop was given the job of making sleds for Vilhjalmur Stefansson's third polar expedition. Stefansson had talked to Lafortune about making sleds during the summer of 1912, and on 22 February 1913, he placed an order for six, designating generally what he needed, but giving Lafortune and the Eskimos a free hand in designing them. Work was begun on 17 March, and the six sleds were finished on 15 May, but on 21 June, Stefansson ordered four more.[12]

By the middle of July all were built, and on the eighteenth Stefansson stopped at the rectory and paid his bill of $505.

Stefansson wrote in *The Friendly Arctic* (page 221), "In Nome I had had several sleds made with toboggan bottoms," but nowhere does he credit Lafortune and the Nome Eskimos as the builders of the sleds that apparently had given him complete satisfaction.[13]

In the midst of all this activity, year after year, it appears that Lafortune never took a whole day off, except for his annual eight-day retreats. His whole time was consumed with Church and missionary affairs, the only exceptions being an infrequent picnic with school children or giving a dogteam ride to the Sisters when he was in Nome.

Sleds made in the Eskimo workshop, Nome, 1913, under Father Lafortune's direction for Vilhjalmur Stefansson's expedition. *(Oregon Province Archives)*

5 / The Mission at Pilgrim Hot Springs and the Influenza Epidemic, 1918

By 1917, Lafortune no longer regarded Marys Igloo as a suitable center for grand-scale missionary activity, and began negotiations to acquire the Hot Springs ranch on the Pilgrim River, some eighty miles north of Nome. On 13 October 1917, James F. Halpin, representing the Halpin family who had bought the property with the intention of giving it to the Church, gave the Hot Springs to Lafortune as a gift.[1] On 26 October 1917, Post wrote Crimont—who had become the first bishop of the Vicariate of Alaska on 25 July—about plans for the Hot Springs. "Mary's Igloo will be transferred to the Springs and with God's help and the assistance of friends we expect to make the Springs for this part of Alaska what Holy Cross is on the Yukon." The Holy Cross mission, with its productive vegetable gardens, was regarded far and wide as the "garden spot" of the Yukon.[2] The mission, which was a combination boarding school and orphanage, was to serve as Lafortune's model, and at last he could have his dreamed-of center for the natives, away from white influence.

The Hot Springs ranch lay in a roomy valley between mountains—the snowcapped Kigluaik Mountains (Sawtooth Range) to the south, peaking at an elevation of 4,714 feet, and Hen and Chickens Mountain, 748 feet high, to the north. The Pilgrim River (also called Kruzgamepa), about a quarter mile from the ranch, was fringed with cottonwood and willow trees, and the springs ran warm all year long. It was truly an oasis, and Lafortune—as a zealous missionary—saw it as

Mission buildings at Pilgrim Hot Springs in 1972. *(National Park Service)*

View of Pilgrim Hot Springs from the southwest, early 1920s. *(Oregon Province Archives)*

A dogmobile on the Seward Peninsula Railway, 1914. *(Photograph by H. G. Kaiser. University of Alaska Archives, Lulu Fairbanks Collection)*

a place ideally suited for the re-creation and building up of the whole man—body, soul, and spirit.

It was, nevertheless, a place subject to sudden and violent wind storms, and on hot summer days mosquitoes swarmed in clouds over the marshy lowlands. Spring floods occasionally washed out newly planted crops, and early autumn frosts sometimes blackened a whole season's vegetable harvest in a few hours.

Lafortune moved to the Hot Springs in the spring of 1918 and immediately planted a garden. During the summer he dismantled a prefabricated church building that Bernard had built at Marys Igloo in 1911, and moved it to the Hot Springs. During August he went to Nome on business and sent back an assortment of livestock: a horse, "driven by Kattak with Attinik as guide and assistant," two cows, and a little bull, which reached the Hot Springs in four days. On 22 August, William Bailey and an Eskimo named Anaulik took four goats on their "dogmobile" (a cart fitted for railroad tracks and drawn by dogs), and started for Iron Creek, a "railroad station," about eight miles from the Springs.[3]

On 12 September, Lafortune and a companion, August Homburger, left Nome by dogmobile for the Hot Springs. Lafortune, having been away for five weeks, was eager to learn how the animals and the gardens were faring. He made the first entry in the house diary on 14 September: "We begin the foundations of the barn. After clearing the ground we carried sand to level it. Mr. Homburger is the master mechanic and Mr. Carey the chief cook and stock superintendent." Several Eskimos, Philip and Charly Ikiguanna, Ullak, and Fred Kiktoraklek, nicknamed "mosquito," were also part of the work force.[4]

The next day after Sunday services they made a tour of the grounds and found wild rice and a "beautiful patch" of hay for their stock. They began to cut the hay, but as it rained on the sixteenth, they fixed up the cellar of the bath house for storing vegetables and gathered wood from the stands around the springs instead. In addition to the disagreeable weather, they had to battle mice, which had got into the flour sacks, the milk, and the cranberries. They made and set traps, and by the next day, "four mice have lost their lives and their death finds no pity."

By 24 September, they had harvested enough vegetables to share with others, and Lafortune and Charly Ikiguanna took a dory full to

Lost River and Teller. When they returned, on 1 October, they found considerable progress made on the stables and great quantities of hay and bedding cut for the livestock.

They harvested the main vegetable crop during the first week of October—tons of beets, carrots, turnips, cabbage, kale, rutabagas, rhubarb, onions, and potatoes, and stored a ton of oats and a quantity of dried fish for Lafortune's dogteam in the loft of the new barn. Work on the stables progressed as rapidly as conditions permitted, but the boards, being old and full of nails, were hard to saw.

Lafortune's dogs were attracted to the livestock. On 3 October, he wrote, "A very sad accident occurred last night. One of my dogs, led by the devil, got loose and went for our goats. The brute wounded our two angora goats badly enough." Two days later he reported that the dog broke his chain and attacked the two goats that he had not seen before. "Luckily he was caught in time. It was the last of his mishaps. The only place for the brute was beyond the great divide, so we divided. Consequently, Philip is given the office of executioner. He fulfilled his duty in a masterly way; and Skookum went to where he belongs."

Lafortune, the able farm boy from Canada, was again in his native element as he harvested the crops, repaired the buildings, prepared for winter, and worked on the plans for his school and orphanage. Little did he suspect during this idyllic period that he was enjoying the calm before the storm that was about to break upon the Seward Peninsula, bringing him orphans in numbers he had not anticipated. Tragedy was on its way, literally, to Nome. The Spanish influenza epidemic was raging in the states when the *Victoria* left Seattle for her last trip of the 1918 season to Nome. As a safeguard, Nome's Holy Cross hospital, which had recently been closed, was reopened and made ready to receive the passengers for quarantine.

The year 1918, in many respects, marked a turning point for the Catholic Church on the Seward Peninsula. The white community of Nome had been on a slow but steady decline for more than a decade, and although the Catholic Eskimo community was increasing and flourishing, the ranks of the white Catholics had decreased so much that the Sisters closed the parochial school on 29 May 1918, and the hospital in September, partly because of the competition of a recently opened hospital under the auspices of the Methodist Church. All of the Sisters had left Nome by 20 September.[5]

The *Victoria* arrived on 20 October, and the passengers were quarantined although they appeared to be in good health. The quarantine was difficult to maintain, however, so after five days it was lifted. Meanwhile, cases of influenza were reported while the *Victoria* was still in the roadstead. Because of the lateness of the season, unloading had begun immediately, and as a result, afflicted members of the crew came into contact with the people of Nome. Walter C. Shields, superintendent of the northwest district of the Bureau of Education, was one of the first to die, and Dr. Daniel Neuman, the only resident physician, was very ill at the height of the epidemic.

On 30 October, just two days after the *Victoria* had left Nome, Lafortune arrived from the Hot Springs, much to the relief of Frederick A. Ruppert, S. J., who had arrived for the Nome Church with a companion, Hugh Ibbetson, on the *Victoria* only the previous month. The forty-year-old Ruppert, though anything but a robust and practical person, had volunteered for the Alaska mission after finishing a three-year term as rector of Loyola College in Los Angeles. Lafortune was unaware of the influenza until his arrival in Nome, which he said, "was in one way providential [so he could help]. I struck Nome at the beginning of the epidemy. . . .The natives were simply mowed down."[6] (At that time there were about 500 white persons and an equal number of Eskimos in Nome.)

On 31 October, G. J. Lomen, the mayor of Nome, called a city council meeting, at which it was decided that all churches and public meeting places were to be closed, and that Holy Cross hospital should be used for the sick, with Father Ruppert in charge. Lafortune, E. D. Evans, the acting superintendent of the Bureau of Education at Nome, and the Reverend William F. Baldwin, a Methodist missionary, were asked to take charge of the Eskimos.[7]

Ruppert's entries in the Nome diary give a grim outline of the first nineteen days of November:

> Nov. 1—Nearly whole congregation ill. Announced at mass time discontinuance of public services for a while. Hugh [Ibbetson] starts to heat hospital as engineer. Weather below zero.[8]
>
> 2—First patients arrive about 1 o'clock. At evening 17 being cared for. Entire Eskimo population is stricken.
>
> 3—Sunday. We both say masses in private. Fr. Lafortune gives last sacraments and brings relief to the natives all day.

4—Several natives succumb. Hospital increasing number of patients. Weather below zero. Natives perishing for want of fuel, food and inability to help themselves. Conditions among them most deplorable. Father Lafortune works on coffins.[9]

5—We take in Eskimo woman in last stages of pregnancy and stricken with flu, and several more patients also. More misery among natives discovered, who are dying fast of cold, starvation and sickness. Whole families perish, though several are rushing relief. Fr. Lafortune evokes universal admiration. . . .Practically all my flock ill. Fr. Lafortune working hard to help natives.

6—Eskimo woman gives birth to child. . . .Some patients dismissed, others taken in. Ravages of epidemic without parallel in Nome.

7—Eskimo woman dies at 5 A.M. . . .Fr. Ruppert makes sick calls, baptizes two Eskimo babies in dying condition at other hospital, baptizes dying woman in hospital. Fr. Lafortune slaves to help natives from morning to night as usual. About 60 deaths among natives.

8—*De More.* [''the usual,'' a phrase frequently used by Jesuits keeping diaries. Here, of course, it has a ring quite out of the ordinary.]

9—One more case taken to hospital and two more deaths.

10—Sunday. No masses for the public. Eight new cases and one Eskimo assisted. . . .

11—Two whites and one Eskimo die. . . .

12—Healthy Eskimo babes to be moved to Holy Cross. Evans warns of threatened removal of orphanage from Sinrock to Nome.

19—Eskimo children placed temporarily in hospital and to be committed to our care with the support of government. Patients coming and going and dying.[10]

The last six weeks of that tragic year 1918 are merely summarized in the next diary entry. Under the date heading of ''Nov. 19 to Jan. 1st,'' Ruppert wrote, ''Whole time was spent in hospital. . . .Hospital was closed to white patients at midnight of Dec. 20th. On Xmas day we had midnight mass without music or singing in the parish chapel. The small place was crowded. . . .A Xmas tree was given the native children in the afternoon of Xmas day. The influenza having broken out at the Igloo about Nov. 15, Fr. Lafortune left Nome, where the natives were all either dead or in the hospital, about Nov. 24. His presence was sadly needed at both the Igloo and Hot Springs. About Dec. 20 he paid a flying visit to Nome to bring Xmas gifts to the orphans up there."[11]

Lafortune left Nome to minister to the people in the Marys Igloo-Hot Springs area. The Hot Springs diary gives a day-by-day account of the course of the epidemic:

> Nov. 28—I started back for the Springs in company with Mr. T. Gaffney to help our natives up here. Death made already 21 victims. On the 27 we met Mr. [H. D.] Reese [a teacher] and made up our minds to take as many patients as possible to the Springs. The only [way] to [do] them good is to gather them and attend to them. Away from their homes made so gloomy by the visit of Death and well fed, they have a fair chance to recover. Today we have 14 patients. The number will go increasing. Moreover, we attend to 3 families at [Davidsons] landing.
>
> 29—Thirteen new patients come to our improvised hospital. Atajok receives the last rites of the Church. Her condition is precarious; she is not expected to live long. Mosquito (Kiktoraklek) is improving. Stanislaus Anayok is very weak. Koyanglaluk died in his parents' igloo near our landing.
>
> 30—The day opens by the death of Atajok and closes by the death of Stan. Anayok. Two more patients come to take their place. They are Tullik and Rita, the daughter of Sango. News came by telephone that 60 people died in Teller and all those who were at Aghiapok.
>
> Dec. 1—Death continues its ravages. Tullik passes away at about 7 p.m. Ubleneak receives the last sacraments. He is not expected to live long. . . .I go to the Igloo after mass and come back with two new dogs, one reindeer carcass, about 100 lbs. of fish and medicines of all description.
>
> 2—The list of deaths becomes longer still. Ubleneak and the infant of Uzirvik die. . . .
>
> 3—The children assist at mass: they begin to revive. . . .We chop wood, carry water and hay. No death, thank God.
>
> 4—Annaolik and his wife give us serious fears, as does the boy Atajok.

5—Death goes away with 2 more victims, the mother of Ubleneak who died of old age and the infant child of Atajok; the one 80 years old, the other about 10 months. . . .

6—No death today. The survivors improve. Mr. Isidore [Isadore] Fix pays us a visit and makes preparations for the burial of the dead. The spot selected is the S.-W. grove of cottonwoods. . . .

8—All hands were on deck this morning. All our sick came down in the chapel. The gloom of death seems to be lifted up.[12]

On that same 8 December, Lafortune wrote to Sister Joseph Aloysius in Wheeling, West Virginia (OPA): "Your kind letter finds me in a deluge of occupations. Were it within your power to pay me a short visit, you would find my house filled with orphans and sick people. Near by, in a tent, you would see seven corpses. At six miles from here, scattered in different igloos, you would see forty other corpses. You are horrified? If you go to Nome, you will find 160 corpses, at Teller 60, etc. . . .

"Hardly was the ordeal over in Nome, when I learned that my flock up here [Hot Springs] had the disease. I hurried up to their help. Twenty-three were already dead. I gathered thirty in my house. Seven died on my hands. The others are convalescent. I am alone with a good man, but one old and feeble. No Brother, no Sister. It is awful. I do not know how to take care of babies and small children. We feed them as best we can. We see to it that they are not too dirty. What else can we do? What consoles me is that they surely are better [off] than they have ever been at home.

"The money which you so kindly sent me will be used to buy clothes for those poor little ones. Our thermometer is down to -30. One needs warm clothes to stand that temperature."

By 10 December, the sick at the Hot Springs were "going very nicely."[13] Despite the recent tragedy, Lafortune plunged into Christmas plans with great energy. On the fifteenth he went to Marys Igloo to bring back "the organ, a stove, some muktuk [edible whale skin], etc. etc., preparatory to Xmas." The next day he set out for Nome "to buy necessary things for Xmas such as toys and candies." While there he heard that the village of Wales had been "nearly wiped out of existence" in the epidemic. On the twenty-second he took Christmas presents to those still living at Marys Igloo, and brought back "a load of junks necessary here for Xmas: the concert box, the crib, the Xmas tree, etc. etc."

On the day before Christmas he went again to Marys Igloo to visit the sick and to provide things needed there for the Christmas crib and tree, returning to the Hot Springs in the afternoon, when he and his lay assistants set up a Christmas crib. "That gives an air of festivity to our house." He then rehearsed his choir ("a few orphans and survivors") in Christmas hymns. After the midnight service, a lunch was served at this first Christmas celebration at the new orphanage, and by two in the morning all were in bed. By eight, all were up again; there was a Christmas tree in the afternoon, and more Christmas hymns in the evening.

The woodpile and two fish traps occupied the better part of Lafortune's free time during the rest of 1918, but he also milked cows, something he had not done for at least twenty-eight years. On the last day of the year he wrote in the diary, "The year 1918 is gone. . . .In the beginning of the year there were a good many Eskimos alive. The world was at war. At the end of the year, the world is in peace but the influenza continues to kill. Our natives have been mowed down like grass. Between 400 and 500 have disappeared in different localities.[14] The world was mourning over the ravages of the war. The world is still mourning over the ravages of the malady. O, the depth of the judgments of God."

Hugh Ibbetson, who worked and traveled with him at this time, said that Lafortune was "absolutely tireless and completely generous with his time. We often worked in the winter from before daylight until seven and eight at night. In the summer ten or twelve hours."[15] Passages selected from Lafortune's diary entries, between January and June 1919, give an idea of the work needed to operate an orphanage in the Alaskan wilds: "We carry wood the whole day. . .I go to the Igloo to see Sango who is sinking slowly . . .We chop wood. . .Our angora female dies, apparently of blood poison, due to the mauling of one of our dogs. . .We carry hay the whole day. . .We have to kill our beautiful calf. On account of lack of proper food the cow could not give milk enough to feed the calf properly. . .I start for Nome. . .I come back from Nome in company with Fr. Ruppert and Hugh Ibbetson. Both deserve a good rest after their trying work during the epidemy. We cross the Golden Gate divide facing -30 degrees and a good wind, and now our faces will take a new skin. . .We lose one of our horses.

Church at Pilgrim Hot Springs in 1972. *(National Park Service)*

Interior of the church at Pilgrim Hot Springs. Note painting above altar showing Our Lady of Lourdes—to whom the Hot Springs mission was dedicated—appearing to St. Bernadette. *(Oregon Province Archives)*

Old age . . .The thermometer around -50 degrees. . .One of our cows was taken sick. . .The thermometer registering -60 degrees. We do not go too far from the house. It is too cold for dogs and men. We chop wood, thrash wild rice. . .The thermometer is still going down, -68 . . .I go to Igloo [on 1 Feb.]. . .I leave for Nome[16] to give service to the Catholics of Nome, Fr. Ruppert not being well enough to go back. . .I come back from Nome after passing 3 days at Iron Creek storm bound. . .I chop wood the whole day. . .Our bull dies and one of our cows is on the brink of death. . .Our cow "Victoria" dies. God's will be done! . . .I buy 250 pounds of dry fish from John Kakaarzuk at 8 cents a pound. . .The storm which broke out last night nearly caused the roof [of the bathhouse] to flounder. . .I go to Igloo. . .I carry and chop wood from the neighbor grove. . . The weather is exceedingly mild [22 Feb.]. . .My two new dogs give proof of being really good dogs. . .David Tutmaarzuk gave us a reindeer. . .The bathhouse is working like a charm. . .On the 7th [of March] I left for Teller. . .The billy goat covered the two females and the little ones are due in the last part of July. Good for billy. . . [On 1 April] we begin the work in the greenhouse. . . Fr. Lafortune returns from Nome with Hugh. An extraordinary weather [on 7 May] prevails. . .It is nothing less than the breakup . . .Two days ago we put a net in the slough. We now have all the fish we want. . .The weather is ideal."

Concerning one of Lafortune's mundane activities, wood gathering, Ibbetson recalls: "During the winter we used wood cut along the river for heating and cooking. It had to be hauled to the mission on a bobsled pulled by the dogs after the snow fell. One day Father and I went to get a load. The wood was piled among the willows on the river bank. The snow was about two feet deep. We stopped near the piled wood and carried it to the sled. Father, as usual, was not satisfied to carry an ordinary armful, but stacked it in his arms as high as his face so that he was unable to see where he was going. About the third load he tripped over a snag under the snow and went flying, the wood all over, and landed head first up to his shoulders in the snow. He got up digging the snow from under his collar, brushing it out of his parky, and said, 'Son of a gun'—only that is not just what he said. Then back to work, not quite so much wood at a time."[17]

Ibbetson also wrote: "He was always in a hurry. A 12-hour day very seldom gave him enough time to accomplish all that he had in mind. Nothing ever stopped him once he got started. One day in the early spring, before the snowbanks were thawed, Father, Gus Wheeler, the mail carrier, and I were going north from Nome, when we came to a snowslide from the side of a mountain to the river. We decided to take the sleds across one at a time, so we hooked both teams to a sled and started. Gus was at the front of the sled pushing up; I was above with a rope to hold it from sliding down; and Father was behind pushing. He couldn't see ahead. I slid down under the sled. Gus said, 'Whoa!' Father said, 'It's all right, it's all right. Let's go!' Gus said, 'It's all right, is it? Hugh is under the sled. It's all right?' He was always in a hurry.''[18]

Although some children had come to the orphanage at the end of 1918, Lafortune and his helpers were not prepared to care for the many who had been orphaned in the epidemic. There was neither the room nor the personnel to handle them. Father Ruppert wrote to his Father Provincial: ''The children have been handed over by the Government to such institutions as were ready to receive them . . . .If only Hot Springs were ready! But without houses, and without Sisters, what can we do?''[19]

In June, Father Post returned from a trip ''outside'' and took charge of the mission at the Hot Springs, and although this freed Lafortune again to be a missionary at large to the Eskimos, he continued to work

Nuns and orphans at Pilgrim Hot Springs, June 1922. *(Oregon Province Archives)*

at the Hot Springs for the rest of the year. On 3 July, with the help of Bailey and Ibbetson, he began "to prepare quarters for a larger number of orphans," and on 4 August a dozen more orphans arrived at the mission, "drenched to the skin but all looked happy. They were given a warm meal and felt better. They were given sleeping quarters and had to remain abed till their clothes were nearly dried as we had no change for them."

On 15 August, Brother John Hansen, S. J., arrived, and the next day "marked a notable event, the arrival, namely, of 5 Ursuline Nuns who come to look after the little orphans." On 14 October, Lafortune went to Iron Creek Station to bring Brother Peter Wilhalm, S. J., to the mission. The Hot Springs staff was then complete: one priest, two Brothers and five Sisters, in addition to the lay help. On 3 December, Lafortune left for Nome.[20]

6 / Nome, 1920-1928

Lafortune's headquarters for the next nine years were in Nome, but during the winters, he spent a large amount of time on the trail, visiting his widely dispersed parishioners, especially at the Hot Springs where he was always warmly welcomed. Lafortune was alone at St. Joseph's during the winter of 1921-22 because Ruppert was ordered to go to Holy Cross. "The little Father" settled into the routine that he had maintained for nearly twenty years, especially in having groups of from twelve to twenty Eskimos gather for instruction.

"They take interest in it," he wrote in the "Litterae Annuae Domus" (annual letters of the house to Superiors). "Although games are at their disposal, as soon as we begin to get ready for religious instruction, they forthwith quit their games and show themselves very attentive."[1]

The makeup of both Nome and St. Joseph's Church had changed in twenty years. Lafortune wrote to the Father Provincial: "The camp being on its decline, our ministries are also on the decline. The white Catholic population has become so small that, were it not for the natives, we might just as well close our doors and make of this place a visiting post. The native population is on the increase. Quite a few have quitted the islands where there is no school and came to Nome to give a chance to their children to learn something. . . .About three times more natives than whites come to church. They have their own choir and the nine o'clock Mass is for them, but the whites are not excluded. . . .In summer, when the islanders come to swell our congregation by about two hundred, we use the large church for the natives and our chapel for the whites. . . .If the white population keeps on decreasing, this place will have to be supported some way or other.

There is no possible way for a priest to be self-supporting here. He would have to go mining and even then he would be starving.''[2]

On 16 June 1922, when Ruppert came back from Holy Cross, Lafortune returned to his work with the Eskimos.[3] He had, however, the responsibility of St. Joseph's choir, of which he was very proud. He trained his own organists, and was a very demanding choirmaster. He was never satisfied until the notes were sung exactly as written and the various voices blended harmoniously. Often he would sing along in a ''delightful, deep singing voice.''[4] Toward the end of 1922, however, the choir had become a source of concern and he wrote to his bishop: ''My parish is going down all the time. When the *Victoria* has left, there will not be one single member of the choir left. A new choir will have to be organized and the Lord knows where I will find the material. I have a pretty good Eskimo choir, but the whites would feel hurt if I have the natives sing in their place. I will let them without music for a few Sundays and I will see what they will have to say. I have to be very careful. There are a few snobs in the parish. They do not want the natives to go beyond a certain limit. Instead of giving them the example of charity, they brush them aside. That sets my blood a boiling sometime.''[5]

The weather of 1923 was unusual from the very beginning of the year. Natural signs—rings around the sun, flamboyant northern lights—seemed to portend tragedy. ''The new year,'' said Lafortune, ''was ushered in by a blizzard.'' In February, after he returned to Nome from a visit of fifteen days in Teller, he was called back by the death of W. Marx who, ''in returning from Ear Mountain fell down a very high bluff, buffeted by the storm, was hurt badly and froze to death.''[6]

In March, ''very mild weather'' prevailed for a few days and traveling became difficult. At the Hot Springs, on 25 April, Post wrote in the diary that it was ''quite cold during the night. There were 3 rings about the sun—pointing in different directions about 11 this morning. 2 disappeared shortly and one around the sun remained greater part of afternoon.''[7]

The breakup of the ice was early that spring and the summer was beautiful, ''the best summer since 1903,'' wrote Lafortune. Yet, ''some miners complain that it is too dry.''[8]

In the middle of September, Lafortune again commented on the extraordinary weather conditions. With some foreboding he wrote: ''The summer keeps on. The nights are warm. We learn of the destruction of

Yokohama and Tokyo [earthquake on 1 September]; but here the weather is splendid. We heard that it snowed in Chicago and the middle states. Here there is not even white frost. It is most extraordinary. Some people are apprehensive."[9]

In October the northern lights were unusually beautiful three nights in a row. On the seventeenth, Father Post wrote, "Last night we had again northern light display, the most wonderful I had ever noticed—four different semi-circles—all in motion in wave and ribbon form. The whole night proved clear as if the moon were up in all its splendor. Even in the early morning the lights were still to be seen."[10]

On 8 October 1923, Father Ruppert, James Halpin, and Bob Ummaok, the mail carrier, left Nome for the Hot Springs,[11] and on 15 October, Ruppert began his retreat. After his retreat he gave eight-day retreats to the Sisters and to the Brothers, separated by a three-day retreat to the children.

On the morning of Thursday, 13 December, Ruppert and Aloysius, a young man from Nome, left the Hot Springs for Nome, each driving a dogteam (Ruppert was using Father Lafortune's team). They were followed an hour later by the mail carrier's team. Although it had snowed a little the night before, the trail was in poor condition for lack of snow. On the fourteenth, the weather was "cold, but dry," and on the fifteenth it was thirty degrees below zero Fahrenheit, and clear; but on the sixteenth, Sunday, it warmed up, and the wind began to blow. It blew all night, but by then the people at the Hot Springs assumed that Ruppert had arrived safely in Nome.[12]

On Monday afternoon, however, one of Ruppert's lead dogs, Mudd, returned to the Hot Springs, half-starved. A little later, "Old John" Kakaruk arrived with the news that he had seen tracks of a man and two dogs, which seemed mysterious to him. At daybreak the next morning, Old John, Brother Wilhalm, Brother Hansen, A. Carey, and Eddie Maloney set out to investigate, the Brothers returning a little after three o'clock with the news that they had found Father Ruppert's frozen body, carefully watched over by faithful old Mink. This dog did not recognize them at first, and though cold and shivering and nearly starved, had stayed near the body. It had not touched Ruppert but had eaten the fur lining out of his cap.[13]

On 22 December, Fred Topkok, who had been hired by Father Post, left by dogteam to take letters to Lafortune in Nome, telling of Ruppert's death.[14] Topkok arrived in Nome on the twenty-third, and by Christmas Eve, news of Father Ruppert's death had spread far and wide and had captured headlines in the world's leading newspapers: "Priest Dies Martyr of Charity," read the headlines of the Paris edition of the *New York Herald Tribune*.

The finding of Ruppert's body posed many questions. Why was he found four miles upstream when the mission and Nome lay in the opposite direction? Why was he in shirt sleeves, wearing only a short, sleeveless sweater? Where was his parka? Where were his sled and the other dogs? And why did the two dogs accounted for have no harness—Mudd, not even a collar?[15]

The tragedy, so far as can be pieced together from letters and diary entries by those close to Ruppert at that time, had resulted from the actions of an impetuous, daring man who was a poor dog musher. The driver and team who accompanied him and the mail carrier, Ummaok (accompanied by his brother Norbert and a boy named Stanislaus), had been ordered by Post to go with Ruppert all the way to Nome because of his reputation as a man who frequently got lost, and who would take grave risks—he would not hesitate to hike alone on a cross-country trek or to swim the icy waters of the Pilgrim.[16] Post, in letters to his Superiors, and also for Lafortune's benefit, stressed the point that Ruppert had more than adequate escort. Lafortune had a very low opinion of Ruppert's dog-mushing abilities and had earlier asked the mail carrier "to bring him in [to Nome]."[17]

The travelers had spent the night of the thirteenth at Duffy O'Connor's roadhouse, about twenty-five miles from the Hot Springs. There they found a box of oranges, which Ruppert himself had brought from Nome in October, but could not take all the way to the mission because of the poor trail. Ruppert was determined to return and take the oranges to the mission, although his Eskimo traveling companions, following the instructions they had eceived from both Post and Lafortune, made every effort to talk him out of starting for the Hot Springs alone. But he insisted and started out alone.[18]

This was the first in a chain of mistakes which, added together, became a fatal error. For some reason his Eskimo escorts did not accompany him. It might have been out of exasperation at his foolhardiness at returning on so flimsy an errand. More likely it was because they took all too literally the order that they were to accompany Father Ruppert to Nome.

Lafortune wrote, "He was not a dog driver and he knew it; he was hampered by his glasses and he knew that it was a great drawback. He knew also that there are always deers on the mountains and my dogs were wild for them. Finally, he knew that the children had all the candies and pies and nuts that they wanted. What possessed him to go to the Springs anyway is more than I can say. He had to die on the banks of the Pilgrim River and he could not dodge it. . . ."[19]

Ruppert's sled was found in September 1924 on the old trail that led from Iron Creek to Nome via the Golden Gate pass. Brother Hansen made the discovery as he was on his way to a dental appointment in Nome. So, after leaving the roadhouse, Ruppert apparently had traveled about twelve miles, then unhitched the dogs, tucked the dog harness under the bow of the sled, and started to walk toward the mission. But having walked six miles on the trail, he came out on the Pilgrim River above the mission, instead of below; and with darkness coming on, got lost in the willows, which are very thick in that area.[20] Ruppert's parka and two sacks, one containing two hundred dollars in paper bills, were found about fifty feet behind the sled, but the box of oranges was never found.

There was much speculation as to why he had unhitched the dogs and started to walk to the mission, although it was generally agreed that the trail was poor with only a little soft snow. Possibly he thought the dogs were becoming tired halfway to the mission, and so let them loose because it was getting late. Some persons surmised that the dogs had begun to chase reindeer, but the investigations proved that this had not happened.

Other unanswered questions were—why had he taken off his parka and left it behind in such cold weather, and why had he not made a fire? At the time it was thought that he had taken off his parka because he was warm from walking, or because a person who is freezing to death sometimes is deluded into believing he is hot and takes off his clothing.

In the short time that he had been on Seward Peninsula, Ruppert had been liked by all. During the 1918 influenza epidemic he had worked hard day and night. The people at the Hot Springs enjoyed his visits, and as the Mother Superior once said, "It seems as if nothing can go wrong while he is here." *The Nome Nugget* praised him for the good deeds that he had done for others regardless of race, color, or creed, and even Lafortune, Ruppert's severest critic, said that he "was very good and bright in many ways, but his utter lack of practical sense was the cause of his death, nothing else. . . . His intention was good but how impractical.''[21]

In 1924, Lafortune was the only priest in Nome, except during the summer, when Martin Lonneux, a young priest new to Alaska, was his assistant. In 1925, although still alone in Nome, Lafortune spent most of April and May on the trail. The summer months were ''tough,'' he wrote to Lonneux, who was then at Akulurak. Not only had he been alone the whole summer, but he had had ''a heap of unusual work: sickness, deaths, visitors, orders from all sides for hides, ivory, mukluks, etc. etc.'' He even ''had to brush up and cook three weeks'' because three of his visitors were nuns who could not cook. At the same time, ''people were sick and dying down [at] the Standard Oil [where Eskimos were camped], in the hospital and at home. I attended to them all, but I had to be on my feet, believe me.''[22]

In December of 1925, his burden was lightened when Post returned from the Hot Springs to take Ruppert's place.

By 1925, Lafortune had been in Alaska twenty-two years, and though he had met frustrations, setbacks, and tragedies, he was inseparably wedded to the north country. He wrote to Lonneux, ''When we come to this country, we become glued to it in such a way that we cannot quit anymore. Even poor Father Jetté had to come back. They did not make a steel rope strong enough yet to pull Fr. Tréca out, and you just as well move the Kusilvak mole [Kusilvak Mountains, Yukon-Kuskokwim delta] to the sea as to transport Fr. Robaut. That will be the way with you. You will become 'entiché' *[sic,* ''wedded to''].''[23]

The next year, commenting to his niece, Sister Marie-Flavius, on the mild winter on Seward Peninsula, he tried to explain what the country meant to him. ''What a shame that you are so far away from me. I would take you on a trip that you would never forget. I have been here for 23 years, and I have never seen such a winter. It is simply a pleasure to travel. . . .Those who live in the cities and towns have no idea of the marvels of nature. What you see in the movies is absolutely insignificant when compared with what we see on our trips. If the poets had traveled to Alaska, they would have thrown their pens into the fire out of despair, and the painters would have lost their minds. God knows how to compensate us in our miseries.''[24]

On 29 March 1925, the Catholic Eskimos of Nome had formed ''a society for the spiritual and temporal betterment of its members,'' called "St. Joseph's Society," which met on the last Sunday of every month. In December the Society held a meeting "in which was discussed the advisability of opening the native building for native dances. The idea back of it is to knock the Hunter Saloon dancing hall in which young squaws and the scum of the white population meet and dance the white man's dances." It was decided, however, to leave the decision up to the women, and in a meeting on 3 January 1926 they voted unanimously to open the native building for dances. Non-Catholics were to be invited on the condition that they behaved perfectly —"therefore no boozing, no familiarities between different sexes."[25]

In 1926, Lafortune and Post met several famous visitors who had come to Nome: Roald Amundsen, the Norwegian polar explorer, Lincoln Ellsworth, financier, and Umberto Nobile, the Italian designer and pilot of the dirigible *Norge*, which had brought them over the North Pole to Teller; and Aleš Hrdlička, a physical anthropologist from the Smithsonian Institution.

Nobile, in his book, *My Polar Flights*, said, "Waiting for us were Father Lafortune and Father Post. . . .The whole population greeted us very cordially. The two missionaries, delighted by a message that I had brought from Rome, from the General of the Jesuits, Father Vladimir Ledochovski [Wlodimir Ledochowski], and all the more so because it was the first and only letter that had come from Europe to America by such an unusual route, could not do enough for me.

"They were my favorite company during the fortnight I stayed at Nome, especially Father Lafortune, a Canadian who had dedicated 25 years to educating the Eskimos. He knew their minds, their habits, their needs, and their language better than any other man."[26]

On 5 June, the Catholics of Nome entertained Nobile and his crew with a splendid banquet in the parish hall, and before leaving Nome the visitors enjoyed several restful days at the Hot Springs.[27]

Hrdlička arrived one month after Nobile's departure. He had prolonged visits with Lafortune before leaving on the *Bear* on 23 July to go north.[28] In his *Alaska Diary* Hrdlička wrote: "After breakfast go to meet Brother Lafortune. Find a sturdy but lively short Frenchman (by origin) of about 50. Speaks the Eskimo language. . . .He is a matter-of-fact, always ready to help, natural he-man, rather than a priest or a teacher, and a great practical helper to the natives, all of whom are his devoted friends; worth, in these parts of the world, ten in a pulpit. Not long ago, others tell me, carried a dead Eskimo on his own shoulders to where the body could be taken care of."

Hrdlička attended "a little service, for the natives mainly, at the Church of Fathers Post and Lafortune. Church poor, service simple, but sincere."[29]

John A. Concannon, S. J., arrived on 27 August to replace Post, who had returned to the Hot Springs.[30] Concannon, who stayed in Nome only a year (he was replaced in September 1927 by Patrick F. Savage, S. J.), wrote in his reminiscences that on his arrival in Nome, Father Lafortune insisted on carrying his baggage. "That was typical of him, I soon found out. He would do the work! Later on when I tried to wash the dishes, or bring in the coal, or sweep, or rise early to start the fires, merely hoping to be helpful, he gently let me know how little there was for him to do. The old sourdough had done all this too many years to be content to do less.

"Short of stature yet sturdily built, cheerful but withal serious—it wasn't long before he left an indelible impression upon me. He was respected by all who knew him, and warmly admired by all who knew him well. He was friendly to everyone but encouraged no one's particular friendship. They were all 'God's children' in his eyes.

"Perhaps I remember less what he said than what he did. He was a 'do'er of the word' rather than a talker. Not a good conversationalist —he was too self-effacing for that and too remote from worldly affairs—he would chat on occasion when primed by a leading question. Even then he seemed reluctant to speak about himself, and his words were few.

"Totally disinterested in himself, he was vitally concerned with those committed to his care."[31]

In July 1928, an epidemic of smallpox broke out among the Eskimos—mostly King Islanders—and Lafortune was kept busy visiting them, dispensing remedies, or acting as interpreter for the doctor.[32] Lafortune wrote to his niece, "The summer is passed and I am not sorry. I have never run so much. All the Eskimos were sick with what our doctor called 'chicken pox.' Whatever that epidemy was, it robbed me of seven Eskimos, and the others, especially the adults were sick as dogs *[comme des chiens]*. . . .In the end my legs refused to move, but that did not last long. I am now ready again to make forty miles a day."[33]

Lafortune's assistant, Savage, proved to be a man poorly suited for work in the Nome area. After having addressed so many pleas to his Superiors for an able assistant to help him with the Eskimo mission, Lafortune must have found it extremely trying to have been sent a man like Savage; yet, he never showed his impatience with Savage's shortcomings, especially with his inability to learn the Eskimo language and to cope with missionary work in the North. Proof that he had masked his opinion of Savage is found in the latter's written comment that Father Lafortune "is a very kind Superior and an agreeable companion, and has done much to make my work here very pleasant."[34]

The year 1928 marked the silver jubilee of Lafortune's missionary life in Alaska, but he apparently did not pay the slightest attention to it. His fellow Jesuits in Alaska, however, had become increasingly aware of his total dedication to his Eskimo apostolate and of the good results he was obtaining. Accordingly, in 1928 and 1929, higher Superiors in Alaska, in Portland, Oregon, and in Rome exchanged letters concerning the timeliness of officially recognizing his work. The General Superior of the Alaska mission, Philip I. Delon, S. J., wrote on 30 July 1928 to the Jesuit Provincial, Joseph Piet: "Do you know that this is [Father Lafortune's] silver jubilee of missionary life in Alaska? Were he in Holy Cross, we would certainly do something to show the appreciation of the Society for his tireless labors and devotedness, and for the results that he has obtained. . . .Someone has suggested that, in reward for his missionary activities, he could and should be given the Profession of four vows, on the technical plea of *peritia linguae indigenae* [expertise in the native language]."[35]

This meant that Lafortune would be permitted to pronounce the four solemn vows that would admit him to the ranks of the Solemnly Professed Fathers of the Society of Jesus. In the Jesuit Order, this permission is rarely granted to one who has, as Lafortune had, already pronounced his final vows. It is granted for only a limited number of reasons: exceptional ability to govern; some superior intellectual achievement; manifestations of outstanding virtue over a long period of time; or a combination of some of these. The Society of Jesus does not often reward its members with honors since it is presumed that they are motivated and guided by its motto, "all to the greater glory of God." In the case of Lafortune, though, Delon, supported by others, felt that recognition and honor were more than amply deserved, and the Father

Provincial in Portland and the Father General in Rome concurred with him.

Both Eskimos and whites agreed that Lafortune was extremely proficient in the Eskimo language. Some of the Eskimos had told Concannon that "he knew it better than they," although he spoke it with a "stiff tongue" (French accent). Lonneux, who also learned to speak Eskimo well, said that "Father Lafortune knew his Eskimo language as no one else ever did so far." Lafortune always read the Sunday gospel in Latin first, then translated it into Eskimo "just like he'd be talking to the people," said one of his Eskimo parishioners.[36] Sometimes the Eskimos had difficulty understanding him because he spoke too rapidly. Eskimos who remember Lafortune said that he always spoke "re—al fast," and Joseph McElmeel, S. J., wrote that he spoke "the Eskimo language fluently, and ten times faster than any Eskimo."[37]

For Lafortune, speaking the language was a tool to use in his work among the Eskimos, and his Eskimo writings—hymns, catechism, a life of Christ, a dictionary, and a grammar—were intended solely as a mnemonic device for him, and as a benefit to a successor.[38]

On 16 July 1929, Lafortune made his Solemn Profession of the three vows of poverty, chastity, and obedience, and of a fourth vow—special obedience to the Supreme Pontiff. For Lafortune this profession was purely honorific, making no visible difference in either his internal or external life. What Concannon described as a "signal honor," Lafortune acknowledged in a letter to his Father Provincial, Piet, on 24 July: "Your Reverence granted me a very unexpected and unmerited favor by admitting me to the four vows of the Professed of the Society. Had my consent been asked, I would have refused, not because I don't value those vows, but because the Society expects from its professed a service that in many instances I cannot render. I will do the best I can; that is all what I can possibly promise."[39]

7 / King Island: Developing Plans

Less than two years after his arrival in Nome, Lafortune was agitating to have a mission established on King Island, and in a letter to Crimont in 1906 he outlined his ideas (see Chapter 3), saying that he was "ready to go" to King Island. By that time there were already a number of Catholics among the King Islanders, whom he had baptized in Nome.

The King Island people seemed to have enjoyed a very special place in Lafortune's life from the first time he met them in 1904. In 1929 he began his house diary, "History of the Mission of King Island," by writing a brief account of his initial encounter with them and of their subsequent conversion and fidelity to Catholicism before he lived on the island.

Lafortune attributed their rapid conversion to the leadership of their "chief," Andrew Aresac, who, upon seeing "the behavior of the Catholics in the church. . .made up his mind to belong to that religion."[1] His conversion, however, seems to have been based on more than just approval of Catholics in the church. It seems to have been motivated also by a somewhat apocryphal event, the circumstances that surrounded the death of his daughter (or his niece) in 1905. One day, her father put a clock in her hands and asked her when she would go to heaven. She pointed to three o'clock, and at three o'clock she died. "That settled it with the King Islanders," wrote Lafortune, "The years after they entered the fold by gangs, till they all became Catholics." Aresac's house then served as a kind of chapel where the people gathered on Sundays for prayers.[2]

History of the mission of King-Island.

Ever since the beginning of the gold mining camp of Nome, the King-Islanders were wont to pass ne part of the summer in Nome, their primary object being the selling of their goods and the buying of their provisions and clothings; and the secondary to enjoy the excitement of a white man's city. As by enchantment the houses were multiplying along more or less regular streets; machinary of all sorts was landed and put into action without any delay. To their great amazement, gold was found on a beach which their ancestors had treaded for centuries.

But in all that activity Almighty God had his plans, very much unsuspected by the gold seekers. At the corner of Steadman Ave. and Kings way a church was built with a high spire surmounted by a cross electricaly lit at night. The King-Islanders noticed a pretty good size congregation frequenting that church. They understood it was a place of worship.

In 1902 Fr. Cataldo, although very old and sickly, began to evangelize the Nome natives. His devotion drew quite a few of them. Naturaly they became apostles in their turn and spoke to all the natives about the kind of worship which was takeing place in a catholic church &c &c. In 1903 a young father was sent from Canada to Holy Cross, (for then the Alaskan mission belonged to the province of Canada). Father Cataldo stopped him in Nome and by order of the superiors, he succeeded Fr. Cataldo in the apostolate of the eskimos. That was bruited abroad and in the summer of 1904 a bunch of King-Islanders showed up and was received very cordialy. Some of these had been to a protestant

First page of Lafortune's "History of the Mission of King Island." This diary was begun in October 1929. *(Oregon Province Archives)*

Almost every year from then on, Lafortune made his desires and dreams about King Island known in letters and reports. On 4 December 1907, he wrote to Crimont again, urging action on behalf of the King Islanders: "We have now 60 Catholics in that island, i.e., a good majority. There is no government school as yet, and if we could be there before the government, we would be absolute masters of the place, and I consider it as an immense advantage. Of course, it is not anybody that can be sent in that exile."[3]

The specter of a "government school" on the island was a threat that constantly urged him on to the building of a mission. A government school, as Lafortune saw it in the context of his French Canadian Catholic training, was either a godless institution or a Protestant Bible school supported by the government. For this reason he was vehemently opposed to the establishment of schools—except for a certain type of Catholic school. Also, he believed that the Eskimos at that stage of their acculturation had no need for schools, which might cause them more harm than good.[4]

In 1908 and 1909, he repeated his desire to go to King Island (and also to Little Diomede Island where some Catholic Eskimos lived) but, without a boat, he complained, "our work is paralyzed."[5] In 1913, he visited Little Diomede for the first time, on the maiden voyage of the *Immaculate II* (see Chapter 4). His stay was very short because of the dangers of floating ice, but he said that "the natives were delighted with our visit; they begged us to come again and build a church and house for a priest to abide with them."[6] He could not get to King Island, however, because they could find no lead through the ice.

Finally, in June 1916, Lafortune visited King Island. Post wrote in the "Historia Domus" (Nome): "In the month of [June], by a special favor of Captain [C. S.] Cochran, skipper of the U.S. ship *Bear*, Fr. Lafortune visited King Island for 8 days. He returned on the same ship greatly pleased with the good disposition of the natives."[7]

He administered baptism to a large number, so that all on the island were Catholic when he left "with the exception of two (2) stragglers," a success that was largely due to Kattak, a young man who had been baptized the previous year in Nome, and had in his fervor on his own initiative acted as catechist and prepared quite a few for baptism.[8]

That year Aresac died, and his house where the people had gathered for Sunday prayers passed into other hands. The Eskimos then built a temporary chapel out of lumber given them by the priests of Nome.[9]

Aerial view of King Island. *(Oregon Province Archives)*

King Island, in 1916, except for the houses, was probably much the same as when it was seen for the first time in 1732 by the Russian surveyor, Mikhail Gvozdev, who had sailed from Kamchatka to the Bering Strait. This island, which was called ''Okibian'' on a map drawn in 1743 by Gvozdev, was officially discovered and named King Island by Captain James Cook of the English Royal Navy, after his executive officer, Lieutenant James King.[10] The village on King Island is still known as ''Ukivok'' on the maps of Alaska. This name, variously transcribed *ukiuvok* and *ugiuvuk*, means ''big winter'' or ''winter home'' and reflects the traditional yearly cycle of the Bering Strait Islanders who spent the winter months in isolation and the summers traveling along the mainland coasts.[11]

King Island—only two and a half miles long, a mile and a half wide, and from seven hundred to twelve hundred feet high—rises abruptly out of the dark blue-green waters of the Bering Sea, thirty-five miles from Cape Douglas on the coast of the Seward Peninsula, and some ninety miles northwest of Nome.[12] The longer axis is oriented east and west, and sheer cliffs ring the island except for the slight embayments in the southern and northwestern shorelines where the slopes are somewhat less steep. The island has no beaches, and granite boulders rounded off by the waves provide landing spots in only three places.

For eight months of the year the inhabitants were totally isolated. Almost all of the white persons who have visited King Island describe it as a wild, rugged, desolate, and isolated pile of rocks,[13] but Lafortune described it as ''a true paradise. Wherever you look [in the spring] you see nature, immense, wild, without a trace of human efforts to improve it, and the whole covered with a vegetation that God alone controls. In the distance you see the coast of Siberia, the Diomede islands, the chain of the Sawtooth Mountains and Sledge Island near Nome. Above your head you see thousands of sea birds circling in all directions and creating an infernal racket."[14]

Bedrock in King Island consists almost entirely of coarsely crystalline and porphyritic granite. On the upland plateau, rows of massive bedrock spires and monuments, like so many ancient megalithic giants, stand above ground level. Generally, the rounded hilltops and steeper slopes are covered with rubble of large granite boulders—some measuring fifteen feet across—while the gentler intervening slopes are surfaced with a rocky, silty soil. About fifty yards east of the village, a small stream, called *kuuk*, drains most of the upland surface through a gully. The stream provides water for the village during the summer and the fall; snow is melted during the rest of the year.

The village was built on the south side of the island on a rock slide two hundred feet wide, with a pitch of about forty degrees to the ocean. Earlier generations of King Islanders lived in semi-subterranean dugouts with a short tunnel. In 1881 there were, in the sides of the cliffs, forty or fifty of these cavelike dwellings which, according to John Muir, who visited the island in July 1881, "rise like heaps of stones among heaps of stones."[15]

King Island people posing on one of their house platforms in 1885.
(From Healy 1887, following page 10)

Ukivok on King Island in the early twentieth century. *(Lomen Brothers photograph. Oregon Province Archives)*

Ukivok in 1974. *(Photograph by Louis L. Renner, S. J.)*

Sometime during the second half of the nineteenth century, a new kind of house was built on the island—a cube-like structure perched ingeniously, but precariously, on tall driftwood poles. From a distance the village looked like a cluster of swallows' nests. Lafortune described these houses as built "on sticks. . . .Out of driftwood they make a sort of platform or shelf. On top of it they build their houses. Naturally they are very small. The walls are made out of rawhides between which they pack dry moss or hay. The roof is made the same way. There is no tunnel in front of those houses, but there is a large storeroom. The whole structure is firmly lashed to the platform with rawhide ropes. When it blows, the whole thing rocks like a cradle. At times it shakes so violently that they cannot sleep at all. One end of the beams of the platform is driven in the holes of the mountain, and the other is fastened to vertical posts varying in length according to the steepness of the mountain. Some of these posts are fifteen feet long. The houses are built at least 150 feet above sea level to be out of danger of the waves. Even at that height the foam of their furious seas frequently covers their houses."[16]

By the thirteenth year after Lafortune's first and only visit to King Island, prior to his permanent move there, a third kind of dwelling was replacing the old dugouts and houses on stilts. These little one-room houses of dressed lumber were described by Patrick J. O'Reilly, S. J., who visited King Island and said mass there in October 1928:

"The entrance to the igloo is through a shelter-porch where the household supplies, besides sleds, guns and fishing apparatus, are stored; then, there is another entrance, strictly private, just large enough for a man's body to pass through. It is operated from the inside, somewhat after the manner of a confessional shutter, but low down on a plane with the floor. My Eskimo host helped me to slide in, and, once inside, I felt like being in a kind of fairy dwelling. The dimensions of his apartment were 8 by 10, and the height 6 feet. There were two small windows in keeping with the smallness of the place, and none of the space was lost by the use of chairs, tables, or beds. A seal oil lamp took the place of a stove, and instead of ordinary beds, the skins of animals were neatly folded at one end of the room, while the smooth wooden floor served in lieu of chairs."[17]

Why would people choose this kind of place for a home? The main reason was because of the island's location in the midst of an abundance of sea-mammal life that provided meat, skins, bone, and ivory for their basic needs. The island lies in the direct route of the annual spring and fall walrus migrations. In the spring the northward-flowing current carries ice floes into the Chukchi Sea, and the walrus —especially the cows and calves—haul out on these floes to rest. In the fall, the Eskimos had another opportunity to hunt as the walrus headed south to their wintering grounds.

Besides seals and walrus, the King Islanders also got whales and polar bears, and fished for crabs, shrimp, cod, and bullheads through holes in the ice. From the upland plateau and the rocky cliffs of the island they gathered large quantities of edible plants and captured innumerable birds—murres, puffins—and their eggs. Although the soil on the island is shallow, it is rich in plant nutrients from the guano deposited over the centuries by the countless birds that nest there every summer; and though there are no trees or large shrubs, many grasses, mosses, sedges, and flowering plants abound—among them at least ten different varieties of edible plants. The island is a natural vegetable garden.

The islanders were rarely faced with starvation because they preserved their food in a natural, year-round deepfreeze, a large double-chambered cave called *kaitco*, located a quarter of a mile east of the village. The food preserved in this cave had often tided them over periods of bad weather or bad hunting.

The King Islanders were also seafaring traders and prominent middlemen for a lively native trade in the greater Bering Strait area prior to the Nome gold rush.[18] In their large skinboats they ranged from Cape Dezhnev (East Cape), Siberia, to Saint Michael, near the mouth of the Yukon River; and from Saint Lawrence Island to Point Hope, beyond the arctic circle. It can thus be seen that they were not the isolated people that many visitors to their island thought, and in the ethnocentric view of all persons who love their homeland, it would have been hard to convince them that the very axis of the earth did not pass straight through the heart of that "melancholy granite rock."[19]

The isolation of that "melancholy" island was one of its most valuable attributes from Lafortune's viewpoint. There the Eskimos would be protected from the corrupting influence of the whites, and there he could carry out his mission in accordance with his plans for an Eskimo "center."

Every year, for thirteen years after his first visit to King Island in 1916, Lafortune hoped that he would be given permission to build a church there. In 1925 he wrote to Jetté, "We have 200 Catholics in

King Island and no priest for them."[20] By 1929 he was almost in despair. "I know nothing of the Superiors' or the bishop's ideas for the next summer," he wrote Lonneux on 5 June 1929. "Will any new Father come? Will they do something for King Island or any other place? I don't know. And I don't care to know."[21]

But Superiors were doing something about King Island, and on 20 June, the mission Superior, Delon, arrived in Nome with the news that materials for a church would soon be delivered at Teller.[22] At last, Lafortune's dreams of twenty-five years were to be realized.

The indecisiveness of Superiors was not entirely their fault because there had been movements afoot at various times to relocate the King Islanders elsewhere. In the early twenties, the Bureau of Education, which was planning to build a school for them, proposed that the people move to Saint Lawrence Island. To make the proposal more appealing, the Bureau offered to give two years' free provisions to all families, as well as easy and cheap opportunities of acquiring tame reindeer. In a meeting held to discuss the proposal, the people were given a specified time to make up their minds. Almost immediately they declared that they did not need any time—"not a single family wished to leave that barren island, which they loved and regarded as the finest settlement in the whole world."[23]

Even Lafortune himself suggested moving all the villagers to a place where he could minister to them more easily—and to pursue his principle of isolation. In 1923 he wrote a friend, "My natives of King Island have left last Sunday on the "Bear" for their cliffs. They are a fine bunch of natives. . . .I wish I could go and pass one winter with them. But I do not see my way to build a house large enough to hold them all. They are about 200 and their country is so steep that I would have to blast an immense shelf to put my house on. Their houses are built on sticks; but they are very small. A house large enough to hold them all could not be built that way. Therefore we have a mind to move them somewhere else. It is quite a problem."[24]

In 1924, he hit on the plan of moving them to Sledge Island, a smaller and less rugged island only twenty-five miles west of Nome. There was a precedent for this scheme. Some King Islanders had already spent winters on Sledge, but they always returned again to their own island, which they preferred. But Lafortune thought that this preference might be counterbalanced by the fact that Sledge Island was nearer Nome than King Island was, and that if a church, a priest, and a school would be provided, it might be an incentive to move. He knew that the King Island people wanted a school.[25]

Lafortune's school was to be private and Church-supported, the kind of school he so often denounced. To all appearances, it would be an ordinary school, but "the schooling," he frankly admitted, "would be only camouflage to teach the children their religion." He justified his proposed school on the grounds that "it would foreclose the danger of seeing the government and a siwash teacher there and destroy our work." The schools that Lafortune found so execrable were the government-supported public schools, which he presumed were often used by ministers of religion to proselytize—the so-called "contract schools."[26] He complained another time, "The government threatens to build a school for them and of course the schoolteacher will be one of those bible peddlers born in Sweden. Why don't we go? For lack of *men* and of *means*."[27]

In 1926, Lafortune advocated moving the Catholic Eskimos of Nome—and presumably also the King Islanders—to Cape Woolley, thirty-seven miles northwest of Nome. "Fr. Post and myself are scheming to take the Catholic Eskimos away from Nome," he wrote. "Nome is a wide opened town. The booze is flowing. Every influence is free to bring about the ruin of the natives." At Cape Woolley, he said, "We must have a tract of land from which we can expel the undesirable. . . .The lazy, sloppy, immoral, drunkards would be fired out of the premises."[28]

But he still wanted, above all, to go to King Island, or at least to be able to travel there. He also wanted to go to Little Diomede because in 1925 he learned that "a Lutheran missionary is establishing himself on the small Diomede where half of the population is Catholic and we have no priest to give to those people. It is galling. My dream is that two Fathers be here in Nome to attend to this place and help at the Springs and do the traveling around and that I be free to go alternately to King Island and to Diomede. Will my dream be realized before I die, God alone knows."[29]

In the years before Lafortune established a permanent mission on King Island, he had close contact with the islanders on their summer trips to Nome. He worried about their hunters, who were often in great danger hunting on the ice; was proud of their success as "expert longshoremen. . . .They unload 50 tons more per day than the whites";[30] and generally admired them: "I have never seen a group of men and women so toughened to endure hardships. They seem not to know what comfort means. To get here they have to paddle a whole night and a whole day. [One year, 1922, he said it took them two days and a night.] Upon arriving at ten o'clock in the evening, they immediately set about unloading their great skinboats. That done, they drag their boats up on the gravel beach, turn them on the side to camp under them. Finally, they brew themselves a cup of coffee, say a few prayers, wrap themselves in a blanket and sleep. I thought they would sleep the whole next day. At six in the morning they were up and in the church.''[31]

At another time he wrote, ''Every spring they all quit the island and come to Nome. When in Nome, they behave splendidly. They mean business. Every Sunday sees them in church and at the communion table. During the week they work like beavers, the men at their ivory, the women at their moccasins and boots. They buy provisions and clothes and go back happy as larks. No boozing, no loafing with those fellows. Eight or nine large skinboats (oomeaks) carry that crowd and about 8 tons of hides and ivory and utensils and dogs etc. etc. That gives you an idea of their boats. The Revenue Cutter takes them back, with all their provisions. There are beautiful souls among those people.''[32]

To his niece, he wrote, ''My people from the islands are truly a special breed. They are good, but they do not know the meaning of discipline. Their clock is the sun. They come to confess at all hours of the day. From 5 o'clock in the morning to noon is their time for receiving communion. It is useless to appoint an hour for them. They come when they want. They are the children of nature and follow their inclinations. But they are religious and edifying. Our whites could well learn some lessons from these poor savages. And as for human respect, they seem not even to know what it is. The women come to church with their babies on their backs. They cry and behave like little imps. The whites cast angry glances about, but the Eskimos couldn't care less. They come to church all the same. The men and women are dressed in the typical Eskimo fashion, and they have no fear whatever of kneeling at the communion rail next to a white lady dressed in silk. They understand that in church they are just as much at home as are the whites.''[33]

8 / King Island: A Mission Established

In August 1929, Lafortune, almost sixty years old, was on his way to King Island. The decision to give Lafortune permission and support to establish a mission on the island was the result of the announcement by the United States Bureau of Education that it was finally going to build a school on King Island in 1929 because the King Islanders had requested a school for many years. On 15 June 1929, Lafortune had written to Crimont: "They wanted a school and that is all. Seeing nothing but government schools all around, they wanted one like the others, but not *precisely* because it was a *government* school."[1] But the King Islanders got both a school and a new church on their island.

After he had been on the island a month, he wrote to his Father Provincial, Joseph Piet: "I wish you could find time enough to visit this place; you would see the wildest country in the world. Every inch of it is wild. It is nature untouched, unrefined, superb, majestic in its roughness. Steep, abrupt, craggy, the island rises nine hundred [1196] feet above sea level. The top is bristling with huge peaks like the steeples of some fairy temple. Here I am for just one month building a church to Christ the King, and I am amazed at the amount of work we have done."[2]

He was the chief architect and head builder of the church, but he had seven Eskimo helpers, "sterling men every one of them. Their efficiency and accuracy is nothing short of wonderful. They have muscles of steel and they work without counting the hours. It is very seldom we meet men so well up to every emergency."[3]

In all of Alaska no church was ever built on terrain more difficult of access and more forbidding than this. The only building site available for the church was toward the top of the large slide on which the village was built. An iron cable was stretched from the ocean to the top of the slide to haul up twenty thousand feet of lumber and about twelve tons of other material. By the middle of September the outside of the church was almost finished. It was built on posts: "the upper ones protrude about one foot above the rocks, the center ones about five feet and the front ones sixteen feet. That gives you an idea of the steepness of the place. You should see the way the natives have to dig among those boulders. Well, that church is as solid as the island itself. It dominates the whole village and puts the public school in the shade. The natives are proud of it"; yet, they ran short of lumber (a supplementary shipment was taken to Seattle because of bad weather), and could not finish the church before the winter set in. They had to use the old chapel, built in 1914, during the whole winter.[4]

The public school, which was under construction the same summer, had a slightly better location farther down the slope. The school was a frame building, twenty by sixty feet, with a total floor area of twelve hundred square feet above a basement, twenty by sixty-five feet. It cost $5717.75.[5] The first teacher for the forty-five children (of a total population of 167) was Arthur Nagozruk, Sr., an Eskimo from Cape Prince of Wales. The Bureau of Education's "godless school, taught by a protestant Eskimo in an exclusively Catholic village," was to be a source of frustration to Lafortune for some time.[6]

Despite the feverish work of getting the church built before the onset of the annual autumnal storms, Lafortune began his "History of the Mission of King Island" during his first days on the island. This handwritten document is a typical Jesuit house diary covering the years 1929 to 1942, and as such, is a complete record of Lafortune's sacramental ministry and of vital statistics. But it also includes many other matters such as weather conditions, game harvests, accidents, visitors to the island, noteworthy secular events, and life on the island in general.

Lafortune had been on the island only a month when he made a general survey of the conditions under which the people lived and worked, and in a letter to Piet he expressed his concern about the health of the people and their future as a group:

"A great many problems have to be solved here and they are serious, since it is a question of the race itself. For many years I wondered what was the cause of the very small increase of the population of this place.

The natives are all Catholics, not addicted to immorality nor to drunkenness; and still the increase is imperceptible. Of course they know nothing about birth control and those horrible abuses that are rampant in many places.

"Since I am here I have observed a good deal, and one of the causes of the small increase in population is that those people work too downright hard, men and women. It is good to work but it is bad to go beyond one's strength, and this is what those people do here. Had I not bought that cable, those men would have tackled the inhuman task of carrying all the lumber, etc. on their backs, up those awful cliffs where one has never a sure footing. It would have taken them two months to do it, but they were resigned to do it.

"Every morning I see strings of women carrying large rawhide bags on their backs, crawling up the flanks of that mountain, slowly, carefully, halting now and then to take their breath. They climb up six hundred feet, cross the island and go down seven hundred feet on the northern slopes to gather vegetables for their winter provisions. That would kill any white woman. The results are premature births and miscarriages. Very soon the young men will follow the same path, but they will go further, five or six miles on the ice, kill one or two seals, pull them back to the island, then load them on their shoulders (a seal weighs between one hundred and two hundred pounds) climb up on the seven hundred feet slant, cross the island and down six hundred feet to the village. That shortens their life. Their old men are not old men but worn out men. What to do? I will do on the northern slope what I have done on the southeast slope. I will put a windlass and not a cable but an ordinary rope. They will hunt more with half the fatigue."[7]

(By 1937, no windlass had been set up on the northern slope, but in the village a stationary engine had been installed to haul up the tons of goods brought back from Nome each year by the King Island people. That year Lafortune estimated that it took less than thirteen hours to haul up fifty-three tons, "thereby sparing untold fatigue to the community. Our idea is to rebuild the tribe.")[8]

Lafortune, though sure-footed and agile himself, felt that the paths in the village should be improved: "One has to be alert to walk in them. They would scare a goat. There is not one boulder that is horizontal. One has to jump rather than walk from one to the other." He planned to organize a "Road Commission" to level the paths by filling in between the boulders. But nothing could be done about the meanderings of the paths, for "there is no climbing straight up except with ladders."[9]

The old chapel (described by Lafortune as "a shack 25 feet long by 18 feet wide, open to the winds and rain") served not only as the church, but also as his bedroom, kitchen, and meeting room during the first winter. The tiny quarters necessitated his having two masses on Sundays and holy days, and catechism taught to a "standing house every night."[10]

Lafortune, the first white man to winter on King Island, did not suffer from the inadequacies of his housing, for "luckily, Almighty God took pity on me and sent mountains of snow that covered my house entirely, so that I wintered practically in a snow house. It was warm and comfortable."[11]

The first Christmas with "the little Father" present on their island was a novel and memorable event for the King Islanders. Before Christmas Eve, Lafortune cooked thirty pounds of reindeer meat with onions and rice, and baked sixty-nine loaves of bread. Most of the flour was supplied by the Eskimos. Lafortune described Christmas Eve:

"At 7 p. m., after the ordinary instructions and rehearsals, we heard the confessions. All went home, but nobody slept a wink. With a baby Jesus left in Nome by the Sisters of Providence and an artificial Christmas tree and some tinsels and some colored candles we managed to put up a crib. Most of the King Islanders had never seen any such thing. It took them by storm. They seemed never to get tired to look at that child. To think that less than 30 years ago those people had their medicine men and their superstitious dances and practices and to see them now kneeling devoutly before the crib and praying most earnestly caused us a great consolation, and we have not the least doubt that Our Lord looked down on the simple faith of these people with the greatest complacency.

"Dec. 25—At 12 o'clock, midnight mass for the men followed by a second one for the women. A surprise was in store. After the gospel of the first mass was heard the rattle of the money in a collection box which the natives had made on the sly. Men and women contributed $34.85 and gave about 10 dollars worth in ivory and mittens etc.

"At 8 a.m. the third mass with the little chapel packed to overflow.

"At 12 began the repast. The women very thoughtfully brought dishes enough for the little ones. With the reindeer meat and the bread and the rice and the candies and about 2½ gallons of tea we filled them up to the neck. They had a good time and behaved irreproachedly."

"I gave them a Christmas," wrote Lafortune to Sister Marie-Flavius, "that they will never forget."[12]

Lafortune's first winter on King Island was a typical one except that it was exceptionally mild until the end of January. The usual hunting was carried on; his diary entry of 20 February reads: "2 polar bears, 5 oogruks [bearded seals] were killed and a few seals." There was "snow galore" in March, but there were no unusual incidents until May. That month there were two deaths; Atkritoac, the wife of Akileina, died on May 22 after a ten-year illness, and Ughitkuna, one of the strongest hunters, drowned only two miles from shore on May 26.

"Just what happened to him, we don't know," Lafortune wrote in his "History." "According to all appearances, he speared an oogruk or walrus, for his kayak was seen half capsized and full of water and his inflated bag standing. He hollered for help, was seen on the ice giving signs of distress. Two boys ran to help as fast as they could. Shortly after, two others started. They all got so excited that they never thought of pulling either the kayak or the bag. Finally, the ice closed in and all disappeared. . . .To allay the grief of the community, we rang the bell. After a short timely instruction we said mass for the repose of his soul. Olaranna [the "chief" of King Island], his brother, was partly insane for about one hour."[13]

Several months later, during one of a series of lectures given by men of the village (started earlier by Lafortune) there was an unusual sequel to this tragedy.[14] The series dealt with social problems as well as religious topics; and that evening, Olaranna spoke on the subject of wife-beating. As he berated those in his audience guilty of this misdemeanor, one of the men suddenly jumped to his feet, shouting a remark that branded Olaranna as one who had attempted suicide. The stunned crowd watched as the accuser ran from the church. This remark referred to the previous spring when Olaranna's brother was struggling in vain down among the floes, and Olaranna could do no more than watch helplessly from the cliffs above. In his despair, he was about to throw himself off a cliff when several men restrained him.

In King Island culture, to accuse a man of having attempted or of having even contemplated suicide was the strongest of insults.[15] Such an accusation implied that the man had considered suicide because he was convinced that he was a man who no longer had the solidary

King Island men in the *kagri agulliit*, photographed by Hubbard, 1937-38. "Chief" Olaranna is sitting in the rear. *(Archives of the University of Santa Clara)*

support of his village faction, and was therefore an outcast. For an islander, to be an outcast was to be as good as dead. To Lafortune the incident presented a challenge to reconcile the estranged parties, and thus was established his role as peacemaker early in his days on King Island.

During his first ten months, Lafortune buried two adults, an eleven-year-old boy, and five infants. This high mortality rate—particularly of infants—bothered him greatly, and he attributed it to the hard life on the steep island where the people worked "like slaves."

There were forty-five hunters on King Island during Lafortune's first spring on the island. The "real big hunting" began on 7 June, a bit later than usual, but despite dense fog the hunters brought in fourteen large walrus, eleven small walrus, and a few seals. "From a distance," he said, "their fusillade resembled the rumbling of thunder."[16]

While the men hunted, and the women trimmed blubber from the carcasses and hides—cutting and storing the meat—the older boys were on top of the island and on the cliffs catching birds and gathering eggs. The girls, too, and even the young children had their assigned work, gathering roots and greens, which were preserved in seal oil, or soured in water for the winter.

On Lafortune's first July Fourth on the island, the *Sierra* arrived with the lumber that had been taken to Seattle the fall before. The villagers finished unloading by 11:15 A. M., and then celebrated the Fourth from noon until three o'clock. "After singing 'America' on the top of the *agulliit* [one of the three men's houses], we had races, absolutely original and giving lots of fun; then shooting for men and boys; then jumping and kicking. Everybody was pleased."[17]

In 1929, at the same time that Lafortune was getting ready to go to King Island, William F. Walsh, a young volunteer priest, had just arrived in Nome from Stockton, California, and was making preparations to build a church in Kotzebue. At that time Lafortune himself had written to Crimont saying that he considered the plans for Kotzebue an important move because the town was strategically located to serve various groups of Eskimos. Little did Lafortune suspect, when he wrote to Crimont, that before 1930 had ended he would be in Kotzebue instead of on King Island, where he had hoped to finish construction of the church and to spend a second winter.[18]

In 1930, when Lafortune arrived in Nome with the King Islanders, he found a telegram ordering him to start immediately for Kotzebue "to give a hand to Fr. Walsh." On 17 July, he left on the revenue cutter *Northland* for Kotzebue and returned to Nome ten days later. (His trip to Kotzebue—183 miles to the north—was the farthest from Nome Lafortune ever ventured in his forty-four years in the Bering Strait area.)

On 25 September, Lafortune, accompanied by Delon, left Nome for King Island on the *Northland.* The next day the two said mass in the chapel, since the church was not yet ready, and by late afternoon the *Northland* had left.[19] As soon as the Eskimos had finished the most urgent work of repairing houses and putting supplies away by October, they began to help build on the church again "with a wonderful zest." The ceiling and plaster boards and slats were put in place "as by magic." Great efforts were made to get the church finished by the feast of Christ the King, to whom the church was to be dedicated on the last Sunday in October.

A contest was held for the making of the permanent tabernacle and altar decorations. "Seven [men] make remarkably good drawings. I will endeavor to have photos taken of them and send the pictures to our benefactors," Lafortune wrote in the "History." "That will show them that the natives are worth working for. The artists are the following: Peter Mayac, Koyuc, Pussuc, Tattayuna, Atanganna, Pitkoganna and Sirloac. The designs are submitted to a board of examiners. After much talking and deliberating and comparing, the majority declares for Koyuc's design. Therefore he is given the job to realize his dream. He sets to work right away with the help of the others."[20]

Plans were being made to open the church and to train the catechists, as well as to start new projects, when on 14 October he wrote in the "History": "All that is blown away like so many cardboard castles," because the *Northland* had returned that day with the tragic news that Fathers Delon and Walsh, along with their pilot, Ralph Wien, had been killed in an airplane crash on the twelfth. The airplane, the *Marquette Missionary*, was a Bellanca Pacemaker, which had been flown from Long Island to Seattle, and then shipped north on the S. S. *Aleutian* by Brother George J. Feltes, S. J., who was officially responsible for it, and who was to pilot it for the Alaska mission to

Bishop Joseph R. Crimont, S. J., blessing the "Marquette Missionary," Long Island, 29 June 1930. At the extreme right are Brother George J. Feltes, S. J., the pilot, and George Pickenpack, the co-pilot. *(Oregon Province Archives)*

whom it belonged.[21] It was the first diesel-powered airplane to fly in Alaska.

Wien, an experienced pilot from Fairbanks, had been engaged by Delon on a temporary basis to act as co-pilot to Feltes on his first tour around Alaska, and to familiarize him with Alaskan flying conditions. On 12 October, Delon wanted to take a trip to the nearby village of Deering to attend to some business and to show Walsh some of his mission territory, but snow flurries blew in just as everything was ready for takeoff, and by the time the weather had improved, it was too late to go to Deering. Since the plane was all set to go, Delon decided to take Walsh up for a short swing around Kotzebue, to show him his mission from the air and to give him his first—and his last—airplane ride.

On 13 October 1930, the day after the crash, a coroner's jury found that "adverse weather conditions, alone, were responsible," but Feltes could not agree with the official finding. He said, "The time, place and weather are all exonerated. The sole cause of the accident was an error in human judgment." He described the accident in a long telegram to Piet: "Ralph took off with the two Fathers and got off nicely. . . .He made a wide turn and flew in a large circle of about a mile and in doing so got into a little snow. . . .He decided to come in to land. . . .In turning to the left he made a very sharp nose high turn and stalled the plane at an altitude of about three hundred and fifty feet. It fell out of control in a wide sweeping turn very much like a spin. . . .About thirty feet from the ground he turned it [the motor] on and went into a straight dive for the ground and struck it head on."[22]

As soon as Crimont heard of the deaths of the two priests, he wired Piet that he had instructed Post, in Nome, to send Lafortune to Kotzebue from King Island. Thus, the *Northland* arrived on the fourteenth with instructions for Lafortune to go to Kotzebue. The sea was so rough that the boat had to anchor at *tununak* ("north [back] side"), which necessitated Lafortune's climbing over the top of King Island in order to leave. He was accompanied by a few young men. "Nature seems to share our sorrows," he said. "The top of the island is shrouded in a thick fog; it is cold and blowing."[23]

Later he wrote to Crimont, "Almighty God did surely play havoc with all our plans. It is bewildering. One feels like not making any plans any more and let the bark go adrift. Had your Lordship seen the scene at King Island when I left, your heart would have split. It was one of the most trying and dismal days of my life."[24]

Lafortune did not arrive in Nome until the eighteenth as the *Northland* did not go there directly, and did not arrive in Kotzebue until the twentieth because, being the only priest in Nome, he had to hold all of the services on Sunday, the nineteenth. On his arrival in Kotzebue he learned that the citizens had wired the bishop to send for him especially.[25] There was much work to be done in Kotzebue, both spiritual and physical, according to Lafortune. The principal religious group in Kotzebue at that time was the Society of Friends, or Quakers, and because of their enormous percentages in tithing, "the entire white population, with exception of T. Berryman, begged us to take possession of the place."[26] Walsh had attracted a number of Eskimos by his cheerfulness, his helpfulness toward the sick, and by the entertainments in his hall. To these, Lafortune began his teaching of catechism.

Lafortune's quarters, a combination church-residence, were, according to him, the coldest he had ever lived in. "There is not an Eskimo shack as cold." He spent two weeks after his arrival caulking the entire building, which was made of six by six timbers spiked together. "Without being bad," he commented in the Kotzebue house diary, which he originated, "the idea is not very good. The lumber being green, contracted in drying and left an opening between the timbers and gave free access to the cold, the wind and the rain." He also found that the stoves were too small. "Undoubtedly, though he did not complain, Fr. Walsh suffered a good deal from the cold."

Lafortune himself rarely complained about the cold and had the reputation of being all but insensitive to it. According to Concannon, Lafortune had "inured himself to hunger and cold. He never made a fire in his room until the thermometer registered 20 below zero. . . . When questioned about the wisdom of such a cold room, he merely replied: 'Well, it doesn't hurt until it gets 20 below, then the blankets get damp—and one must take care of one's health.' On the other hand, he insisted that I have a fire in my room whenever the weather became inclement. One could get pneumonia, you know!"[27]

Throughout the winter of 1930-31, Lafortune was busy in Kotzebue carrying out the usual round of priestly duties and turning his quarters into a habitable residence and a fitting church. In May he wrote, "The Flu visited us. That was a blessing for the camp. Everyone was sick excepting myself, and I don't know who else. That gave me a nice opportunity of visiting the Quakers. They were mighty glad to have fruits, etc. Now all the doors are open to us. One fanatical woman refused my services. Unknowingly she ate some fruits that I had given to another native. When told that those came from me, she made desperate efforts to reject them, and she died."[28]

Lafortune seems here to have been gloating over his own good health and rejoicing over the ill health and misfortunes of others as a splendid opportunity for making converts. But if this is read in the overall context of his long life in Alaska, it is seen simply as a statement of fact made by a man who marveled at the ways of Divine Providence.

Along these same lines, Lafortune wrote: "Two natives from King Island drifted ashore during winter. Severe was their experience. For four days and four nights they walked across floating ice floes, having nothing to eat, and not too warmly clad. Their sole guide was a compass during the day and the stars during the night. One night, on account of the storm, they had to walk at random. All that had a salutary effect on them. It happened that those two fellows were the toughest on the island. One had never consented to be baptized though all his family is Catholic. The other did not frequent the sacraments for a few years, in spite of his having a very good little wife. As soon as he stepped ashore, our pagan asked for baptism, and the other is a good boy now. Wonderful are the ways of the Lord!"[29]

Lafortune saw himself and his gift of good health as being used by God as instruments to bring about the spiritual salvation of the people with whom he worked. "He gives me health of iron. May I use it solely for his greater glory!" he wrote to his niece.[30]

To Lafortune, God was really present at all times. He was a God who often intervened in the lives of others as well as in his own and in the affairs of mankind in general. The God he served was often a stern God with a severe, vengeful side, given to anger and punishment to "teach them a lesson." But he was always a God who had his reasons (sometimes wholly mysterious reasons) for acting as He did.

Lafortune's God was also an impartial God who favored no one. Lafortune himself experienced many disappointments and setbacks in his own life and works. Not infrequently the Almighty "did surely play havoc" with his plans. He found that the ways of the Lord—though wonderful—were also "bewildering." Yet in all adversity—personal adversity included—he saw only the loving hand of God. In his words one finds not the slightest trace of bitterness toward the Lord he served, for there was none in his heart. What supported him throughout the

The Catholic church in Kotzebue and wreck of the "Marquette Missionary," 1931. *(Oregon Province Archives)*

whole of life was the unshakable conviction that God acted and intervened in the lives of men only out of a boundless love to bring about greater good for men. On his part, Lafortune did everything solely out of love for God—for the greater glory of God and the good of souls.

Every day throughout his eight-month stay in Kotzebue, Lafortune had to face the grim reminder of why he was there and not on the island of his heart's desire. Behind the church sat the mangled *Marquette Missionary*. Toward the end of May he dismantled the wreckage and was "amazed how carefully it was put together. Nothing can get loose in those planes."[31]

In the middle of June 1931, Lafortune returned to Nome to attend to the Eskimos there and to return eventually to King Island. Nome was swept by whooping cough. "All the children, whites and Eskimos, caught it, and, as ever, it was much more harmful to the natives. On the heels of the whooping cough came a most severe grip or flu which prostrated all the adults." By the end of the summer he had buried seven, six of them King Islanders.[32]

Some interesting reactions to his sudden leaving of King Island to go to Kotzebue the year before were recorded by Lafortune in a letter which he wrote in August:

"When I came back to them, they revealed their whole soul to me, and, though I had been a long time with the natives, I did not know yet that there was so much pathos among them. Some of their utterances might interest you. Without being questioned at all, an old native told me 'after you were gone, we wanted to take our breakfast, but we could not eat. Then we went to work in the *kazine* (a large place where the men work together) [usually pronounced *kagri* or *kazgi*]. We sat down to work; nobody spoke for a long time. It was hard to work. Our fingers alone worked; our mind was not there. It was like if there was nobody left on King Island. We felt all alone.'

"And the women also shared the grief of the men. They told me: 'After you were gone we went to our houses and we could not speak. We cried till we were tired. In the morning we did not hear the bell calling us to mass and holy communion and we cried. On Sundays we gathered in the new church and we prayed, but no mass, no sermon. It was sad.'

"An old fellow felt some relief, when he felt blue, by making a kind of pilgrimage. He would climb up to the church and walk around it two or three times and go home.

"Another said: 'When you were gone, I felt like if my mother, my father and brothers and sisters were all gone.'

"A young lad, after catching some fish told his mother: 'It is too bad the Father is not here; I would give him some fish.' "[33]

On 24 September, the *Northland* left Nome for King Island. On board were Lafortune, 170 Eskimos, Lafortune's good friend, Captain Thomas Ross, and his daughter, Frances Ross—the first white woman ever to spend a winter on King Island. The trip home was an unusually hard one for the Eskimos because many were still sick with coughs and the flu. The crew helped to make the trip easier by putting the more seriously ill in the sick bay and the rest—who were also sick—under an immense tent on the aft deck.

Lafortune and the ship's doctor were apprehensive about the condition of the natives and the oncoming winter. When the ship arrived at the island on the twenty-fifth, the same sick crowd had to do the unloading. "There was no dodging it." Lafortune wrote to Crimont. "The poor natives submitted to it with a zest that appalled me. You would have thought that all their sickness was gone. But now that the excitement is over, they begin to collapse. I came here just two days ago and three died already. By the end of the winter I expect that ten or twelve will go to their grave."[34]

Lafortune was still intent on isolating the King Islanders against the harmful aspects of Nome. "We have to do all in our power to stop them going to Nome. For that a priest has to be here at least the first summer. The old folks and the women and the children have no business to quit the island and go to take all kinds of sickness in Nome."[35]

The church on King Island in 1938. *(Photograph by Hubbard. Archives of the University of Santa Clara)*

Interior of the church on King Island, 1931. Father Lafortune is standing at the left. *(Oregon Province Archives)*

During Lafortune's Kotzebue interlude, the King Islanders had gone ahead with work on their church, which he described as "large enough, solid, and easy to warm." That winter he had to live in a corner of the church because Frances Ross, who was engaged in anthropological research, had to move into Lafortune's house when she was unable to use a room in the schoolhouse because of "the ill will of the Eskimo protestant schoolteacher."[36]

Early in October the village youths were finally organized into the long-planned "Road Commission." Elections were held and Peter Mayac was appointed "Commissioner." The paths were filled in and leveled with rocks from the creek. On the twelfth the Road Commission worked at the "graveyard," which had been laid out by Lafortune on the fifty-degree slope immediately above the village. A place was prepared large enough to lodge six or seven bodies. This was not a graveyard in the ordinary sense for no digging or burial was possible. When a King Islander died, the remains were placed in a wooden box, which was set on a more or less level spot among the boulders and covered with rocks to protect it from dogs and foxes.

Throughout the month of October, people were busily making final preparations in the church for the celebration—already twice postponed—of the feast of Christ the King (patronal feast of the King Island mission). "Koyuc, Pussuc and Killarzoac have been working at the center piece of the main altar. Those people are extremely painstaking. No detail is small enough to escape their attention. . . .Very few white people would do better work."[37] Tattayuna, the organist, made a stool for the organ, and Sirloac made the confessional. The altar was painted afresh and decorated and the floor carefully scrubbed. The day before the great feast of the formal inauguration of the new church, new damask curtains were hung before the altar. "It made quite an impression." On the day of the feast itself, three children received their first communion and twenty-eight were confirmed.[38]

In 1931, the King Island mission was officially on its way at last.

9 / The 1930s

During the 1930s, Lafortune devoted a large part of his time to serving King Island, the Nome parish, and to establishing a mission on Little Diomede Island. Furthermore, in those years, he was host to numerous visitors to King Island.

The first airplane landed at King Island early in Lafortune's stay there, in April 1932, by prior arrangement with Jesuit Superiors and the Bureau of Education. "Therefore, before Easter," wrote Lafortune, "we prepared a field by chopping off the rough ice at *tununak* and putting coal sacks at the corners. Now the question was, 'Will a plane dare to come and who will be aboard?' The talking and discussing and guessing were rife when, on the morning of the 10th of April a roar is heard from the sky and from below the most formidable shouting and hollering King Island ever uttered. Even the dogs took part in it. The machine passed over the village and turned around looking for the landing field. Presently a stream of people was seen tumbling down from the village and running toward *tununak*. The fliers saw the whole maneuver and understood. They circled around towards *tununak* and made a first attempt to land. But a woman was fishing just in the middle of the field and she had no sense enough to understand she had to get out of the way. Rather than to kill her the aviators soared up and circled again. In the meantime that woman was made to get out by the first arrivals on the field. A second attempt and the big bird landed gracefully and without any mishap. The distinguished visitors were our Rev. Fr. Superior, Father [Francis] Ménager, piloted by a good Catholic aviator Mr. [Arthur G.] Woodley. . . .The joy was universal and intense.

"Fr. Superior had visited all the other missions and he manifested his regret not to be able to see King Island to Mr. Woodley. He took the hint, left Nome in a fog, soared above it and at a long distance (over 90 miles) he could see, in the blazing sunshine, a white cone. He made straight for it and landed here 55 minutes after taking off. They intended to remain here only one hour and a half; but they could not quit the place before 7 hours, so entranced were they at all what they saw. They took numberless pictures, tasted our canned crabs and were delighted, bought some ivory. Father Superior addressed the congregation. We sang a few hymns. He blessed us, and, regretfully, we accompanied them back to the field. It was about 4:30 when the plane, 'The pace maker,' was again in the air, pointing straight for the Springs. May God be blessed in those wonderful inventions!''[1]

Only two months later, on 12 June, another airplane came to the island, and though there was no possibility of its landing since it had wheels, ''great excitement prevails.'' Before long a bundle was dropped. In it was a book, *The Eskimos*, by Peter Freuchen, and a letter from the Lomen Commercial Company containing the information that ''one of the biggest film companies of the States. . .had sent a gang of experts and the Steamer *Nanuk*, and that they desire the cooperation of the King Islanders and other natives.'' Said Lafortune, ''They want 10 of our best hunters to go North with them whilst their families will be well taken care of in Teller. All the King Islanders are invited to proceed thereto for two days of feasting and moving picture seeing; all to be under salary for one or two days. Only the 10 hunters will have their steady salary for 1½ months and their families will be taken care of.''[2]

The plane was to return shortly to learn their decision. ''If they accept the offer they have to signify their intention by making a fire with lots of smoke. If they refuse they will wave a large red rag from a high rock.'' Twelve men volunteered to go, two of whom were discarded by ballot. Lafortune thought that the rest of the islanders would also go to Teller, although some would have preferred to go straight to Nome. ''It is left entirely to them. I have exercised no coercion whatever. If they are sorry, they will have nobody else but themselves to blame.''[3]

Because it was blowing and foggy on the thirteenth, the plane did not come until the fifteenth, but by that time the men were out on the ice for the ''big hunting,'' which was more important right then than movie-making. They continued to hunt walrus for the next five days. On the twentieth the *Nanuk* arrived to tell the hunters to get ready, but she soon left. The ten volunteers never did get the chance to be in the movie because the *Nanuk* never returned for them, going instead to Wales for the actors. According to Lafortune, it was because of a misunderstanding that had resulted from conflicting information given to the moviemakers by the chief, Olaranna, and the schoolteacher, Arthur Nagozruk. Olaranna told them that they would be ready in three days, but Nagozruk said that it would not be before eight days. Because the movie people could not wait that long, they found other actors.

The villagers did not simply swallow their disappointment. Lafortune recorded: "The King Islanders, in a body, wrote to the Bureau of Education to fire out the schoolteacher. If not, none of the children would go to school next winter."[4] (A year later he wrote next to this entry, "N.B. That threat was a bluff.") It is evident from several entries in the "History" that Nagozruk was merely tolerated on King Island. It was partly because of his own personality but largely because he was a "bigoted protestant," in Lafortune's words—unfortunately, an attitude that fostered an atmosphere of suspicion and disrespect toward secular schooling on the island for a long time. Furthermore, Nagozruk was a *Kingikmiu* (a person from *Kingigan*, or Wales) and there had been a long tradition of intertribal hostility between the Wales and the King Island people.

A year later, however, Lafortune was objective enough to write that Nagozruk's intervention was "a blessing in disguise" because the "outfit did not keep its words nor promises. . . .The whole affair was a fizzle."[5]

In the summer of 1932, Lafortune was finally able to get to Little Diomede Island and to establish the mission there, something he had been hoping to do for a long time. He had expected to go there with one of the traders before the Eskimos went on their annual trip to Nome in July, but the weather was so foggy and cold, and the sea so rough, that no trader came to King Island. Not until July tenth were the Eskimos and Lafortune able to leave the island. When they arrived in Nome the next day, Lafortune was able to get passage on the *Northland*. The accommodating skipper, Stanley V. Parker, even stopped at King Island so that Lafortune could pick up some chairs, a lamp, windows, and tools to repair the house, also some items needed for mass on Little Diomede.

Lafortune found conditions on Diomede "simply dismal. . . .The sight of our house in Diomede made my heart go in my boots. . . .Built long ago [by someone else for other purposes], it had never been occupied. The windows were covered with gunny sacks, the original windows having been broken by the snow and the youngsters. The inside was uncovered and black. Chips and pieces of board covered the floor. . . .No stairway of any kind led to the door, which is at about 4 feet from the ground. Entering the house was a good gymnastic."[6]

Captain Parker returned to Nome with a list of materials—tar, felt paper, maltoid paper, kalsomine, which Lafortune needed for repairs—and came back with them a few days later.

"With the help of Umiak and Akkeinga," wrote Lafortune, "I put on the felt paper after fixing the roof. . . .Then I kalsomined the whole interior, put my tabernacle on the table or rather the altar, hanged my gasoline lamp to the ceiling and began the services for good. In seeing the change in the house, the crowd was taken by storm. They began to come, including the Eskimo schoolteacher [Samuel Anaruk] and his family."[7]

Lafortune spent a good part of the summer on the island, teaching catechism and visiting the people with what he thought were favorable results, especially when a young lad, whose parents were Lutheran (the

Little Diomede Island in 1928, with the school in the foreground.

competitive Church on the island), wanted to join the Catholic Church. Lafortune explored the island and compared the living conditions on Little Diomede with those on King Island.

"The living conditions at Diomede," he wrote in his "History," "are not so favorable as King Island's. To begin with, the scenery around the village lacks all beauty. It is nothing but a disorderly heap of boulders interspersed by patches of shaggy tundra ploughed deep by recent landslides. Away from the village, there are beautiful sceneries. The vegetation is somewhat the same [as on King Island]. . . .The sea hunting is easier [there] but not so abundant as here [King Island]. The worst features of Diomede are the lack of good water and of cold storage. On account of the dampness caused by fogs and rains, they have hard time to dry their meats. What they cannot dry they put in pits where it rots. And they have to eat that stuff! It is a wonder they have not all been poisoned long time ago.

"Diomede has one good advantage over K. I. The grade is not more than 5%. Another advantage is the smoothness of the ice. Men and women have not to work half so hard as the K. Islanders. The result of it is that the Diomede women are stronger than the K. Island's, the babies don't die so fast, and the sexes are equally distributed [he is referring here to the fact that in one catechism class on King Island he had twenty boys and only one girl, and in another, sixteen boys and nine girls]. Therefore there is more future in Diomede."[8]

The next summer, 1933, he planned to build a church on Little Diomede with the lumber from the dismantled Nome Eskimo chapel because by then he had sixty-five Catholics on the island and he hoped to spend the winter of 1934-35 with them.[9] But he could not carry out his plans, even though the *North Star*, the new Bureau of Indian Affairs boat, was willing to take the lumber there free. "By order of the Superiors" he had to forego the trip to Diomede. He remained in Nome.[10]

During the summer of 1934, he again hoped to go to Little Diomede to build a church, but he could not leave Nome because he was the only priest there after 25 July. He did, however, anticipate progress toward building a church on the island, as is evident from his 30 July entry in the Nome diary: "Four Diomeders begin to demolish the shop. The lumber will be taken to Diomede and turned into a church." On 23 August, the work of knocking down the building was finished and

"Now St. Joseph has to prevail on the Capt. of the North Star to take all that lumber to Diomede."[11]

Of his having to spend the winter of 1934-35 in Nome, Lafortune wrote in the Nome diary: "It is more than sad to leave those people without a priest for the whole winter [the second since 1929]. I pity those who are responsible for that."[12]

On 26 March 1935, Lafortune wrote Bishop Crimont: "The church in Diomede will not be completed much before Christmas. The material for finishing the interior is not on the island yet. I will ship it in the fall with the stoves etc. etc. I could send the coal and my provisions ahead and after Christmas have a plane take me over there. There is no trouble landing at Diomede in winter. I could come back here at the end of March and prepare the people for Easter, and after Easter attend to Teller."[13] (About six weeks before this he had made his first trip to Teller by airplane in thirty-five minutes, a striking contrast to his dogteam trips of thirty years before.)

Finally, in 1936, a priest remained for the first time on Little Diomede Island throughout the winter. Thomas Cunningham, S. J., who had been in charge of St. Joseph's parish of Nome during 1935-36, left for the island in October. He remained the priest of the Little Diomeders until 1947, when he replaced Lafortune on King Island.

During the years that Lafortune was trying to keep the King Island and Little Diomede missions going, there had been a constant coming and going of pastors in the Nome parish. As a consequence the buildings were neglected. During the forty-four years that Lafortune spent in the Bering Strait area, more than two dozen priests served the Nome parish. Only the hardiest survived conditions there more than a year or two. Lafortune's hardiness at times kept him from his first love, his King Island flock. After the King Islanders spent the winter without a priest in 1934-35, all of the King Island men, with their "chief," Olaranna, went to the rectory while John B. Sifton, the Superior of the Alaska mission, was visiting there. When the men arrived, Lafortune was reading his breviary, and as he did not have enough chairs, they sat down on the floor.

"The Eskimos played a nice trick on my Superior," he wrote to his niece, Marie-Flavius. "I asked the chief what the meaning of all that was. 'I want to see your chief,' he answered. I went and got my Superior. The chief gave him a chair, and sat down opposite him, and here is what he said: 'You are the chief of all the Fathers in Alaska.

Last winter you left us without a priest. Children were born. I baptized them as well as I knew how, but I am not so sure of my baptisms. Some adults died. Before dying they wanted to go to confession and to receive holy communion. I could do nothing. Our children were not as well behaved as usual. On Sunday, not knowing what to do with ourselves, we were tempted to go hunting or to work. We want a Father for next winter.' And all applauded. The Superior was caught. He promised them a priest. That is why I will go to King Island."[14]

So, after an absence of fifteen months, Lafortune returned to the island in October 1935. By this time the *North Star* took the people back to the island each fall. They no longer had to rely on a revenue cutter. A long entry in the "History" gives an idea of how complicated this yearly migration could be, even on a special supply vessel. On 12 October, the Eskimos were told to load their umiaks so they could go out to the boat, which always anchored about a mile from shore because of the shallow water, but some were slow and had to be left behind when a southeast wind began to blow. When the boat arrived at King Island, only part of the passengers went ashore because it was too windy to unload the freight.

"All those who came on this trip are in a mess because their outfits are on the *North Star.* Many have hardly any bedding and kitchen utensils. One thing that they miss more yet is their *tobacco.* But they all take it bravely. My satchel is on the boat. My beard is growing alarmingly and my razor is in my satchel. Punuk is in Nome, his children are here and his wife is on the boat. Now that boat is gone. When is she going to come back is the question."

Finally, by the twenty-second of October, the sea had grown calm enough for the *North Star* to return to King Island with the stragglers and all of the islanders' goods, provisions for two stores, twenty-five tons of coal, and provisions for the new schoolteachers, Mr. and Mrs. Sullivan Coan. All of this was unloaded in less than eight hours with the crew of the *North Star* visiting and observing the work "to their great amazement." The islanders proceeded with their tasks "as if no stranger were on the island. There was no waste of time talking."[15]

The Nome congregation greatly welcomed Lafortune's next sojourn in the Nome parish, during 1936-37. Father Segundo Llorente, S. J., of the Nome Church, wrote, "Some complained that since Fr. Lafortune moved to King Island they felt they might as well forget all about the Church. The frequent change of priests made them feel dizzy."[16] A good example was the situation in the parish at that time. John Concannon was in charge of the Nome parish during 1937-38. While Lafortune was in Nome during the summer of 1938, he and Cunningham, in from Little Diomede, renovated the Nome chapel. When Concannon left on 2 September 1938 on the *Denali*, with the Hubbard party (see below), and Lafortune and Cunningham went to their islands, the Nome Church was without a pastor until the Father Superior of the Alaska mission, Joseph McElmeel, arrived to take charge on 2 January 1939.[17]

In June 1937, Lafortune came closer to leaving the Seward Peninsula area than at any other time since his arrival in 1903. Since Bishop Crimont was approaching his eightieth birthday, the Jesuit Superiors considered it time to call a Mission Consultation for the purpose of "selecting a *terna*,"[18] that is, of drawing up for Rome's consideration a list of three names of possible candidates for the post of Coadjutor Bishop of Alaska. The Consultation was scheduled to take place at Holy Cross.

Lafortune was one of the four Mission Consultors, but he never attended. The reasons he gave for absenting himself from the Consultation were that he was utterly ignorant of all the rest of the missions and their needs, having never been outside the Nome district during his entire stay in Alaska; that he did not know the men, in or out of Alaska, who might supply those needs; and that the distance was too great, and travel too slow. In brief, Lafortune felt that this added up to more money and time than he could afford, and that his presence at the Consultation would be only an expensive, useless gesture. Consequently, the *terna* that led to the naming of Walter J. Fitzgerald, S. J., as Coadjutor Bishop of Alaska went to Rome without any input whatever from Lafortune, and his record of uninterrupted service in far western Alaska remained intact.

In the spring of 1937, the first boat of the season brought to the King Islanders and Lafortune the beginning of a year of excitement without precedent when the expedition of Father Bernard R. Hubbard arrived. On the seventh of June, Lafortune wrote in the Nome diary that the *Northland* had arrived with Fr. Hubbard, S. J. (the "Glacier Priest"), his "two giant companions," Kenneth Chisholm and Edgar Levin, and Hubbard's nephew, Bernard Stanley, a radio operator, en route to King Island where they planned to build houses and to live, along with

Father Hubbard's party on King Island in 1937. Left to right: Kenneth Chisholm, Bernard R. Hubbard, S. J., Edgar Levin, and Bernard Stanley. *(Archives of the University of Santa Clara)*

Ukivok after the school, church, and Father Hubbard's buildings had been built. *(Photograph by Hubbard. Archives of the University of Santa Clara)*

their "two beautiful dogs, the faithful guardians of the party, Mageik and Wolf."[19]

On the twentieth, the *Northland* left for King Island with Hubbard's party, his boat, and dogs, as well as Lafortune, to familiarize them with the island and to show them where they could build. "Two skin-boats came to meet us and directly the natives began to unload the 10 tons of stuff that was aboard for Fr. Hubbard's expedition."

When Hubbard moved, he moved on a truly grand scale. A short time later another hundred tons of freight were unloaded from the *Derblay* for the Hubbard expedition. In October, the Hubbard party, along with the King Islanders who had spent the summer in Nome, sailed to King Island on the U.S. Coast Guard Cutter *Duane*.[20]

Hubbard had received the name "Glacier Priest" from guides who had assisted him on climbs in the Tyrolean Alps prior to his ordination to the priesthood in Innsbruck in 1923. He had gone to Alaska every summer since 1928, not as a missionary but as an amateur geologist and explorer and superb photographer.[21] Working out of Santa Clara University in California, he followed the same routine for almost thirty years—spending his summers in Alaska on various expeditions and the better part of his winters on lecture tours around the nation. But his 1937-38 expedition to King Island was, by all accounts, the most ambitious undertaking of his career.

According to Sergei Bogojavlensky, an anthropologist who lived on the island in the 1960s, "The sojourn of Hubbard's party during the winter of 1937-38 was the first intensive encounter with a group of white men during the winter for the islanders."[22] From the outset the party's presence on the island had a pronounced impact on the entire community. Much new material was brought in, new buildings were erected, the island and its people photographed, and generally, there was a rearrangement of various activities. Lafortune wrote in his "History":

"There being no warehouse in this part of the globe, the perishables had to be stacked in the church and my house became the dwelling of the party. . . .Fr. Hubbard has a whole moving picture outfit with him and a powerful radio with transmitter and all; even a radio phone. That necessitated a first class and powerful Kohler engine, that is used also to light the house and the church and part of the village. Besides that, the Father has 5 Johnson electric plants. These are to be used in the 3 *kazines*. It is a good reward for the work the men have done. It will

save the oxygen of the *kazines* and allow the men to breath purer air . . . .In the church will be installed a large oil burner stove. That will be much cleaner than coal. To encourage the youngsters to work, the Father gave them already a few very interesting moving picture shows."[23]

Besides building a house to live in, Hubbard decided to construct a community hall under the church because none of the ceremonial houses was considered large enough to show the movies and to hold the other events that Hubbard was planning. By the evening of 21 October, the foundation and floor were finished and the studding put up, and by the twenty-second, Lafortune could write that the "work. . . has been progressing so rapidly that we were enabled to have the first movy and talky show therein this evening. The hall is plenty large enough for the crowd. When finished it will prove very valuable and useful for many different purposes." On the second of November, the children helped Hubbard carry his films from his house to the new hall.[24]

In that hall Hubbard showed the many films that he had brought to King Island. They were very popular and were even added to the traditional bear celebrations. Lafortune said that Hubbard was kept busy "giving shows to the natives. Every successful hunter wants a show when he bags a bear, and he is given a show, with the whole crowd, of course."

The Christmas holidays had many evenings of movies, including a newsreel showing the Magi visiting the infant Savior. On the sound track of the film was the carol, "Holy Night," which was carried far out over the Bering Strait at midnight, Christmas Eve, by amplifiers placed outside the church. This "miraculous" sound was soon explained to the islanders. Needless to say, no one was absent from midnight mass.

Father Hubbard not only gave "movy and talky shows," but "took" them. Probably no other group of Eskimos has been so intensively recorded on film as have the King Island people by Hubbard. He had barely set foot on the island when Lafortune wrote, "One can hear the click of the camera at any hour. What is commonplace to me is wonderful to Father Hubbard." Hubbard made several long documentary films and took thousands of still pictures of almost every aspect of King Island life. On 20 October, he even filmed the funeral of Nerizuc, with the whole community in attendance. Wrote Lafortune:

"Fr. Hubbard movypictures the whole ceremony. The weather is in keeping with the circumstance, i.e., none too good."[25]

On 31 January 1938, Hubbard was permitted to photograph, in the *nutaat* ceremonial house, the celebration dance of Pullac's success at bear hunting. Pullac had the distinction of having killed more polar bears than anyone else so far that season. "Father Hubbard," wrote Lafortune, "after flooding the place with light, takes movies of the whole affair."

Bogojavlensky and Robert W. Fuller, who published a number of Hubbard's still photographs in 1973, praised their high quality. "The ethnographic and historical significance of these photographs is enormous. . . .To our knowledge, there exists no comparable photographic record of an aboriginal sovereign state in all of Arctic ethnology."[26]

Despite the unusual activities, everyday life kept on—hunting, getting the provisions (including fifty drums of oil and large windows) up the steep slope with the hoist attached to their "amazing economy engine," school, New Year's festivities, and repairs. In April, repairs to the boat-landing place (below the rock, *iyac*) almost created a crisis in the village and again reflected the friction between the government teacher and the Catholic priest. The poor condition of the landing place had bothered Lafortune ever since his arrival on King Island, and Levin decided to work on it before spring hunting began. He planned to blast the rocks with dynamite. After a talk with the people, "the work started with a zest," and nine holes were bored in two days, mostly by the youngsters, since the men were busy working on their boats.

"Now two or three sneaks," wrote Lafortune, "busy bodies (there is that kind of vermin in every community) wanted to hamper the work. To that effect, they went to the schoolteacher and told him that the village was in danger; that Ed. Levin knew nothing about dynamite etc. etc. Now the fact of the matter is that Ed. is a real expert in handling dynamite. He has been using it for over 20 years and without one single accident. As to the danger for the village, that is childish. All that talk was dynamite for Ed. He could not wait till all the holes were bored, and burned to give a lesson to the teacher and his pals. Yesterday (May 7th) a succession of blasts were heard. The rocks flew from their place in a hurry. At first the natives were panicky. Even the men would not dare go around, but soon they got used to it and learnt everything. Now they will be able to use dynamite and make a road to the cold storage, a thing they want for many years.''[27]

By 9 June, the beach below *iyac* was ready for the cement work, and by the eleventh the concrete had turned the landing into a ''very convenient place. . .'' but Lafortune wrote that more work had to be done before it was ''perfect.''

Levin, a former professional prizefighter, had also developed an athletic program in the new community hall. Lafortune said that all of the boys and girls needed ''to be strengthened'' and were taking to boxing ''like ducks to water. Lots of other physical exercises are also given them. The girls have also their share. . . .When in Nome the boys will not look for trouble, but they will not run away from it. They will be able to knock spots off the booze sellers and protect their girls from the rif-raf of the town.''[28]

One of the most enduring contributions of the Hubbard party to King Island was a large bronze statue of Christ the King, about six feet tall, which was placed on the top of the island. Hubbard's gift had originally been made in clay by Samuel J. Kitson in 1904. (Kitson died in New York City in 1906.) Early in 1937, Hubbard asked Hilda Gavin of Boston if she would bear the expense of having the statue cast in bronze. She consented, and Hubbard brought it with him to the island. On 17 October 1937, the statue, which weighed about 900 pounds, was hauled up 700 feet of a 50° grade by almost all of the men and boys of the island in about an hour and a quarter.

The last day of October was a Sunday and the feast of Christ the King, ''a day that the natives will not forget for many generations. The statue of Christ the King is put in place and blessed by Fr. Hubbard. The whole population was present with the exception of a few sick and one or two cranks. Right after, the hymn 'Be Thou King, O Lord' was sung, then the consecration of the island to Christ the King was read, then the hymn, 'Blessed be God.' The weather was good enough to allow Fr. Hubbard to take lots of pictures. Our wireless gave the news of the proceeds to the Catholic world.''[29]

During the rest of their years on the island, Lafortune and the King Islanders regularly made ''pilgrimages'' to the statue, to the foot of which Lafortune transplanted ''every kind of plant and flower that grows on the Island.''[30] This piece of sculpture seemed to be more than just a statue to them; it was Christ the King himself, physically present

Statue of Christ the King. *(Photograph by Louis L. Renner, S. J.)*

Louis L. Renner, S. J., standing before Christ the King statue on King Island, 1974.

there, robed in a mellow patina of weathered bronze, arms outstretched, looking protectingly down upon the village hundreds of feet below. Lafortune liked to take guests up to the statue, but also to the top of the island for its own sake. Especially on a clear day, a rare sense of elation invariably overcame them as they looked out from the island's heights.

"It is my duty," Lafortune wrote, in 1940, to Ed. Coyle, a Jesuit seminarian, "to draw their attention to the marvels of the creation that surrounds them and, consequently, to the power, the beauty, the prodigality of the Creator."[31]

The Hubbard party left King Island in June 1938, but the effect of their visit on the islanders was talked about for a long time. On 18 November 1938, Joseph McElmeel, the General Superior of the Alaska mission, wrote an official letter to the Very Reverend Wlodimir Ledochowski, the General of the Society of Jesus in Rome: "Just at present Father [Lafortune] has the task of overcoming the bad influence of the Hubbard party on the island last winter. The seculars with Father Hubbard should never have been taken there. Father Hubbard has admitted to me that he can no longer control them as he used to. Even non-Catholics in Nome spoke to me about the danger that the King Islanders would be affected by the stay of the Hubbard party. The too frequent moving pictures developed a craze for pictures in the Islanders. On their visit to Nome this summer it was observed by seculars that they were no longer as simple as they used to be. Father Hubbard is a hard-working man, but he should not be permitted to come to the missions with the type of men he brought this year."[32]

The accusations, however, apparently were not very serious because Hubbard and four others, including Edgar Levin, were welcomed back in the summer of 1940 for more photographic work, and to make further improvements to the village. They arrived on 5 July, but the weather was too dark and rainy for photography until the first of August. Meanwhile, they helped unload the winter's supplies and build houses ("New houses are growing everywhere like mushrooms"; in all, thirteen new houses and a store were built). Especially Levin prepared the ground for a large warehouse, 40 by 25 feet, to be built at the head of the cable. They left King Island on 30 August on the *Aurora*.[33]

Lafortune's policy of isolating Eskimos from the undesirable effects of nonnative culture was still very much alive in his own thoughts in the 1930s. He cherished a plan for keeping the King Island people on the island permanently—never mixing with the rest of the world—and he wanted to relocate other Eskimos to places where they would not be contaminated by white culture. Uppermost in his mind in 1937 was his old plan of 1926 of relocating the Eskimos of Nome at Cape Woolley and establishing a mission there. He outlined his plans to Crimont. At Cape Woolley, he said, there once were two villages, both of which were destroyed by the influenza epidemic. At that place, "all the winds of creation seem to gather, and, on that account, even in winter there is open water all the time, and that is just what the hunters want. The winter hunting is good. In the spring of the year the birds fill the air and the fishes come by shoals in a large lagoon back of the village. The seals and the belugas follow them and can be killed in large quantities. By means of outboard motors or inboard, the walrus can also be procured. In the hills the berries are plentiful and the greens also. If the driftwood runs short, oil can be used for heating, not diesel oil, but seal and oogruk oil.

"The place is well known to the natives. They all speak well of it. The islanders who are too weak to hunt in the islands would willingly come there and make some kind of living. The question is 'How to open that place?' There is not a house left. First, we would need a practical Father, with some experience in that line. Secondly, we would need money enough to build on a small scale a house for the Father and five or six houses for the first comers. These could use those houses at a condition. Within 2 years they would have to build houses for their own selves, and our houses would become open again to other newcomers. In a few years a village could thus be built. Then would come the question of a school (day school). A small boat to carry wood and fish and hunt would also be needed. . . .At least $3000.00 would be needed. That would be a great work.

"The people of Nome, who are sick and tired to see drunken natives and the jail full of them, would appreciate that work immensely. Perhaps more than the whites the natives would be happy to quit this Babylon [of Nome]."[34]

10 / Lafortune's Notes on Hunting

Father Lafortune faithfully recorded hunting experiences, ice conditions, and tragedies, year after year on King Island. Many of his entries are repetitious—"good hunting," "bad hunting," "unusually bad winds," "two polar bears," "ten walrus"; but his comments, when combined topically, give a valuable, first-hand picture of a subsistence way of life that has almost disappeared since the island was abandoned in 1966. (No one lives there permanently now.) Lafortune was a rare person; he lived with the Eskimos as a priest devoted to their spiritual salvation, yet objectively recorded the minutiae of their everyday life.

Everyday life on King Island, however, was unlike everyday life anywhere else. A large part of it revolved around the ice and ice conditions, for it was on the ice that most of the hunting was done, and from it came most of the King Islanders' food and clothing.

When the King Islanders returned from Nome every October (in the early days on a revenue cutter, and later, on a Bureau of Education or Bureau of Indian Affairs boat), thin ice had begun to form on the ocean. In October, weather conditions were so unsettled and changeable that the hunters did not venture far out to sea, and few marine mammals migrated at that time.

In November, called "the month when one climbs up over the cliff," the hunters no longer hunted below the village on the south side of the island where the sea was usually still free of ice, but climbed over the island to the north side where the prevailing northerly winds had piled up enough ice to make seal hunting possible.[1] This is where the winter hunting generally took place. Each year the people waited for the pack

Village of Ukivok on King Island. *(Alaska Sportsman, February 1969)*

Typical ice conditions near King Island. *(Alaska Sportsman, February 1969)*

ice. One year Lafortune wrote that it had come on 25 November; another year, it came on the twenty-seventh, but once it did not arrive until 8 December. At this time Lafortune recorded in his "History": "The whole village feels good. About one ton of food was the result of the first real hunting of the season. Five oogruks were killed and quite a few seals. Every bit of the meat was taken to the village. I was given a good share of the spoils."[2]

By January, an extensive apron of shore-fast ice surrounded the island, but the winter hunting was not done on this stationary shore ice. The men hunted on the moving, churning slush and pack ice (formed both by the winter's cold and the ice pack driven by winds from the Arctic Ocean), and in the constantly opening and closing leads in the ice field where the wintering seals and a rare young bull walrus surfaced to breathe and to rest on the ice floes. This vast, desolate world of water, fog, and ice; and of wind, cold weather, and short days was the extended environment in which the King Islanders found a great part of their livelihood.

Lafortune wrote, "Of all hardships, I think those our Eskimo have to face are the hardest. I cannot see what could be harder. Hunting is their daily life, their daily bread. Early in the morning, irrespective of darkness, cold or storm, you see them climbing down the cliffs with guns, knapsacks, snowshoes, spears, ropes, packed on their back. And do not imagine they are going for the mere sport of it or for an easy walk. The ice is always moving and covered with hummocks varying between five and twenty feet in height. The currents are most treacherous. They walk for miles in search of some sea animal such as seal, walrus and polar bear. Now comes the worst part of the work. The animals they kill have to be dragged back to the island. When you consider that the lightest of all weigh at least 120 pounds and the heaviest 2500 you have an idea of the work. No sled can be used. Only human muscle can do that work. Time and again, on walking among those moving ice floats, they fall through. When they come back home they are as tired as living humans can be."[3]

The King Island men were out hunting whenever wind and weather conditions permitted. The hunters started out before dawn to climb up roughly six hundred feet on the village side of the island; then they walked across the mile-wide plateau to descend more than eight hundred feet to the ice field below. In the middle of winter there were only a few hours of daylight for hunting, and sometimes hunters ventured as far as ten miles out on the moving ice.[4]

There was great worry and anxiety when hunters did not come home when expected. They were sometimes delayed. On one occasion, "on account of the frightful condition of the ice. It was piled mountain high on every side."[5] Another time when a hunter was missing in the dark, and the villagers heard two shots in quick succession (their S.O.S.), Lafortune wrote, "As ever the ice was bristling with thousands of hummocks ranging from 10 to 30 feet in height, thereby forming thousands of angles and holes where a man could fall."[6]

When the leads in the ice began to widen in March, the hunters prepared their gear for early spring hunting; and by June (and sometimes by May) the ice had broken up and was gone.

Extremely low temperatures of thirty and forty degrees below zero F. bothered the hunters only if there was wind. Combined with the cold it often kept the King Island hunters indoors. Wind was one of the topics most frequently discussed, but more to be feared than the wind's chilling effect was its action on the ice floes on which the hunting took place. By grinding the floes one against another or against the shore ice, winds could break them up and turn them into slush ice in a relatively short time. A sudden reversal of wind could also drive the ice floes away from the shore-fast ice, cutting the hunter off from the island by a ribbon of open water and leaving him stranded, adrift.

This may be what had happened to a lone figure that the King Island hunters saw one day in January 1933. Lafortune wrote that they thought he was "probably from Siberia, walking on the ice not far away from them but beyond hailing distance. He seemed to be heading for Cape Prince of Wales—or rather for death. King Island was in full sight of him; he surely heard our hunters. Why did he not come here for refuge and safety? The natives have a reason at hand. Long time ago, the Siberians, just to satisfy their thirst for blood and rapacity, came at night in their skinboats and made a raid on the island. After a good deal of slaughter, they were repelled and compelled to run away as fast as they could. That crime is still preying in the minds of their great grandchildren, and they fear the vengeance of these natives. That poor fellow preferred a doubtful death to what he considered a sure death had he landed here." Was this simply a case of a lost hunter, or a case of a *tiktak*, a "drifter"? The drifter was a self-exiled social outcast, whose fate it was to drift alone, aimlessly and endlessly on the moving ice. He was an island unto himself, adrift in a hostile sea.[7]

During the winter, except for an occasional father-and-son team, the King Islanders always hunted alone on foot, although some hunters took a dog along to help drag game home or to help with tracking in case a bear was spotted. By April, the hunters no longer hunted on foot since leads began to open up in the ice fields, which during the winter had been more or less solid, and seals could be harpooned from kayaks. The discomfort and danger involved in this kind of hunting, the hardiness and daring called for, and the anxiety caused those waiting at home for the hunters' return were written about, time after time, by Lafortune. "When the night comes and some of their men are missing," he wrote, "they blow the fog horn; they have steamers' fog horns. In the same time some walk on the top of the island with lanterns. They have lost quite a few men in the past."[8]

One theme that keeps recurring in Lafortune's entries deals with the accidents that befell hunters on the ice. But this was the nature of the life on King Island, and his writings constitute one of the few records kept by a literate observer which show at first hand, over a long period of time, the extremely dangerous conditions under which the hunters worked to get their food.

In his first winter on King Island, Lafortune was present when a hunter drowned (Chapter 8), but his writings fortunately contain more "narrow escapes" than serious accidents. One January, Lafortune wrote: "An accident that might have resulted in his death happened to Akileina. He was riding on a cake of ice too weak to withstand him. The thing broke in 2 and the poor fellow went down in the brine clear above his head. Luckily 2 other natives were not far and saw his plight. They threw him their grab hook and hauled him to the ice. As it was pretty cold, Akileina had to run as fast as he could all the way home not to freeze."[9]

Concerning somewhat similar circumstances, he reported one December that two young hunters, hunting separately, "learnt a lesson that they will not forget for some time. They are Lawrence Appapayuk and Joe Anarac. They walked on dangerous ice, made so by a very light snow that covered all the crevices. They stepped on that snow and went down clear over their head with their knapsacks and guns on their backs. . . .Their knapsacks filled with water. Before Lawrence reached solid ice, he lost his gun, and to climb on the ice he had to use his cutlass. He could not reach the top of the ice with his hands. It was too high. He had to hurry up home not to freeze. He escaped unharmed. The fate of Joe was worse. After climbing on the ice he lost his bearings and was going away from the island. Had it not been for the presence of mind of Patunnac and Pullac, he would have perished. They drew his attention by firing. They helped him come across open water with their kayaks and packed him home. They know now that it is foolish to go hunting alone. They should have known that before.''[10]

In another January—1940—he wrote about a young man whose inexperience almost cost him his life. Every man of the island was out hunting on the fifteenth, and those ''who had experience apprehended the weakness of the current. At about 1 p.m. a rift was noticeable in the ice in front of the village. The alarm was given by boat horns. In the same time the wind began to blow southward. Soon it turned into a blizzard. Those who heard the horns ran back, but had to go around the opened water. John Anaokazuc lacking experience tried to come straight home. He got into bad ice. It was beginning to be dark. He fired. They hollered to him to go around the widening crack. Did he hear? We don't know.''

The next day, Lafortune recorded that men tried to draw his attention with lanterns until two A. M. The temperature dropped to twelve below zero F. and the wind blew with gale force. ''We have the gravest fears about him.'' On the nineteenth he wrote, ''*Deo Gratias*. For the last 4 days, speculations were rife about the fate of John Anaokazuc. Nome was notified and a plane was to come in search of him. This morning John B. Kokuluk climbed on the top of the island with. . . powerful binoculars. . .and, by God's Providence, spotted Anaokazuc and his black dog at about seven or eight miles from the island, S-E. No sooner had he given the news than a gang of fleet-footed youngsters made for him.''

They took a sled and furs and asked Lafortune for some fruit juice because those who had had the same experience said that they had suffered from thirst more than anything else. He had none to give them but instead gave them about three ounces of mass wine. They were back in two and a half hours. ''He was in awful shape,'' his lips parched and cracked, his tongue frozen from eating too much snow, and he could scarcely speak. The consensus was that another day out on the ice would have killed him. He had had nothing to eat until he killed a seal on the third day, but "the worst was the lack of sleep." He had tried to warm himself with the "heat of his dog but found out that it created too much condensation and was rather detrimental. Now the whole village is happy. . . .John says that he prayed all the time. That is what saved him."[11]

Polar bears and polar bear hunting occupied a special place in the life of the King Island hunter.[12] A polar bear was hunted on foot and a hunter's greatest prestige came from his success as a polar bear hunter. The meat was considered to be very good, and the hide salable to collectors, but the very act of hunting and killing the bear made this a laudable pursuit. Among the King Islanders, polar bear hunting was extremely competitive, and some hunters, especially young ones, took great risks to match or surpass the hunting success of their fellow hunters.

Polar bear hunting was a dangerous undertaking inasmuch as it took place during the shortest and darkest days of the year, and usually under the worst weather and ice conditions. The bear itself often presented a threat. Normally a polar bear runs away from a man, but if surprised, wounded, or winded, it will turn on its pursuer. The wind, however, was the greatest danger to the hunter because, sometimes, without warning, it changed direction, sending the ice and hunter adrift. Many a King Islander, hot in pursuit of a polar bear, was cut off from his home in this way; some returned safely but others disappeared forever. (In 1945, four men, hunting seals and walrus, were driven by a gale toward Saint Lawrence Island, but toward the next morning the wind reversed itself, and they were saved.)[13]

Lafortune's notes in his "History" reveal the competitiveness and importance of bear hunting, and he gives us an idea of the numbers of these formidable animals that were killed. On 29 December 1932, two hunters returned with a polar bear each, and on the thirtieth, "Patunnac was not to be beaten by those 2 fellows. He started in the dark (early in the morning) and found a big fellow watching over a seal hole. He made short work of it."

That winter, especially during the first two months of 1933, the polar bear take was quite large because of the constant northerly winds that drove down the pack ice, the native habitat of the polar bear. On 7 January, he wrote, "two more polar bears are bagged," and on the ninth, "Pullac has a crack at a polar bear, having overrun Atluk and Sabrana." By the tenth everyone was after bears, but none was sighted until the twenty-sixth when Lafortune reported: "The largest polar bear within the knowledge of the present generation was killed today by C. Mayac. Had it not been for his dog, he would never have found the animal. Unmindful of the tracks of the monster, guided only by its marvelous smelling sense, the powerful canine dragged Mayac straight to it. A long range shot broke one of the shoulders of the bear and brought it to a halt." In February, the King Island hunters killed nine polar bears, four of them on one day when they were found feasting on a huge ugruk.[14]

March 1934 was also a good polar bear month—ten bears in five days. On 16 December 1939, the hunters killed seven bears, "*A Record*," wrote Lafortune. They got twenty bears in all that month. In 1940, they had killed twenty-seven bears by 11 February in ideal weather.[15]

In the days before guns, the hunter killed a bear with a spear, but even with guns it was a dangerous encounter. Lafortune described one close call: "This is a day [22 January 1934] that Frank Ellanna will remember a long time. Had it not been for the timely and quick action of Leo Kunnuk, he would have been killed by a polar bear. Although the day was very cold, the boys went to hunt for big game and scattered themselves over a large field not to be in the way of one another. Ellanna spotted a bear and came within shooting distance of the brute. He fired and hurt it but not enough to disable it. The bear ran away and Frank gave him another shot. This time the animal did a thing that very few of them do, i.e. turning *volte-face* [about face] and coming right back on his aggressor. Frank knew he had 3 cartridges in his gun. He first stood his ground and shot the infuriated beast but did not disable it. He shot a 2d time without more effect. Probably due to excitement, he missed his 3d shot. The bear was within a few feet of him. He had no time to reload. Then began a race in comparison of which all the marathon races are childplay. If fear ever gave wings, it was this time. The frightful gnarling of the wounded beast became more and more distinct. The crunching of its claws and its breath could be heard easily. One or 2 minutes more and a slap of its left would have hurled Frank into his eternity. But lo! comes Kunnuk running like a wild deer. In a wink he threw his knapsack on the ice, grabbed his gun, aimed and blazed. The inert mass of the victim rolled within 2 feet from Frank. May the Sacred Heart be blessed forever!"[16]

The daring, skill, and physical stamina needed in bringing back a polar bear were rewarded by a ceremonial, and a successful hunt was celebrated in the most lavish of all King Island performances, *Anirsaak*, or "polar bear dance." According to Bogojavlensky and Fuller, this term is "etymologically derived from a base referring to 'departure.' This refers to the fact that between the time the bear is killed and the night the final ceremonies are performed, the spirit of the bear visits the community, and observances result in a placated soul and a propitious departure which bodes a return in the body of another polar bear."

The skull of the bear was taken by the hunter directly to his *kagri* and put on a bench where it stayed until the polar bear dance, which was held four days after a boar was killed, and five days after a sow. After the dance the skull was taken out on the moving ice, and when the ice made a noise as it moved, the spirit of the bear was regarded as having departed.[17]

The aspects concerning the bear's spirit were somewhat played down after the King Islanders' conversion to Christianity, but Lafortune knew that the dances took place, and from his notes in the "History" he seemed to support rather than oppose them; for example, in January 1934, when he wrote: "Two bears [on the twenty-sixth] paid the penalty for the pranks of their friend of the 22. Patunnac with Pussuc and Peter Mayac had one, and the other Mayac had the other." On the twenty-seventh, "Atluk and Aluuzac returned late at night with another bear. So now the 3 *kazines* [men's houses], according to ancient traditions, will have to give each a dance and the lucky hunters will have to produce *kacpadac* [sour greens with seal oil and reindeer tallow] and *alluit* [snow with seal oil and berries] and *tammoagac* [a mixture of reindeer or moose tallow, dry fish, seal oil, and water] to the crowd."[18]

The hunting of seals and walrus may not have provided the excitement and rewards of polar bear hunting, but it did provide some of the most important food and materials for clothing and boats. Seals were the most important source of food since they were taken throughout the winter at breathing holes through the ice, and harpooned later on when the ice opened. The walrus were hunted on their annual migration north into the Arctic Ocean in June, and again, to a limited extent, on the southward migration in the fall. Ugruks, or bearded seal (a very large seal), and beluga ("white whale") were also hunted. Occasionally a dead or stranded black whale was found on the beach or on the ice.

Lafortune's comments about sea-mammal hunting show the industriousness of the King Islanders and the quantities of food that they were able to obtain. In November 1932, ice and weather conditions were favorable; consequently, "lots of seals and oogruks and one walrus and two belugas, besides all kinds of birds [were taken]." On 12 December 1933, he recorded, "This is one of the biggest hunting days. Every hunter had two or three seals. A few of them had 4."[19]

The "big hunting," however, came in June (occasionally in May) when the ice pack moved back north and walrus and ugruks migrated through the Bering Strait from the south. The generic name, *Odobenus*, of the Pacific walrus means "the tooth-walker" (for when it hauls itself out by its tusks onto the floating ice pans, it seems to walk on its teeth). During the spring migration when the walrus came past the island by the thousands, there was a feverish, round-the-clock activity in the village for both the hunters and the women who cut up the meat and prepared the skins for use. Only Father Lafortune found leisure in an otherwise hectic world. He suspended catechism classes for the children and retired into the solitude of his annual eight-day retreat. "In the spring of the year nothing but absolute compulsion can hold the children and that should not be resorted to unless one wants to make religion odious to these people. Moreover, the children are needed for bird hunting and green culling."[20]

He commented variously on the walrus hunting and its products: "Skins and meat drying everywhere"; "On the 11th [of June 1933] the big hunting began and it is still going on. But it did not last long. The natives however have all the meat and oil and skins they need, but very little ivory. They killed about 50 walruses." On 4 June 1934, he wrote, "The big hunting is going on unabated; but this time it is kayak hunting and the oogruks have the worst of it. Every pair of kayaks come back pulling big fellows." On the next day, "The big hunting is still going on. All the houses are covered with drying meat. Boats and kayaks are coming full of hides and meat and a good deal of ivory." On the eleventh that year they stopped hunting because they ran out of ammunition, but they had had a good season. "Now it remains to dry the skins. That will take quite a little while; there are lots of them. As fast as the women can split the walrus hides, they are made to dry. Most of the oogruks are made to dry with the hair on."[21]

In June 1939, several of Lafortune's visitors saw what walrus hunting was like when he sent them out hunting with the Eskimos:

John Charles Olaranna (standing, right) divides his crew's ivory harvest in June 1938. *(Photograph by Hubbard. Archives of the University of Santa Clara)*

"They had good guns, but they had never seen a herd of walrus. Great was their excitement when they saw the ice covered and the water churning with walruses. At this time of the year the females are dangerous. They have their little ones to protect. Their defenses are long and pointed. If the hunters are not on their guard, they tear their skinboats and cause them to founder. The excitement of my visitors gave way to fear, but the calm of the Eskimos reassured them. Armed with the powerful pistol of the colonel [Douglas B. Wesson], the chief dispatched the most dangerous ones. That was the signal for the slaughter. In an instant the sea turned red. Around 30 walrus were stretched out on the water. Then came the work of cutting them up. Soon the boats had, besides their passengers, at least 10,000 pounds of nourishment and skins and ivory."[22]

In 1940, he wrote that by 8 May, "Over 50 walrus were killed already. The oogruks are not so numerous," and on 11 May, "Heavy hunting. The roar of the guns is heard all over. That is the ivory harvest. But due to the scarcity of boats, there will be scarcity of meat and oil, if the hunting stops now."[23]

The discovery of a dead whale in the ice was always a time of rejoicing, for it provided the King Islanders with the delicacy called muktuk, or the whale skin, which is edible. In one notation Lafortune recorded that nineteen hunters, who had been within hailing distance of the person who had found a whale, converged on it and cut off about a thousand pounds. At another time they found a whale—the body still warm—which had been attacked by a killer whale.[24]

Lafortune often mentioned eider ducks, auklets, murres, eggs, crabs, and fish. His comments certainly made King Island seem like the land of plenty. For example, he wrote one year that the hunting had been very good in November even before the ice pack had arrived. In addition to seals, ugruks, one walrus, and two belugas, there were "all kinds of birds." At another time, "The long north wind brings also the 'kaloet,' blue cod in abundance" [a great favorite, which in February 1934 appeared for the first time in five years]. On 27 January, "John Anaokazuc comes back with a bear. The others have seals, oogruks, blue cod and crabs. There is no danger of famine, thanks be to God."[25]

11 / Lafortune's Concern for the Eskimos and Their Way of Life

The physical and mental health of all of the Eskimos that he ministered to had been constantly in Lafortune's thoughts from the time he arrived in the Bering Strait area. During his earliest years there he felt that they were doomed as a race, and he put the blame on the "baneful effects" of the white people. These earliest impressions accounted largely for his policy of isolation and relocation, which have already been mentioned.

In his earliest writings, Lafortune blamed the whalers, the "whiskey peddler," soldiers, and the "impious and irreligious miner" for the Eskimos' troubles. He felt that they were from the "lowest strata of human society," debauching the Eskimos almost to the point of annihilation. "Epidemies have [also] wiped them out," he said. (The measles epidemic of 1900 and the influenza epidemic of 1918 did indeed take a heavy toll of life, but the population of the Bering Strait region has increased steadily since then.)

"Our poor Eskimos are dying like flies *[comme des mouches]*," he wrote to Albert Bellemare in 1910. "They begin by having the measles, and for lack of care the measles turn into consumption. Within the last two months [in Nome] I have buried about 15 of them, and some more are on the death list." In the Nome diary he wrote, "They all die of consumption," and, "Government statistics declare forty percent of the natives to be victims of syphilis!" (In 1932, however, he wrote that tests taken by doctors aboard the *Northland* revealed that "tests of the same kind [as on King Island] were taken in other places with the most satisfactory result that there is no syphilis among the natives.")[1]

To his niece, Marie-Flavius, he wrote, "I will not leave this country until I have buried the last of my Eskimos; or it is very probable that the Eskimos will bury me before they all disappear."[2] Writing in the same gloomy vein to the Catholic Editing Company, he said, "The Eskimos are not numerous. Previous to the coming of the whites, they have been decimated by frightful plagues. Now consumption and other sicknesses which they have taken from the whites will destroy the rest of them. Nearly every year the number of deaths exceeds that of the births. We assist at the agony of the race."[3]

Lafortune expressed his views in letters and especially in his essay, "Sociability and Customs of the Eskimos," written in 1922.[4] His knowledge of the Eskimos was from first-hand observation—not gleaned from books or scholarly reports—and he made it clear that he wrote only from a missionary standpoint. In this essay, Lafortune said that before the Eskimo first came into contact with the white man and his diseases, he had to rely on his own skills and endurance for his hunting, traveling, and livelihood, which, for the most part, meant a strenuous and hard life. Nevertheless, this traditional life was a more desirable one, not only because it was free, but because it was hard and hardy, calling forth the Eskimo's finest resources and energies, which kept him from sinking into the lethargy that afflicted many of those trying to live in both the Eskimo and white cultures. Although Lafortune endorsed a spartan way of life, he also realized that excessively hard work would have a debilitating effect on people weakened by disease. He was convinced that the Eskimo women's incessant, back-breaking work was one of the main causes of a weakened race and of a high infant mortality.

He also laid the blame for what he thought was the decline of the Eskimo race at the feet of the Eskimo men themselves, especially because of the attitude of the men toward the women and the prevailing marriage pattern. When the Eskimo men complained to him about Eskimo women marrying white men, he told them, "It is your own fault! Eskimo women can notice that Eskimo husbands leave home for days without providing food or fuel for their families; they can notice also that white men who have Eskimo wives never leave without making sure that the family is supplied in their absence." The number of Eskimo men already exceeded that of the women, and yet Eskimo women often married white men.[5]

The vital statistics in his diaries are not complete, but apparently the deaths and births were about equal on King Island until the 1930s, when the population began noticeably to increase despite several epidemics of whooping cough and measles that reduced the infant population. In the winter of 1936-37, eleven babies died of whooping cough, and in 1939, ten babies and two adults died of measles contracted in Nome.[6] But in 1940, there were nineteen births and only two deaths. "So we are 17 to the good," wrote Lafortune. "That general health condition is undoubtedly due to the natives' staying here last summer. The women had none of that grueling fatigue caused by their trip to Nome and by their sojourn there. I hope they will realize it."[7]

For many years he had advocated that the King Islanders stay year round on the island to avoid the diseases and the evil temptations of Nome, as well as the hard trip of getting there. The trip to Nome was no longer as grueling as it had been before Lafortune established his mission on King Island because the people had adapted outboard motors to their umiaks. The trip no longer took twenty-four or thirty-six hours to paddle or to sail; instead, their motors took them there in about fifteen hours. Still, it was a tedious trip, especially if the sea was rough and the weather foggy and cold. The skinboats were always "jammed with people [who] could hardly move, still less sleep," and if the wind was from astern, "the gas coming from the exhaust was nauseating."[8]

After the deaths from measles in 1939, he wrote, "The natives seem to be convinced now that it does not pay to go to Nome. Next spring a very serious effort will be made to hold them here."[9] He did indeed approach the summer of 1940 hoping that none of the King Islanders would go to Nome, but he was realistic enough to see that they would have to go occasionally for medical care, to get new glasses ("Most of the women wear glasses [because] they strain their eyes by sewing, doing beads work and often with poor light"), to buy certain hardware items not carried in the local store, or even to make some money longshoring in the event of a bad hunting season.[10]

But his optimistic prediction written to his niece that "I am going to spend the summer here with the greater part of my flock. . .a new adventure for all of us," did not work out quite the way he thought it would.[11] Old habits were hard to break, and on 14 June, "Pullac's boat stealthily got ready to go and early in the morning, in spite of the fog and poor current, the motor was heard. They were gone, but they missed their bearings and landed at Teller.'' On the twentieth, ''Two more boats leave for Nome, loaded mostly with men. The few women who went with them did it by necessity. We will see what the result of the experiment will be. There is no danger here for the youngsters but there may be danger for the men alone in Nome.''[12]

He felt, however, that the summer spent on King Island had been beneficial, for the health of the people seemed ''one hundred percent better'' than the previous winter. On 21 May 1941, he wrote Crimont, ''I think it is due to the crowd summering here. They were spared the hardship, the sicknesses and the filthiness attendant to their trip and sojourn to and in Nome and therefrom. I think they understand it,'' and he had his population figures, ''17 to the good,'' to show for it.

Still, even on the island, illnesses could be serious, for the people had no professional medical assistance when sick except for an occasional visit by a nurse or a doctor who came for a brief time during the open season. (Lafortune himself never needed to see a doctor because he was never sick!)

Throughout his ''History'' he recorded the illnesses that beset the King Islanders: measles, grippe, influenza, colds, and dysentery, which usually seemed to strike them when they went to Nome or when the first ships arrived at the island in the spring. ''If it were not for that sickness,'' he said, ''it would be perfect here.''[13]

He was constantly trying to get better medical care for the King Islanders, and in regard to dentistry he wrote to Crimont, ''The Coast Guard Cutters do all what they can for the health of the natives, but, as they cannot anchor long at one place, they cannot do dental work except pulling the teeth. That is a calamity that will destroy the health of these people. Would it be possible to have a dentist pass about 15 days here and train a willing young man, just to fill up the teeth that begin to decay? The natives are very clever with the tools. It would be no question of crowning the teeth nor of bridging them, but just to fill them. That would be one hundred percent better than to pull them.''[14]

By 1941, he felt more optimistic about the health of the King Islanders after Dr. Victor E. Levine of Creighton University again visited the island and examined the people. In the ''History,'' Lafortune recorded that the examination ''of the natives by the Dr. reveals the fact they are way stronger than the natives of the other villages. In

1934, Dr. Levine examined the natives. His verdict was rather discouraging. Now he says that he is surprised at the change. The younger generation will be stronger than the previous ones.''[15]

Although he had repeatedly written about the accidents that took off the strong hunters, and the short life span that resulted from a hard life, there were some King Islanders who lived to be old. One, ''the oldest woman of the island and probably of the whole of Alaska,'' died on 14 January 1933. She was Unaleina, the mother of Arnasiak and Sukareak, a woman who ''must have been over 100 years old. She never knew wealth nor sickness. She saw the times when the natives had no guns and ate only native food. She was raised on that kind of food and saw older days than most of those who have partly adopted the white man's fare.''[16]

Native food was one of Lafortune's favorite topics in writing and conversation. Throughout his entire career in the Bering Strait area he was convinced that white man's food weakened the Eskimos. ''One thing sure is that those among them who adopt our ways are losing their strength. Toothache and stomach-ache and rheumatism are becoming frequent among them. Some of them, after trying our ways, went back to their old ways and they feel better.''[17] Lafortune was convinced that the native diet provided all the nutrients necessary for good health, and chose it himself, whenever possible, over the white man's. He relished the Eskimo's food, and on King Island it constituted the major part of his diet. It was a good thing that the Eskimos always gave him a portion of almost everything they caught because had they not done so, he would have had to live still more frugally. As late as 1941 his ''salary'' was only $360 a year, and from this he had to buy fuel for the church, chapel, and his private quarters.[18]

His fellow priests all agreed that he could eat anything an Eskimo could eat. He liked fermented fish (herring, salmon heads, whitefish) which on the mainland was prepared by placing the fish in a hole between two layers of hay and letting ''nature do the rest. In winter they open that hole. The odor is pretty strong, enough to draw the foxes from a few miles, but it is not worse than limburger cheese. The taste is not bad and it is surely very nutritious. They eat a great deal of frozen fish in winter. It is not bad at all if one wants to overcome his prejudices.''[19]

Lafortune thought that the white man's customary opposition to native foods was only a matter of ignorance or of prejudice, and in a strongly worded letter to his Superiors, in which he discussed the type of man suited for the Alaska mission, he said, "One has to learn how to use the food of the country. Woe to the one who is guided by his prejudices. He deprives himself of a better food than anything he can buy on the market. Nowhere in the world can be found better fish and better meats than here. Still some of our Fathers are so prejudiced as not to want even to taste that food. One has to use his judgment and overcome those prejudices, otherwise he makes himself useless and a heavy burden on a mission."[20]

In 1941, Dr. Levine also made a nutritional analysis of the greens and other foods of King Island, which Lafortune had wanted done for years. In October, Lafortune received the report, which was "an eye-opener to me and the natives. As soon as they are all back from Nome, I will take a large sheet of paper, write that report in large characters, explain the whole thing to them and pin it on the wall of the church. That will surely make a change in their diet and in their health [since they apparently had been eating too much 'white man's food']."[21]

Throughout the years, Lafortune's life on King Island was full of a variety of activities, helping his parishioners in many ways other than attempting to get good medical assistance or overseeing their health. He was also mediator, homemaker, baker, cook, innovator, inventor, carpenter, painter, and during one winter, a schoolteacher, but above all, a priest. Although he was first of all a spiritual leader, he was also a very practical man—as he had been in Nome—who was able to cope with, and solve, many of the difficult situations that confronted him on King Island.

He had once proved his ability as peacemaker during his first year on the island (Chapter 8), but he was tested again just after his third Christmas there when it appeared that factional feuding was about to erupt again. "Jimmie Atluk in returning from hunting killed one of the dogs of Frank Ellanna because he was afraid he would kill his own dog. The dogs of Frank are kind of vicious. That was bad enough but worse was to come. The father of Frank, Nerizuc, hearing of that, to revenge himself, went to kill the dog of Jimmie Atluk. That dog had nothing vicious about him. It was mere revenge. Naturally Jimmie wanted his revenge and he made up his mind to clean [out] the bunch of dogs of Nerizuc by killing his two females. Fortunately, Jimmie had sense enough to speak to me of his proposal. It was easy enough to dissuade him. But for such things not to recur, I called a meeting of the men and we passed the following resolution or law: 'Henceforth, in order to be justified to kill a vicious dog three men will have to testify to the chief that the dog is vicious. The chief will warn the owner of the dog to chain the animal. If he refuses, then the complainant will be free to kill the dog.' "[22]

But the physical problems that the villagers had on their island were as important to Lafortune as their social problems. In his "History," he wrote that as "we become more acquainted with the situation. . .we find it bristling with many interesting problems: (1) The housing is wretched. The big boys are forced to sleep in the *kasga* [men's house]. There also the husbands have to pass the whole day if they want to work at all. The family life suffers for that. How to remedy that is more than we can tell for the moment. (2) A 2 or 3 inches pipe should bring the water from the creek to the heart of the village. Besides supplying everyone with the water he needs, that would enable us to clear all refuses and garbage, thereby doing away with a danger of infection. (3) A derrick should be erected that would allow good size wooden boats to be put safely on the rocks every time that the natives come back from hunting or fishing. It would also be very useful in the fall of the year to unload the boats. So far the unloading is simply killing. A derrick in connection with the cable would save lots of lives."[23]

In 1933, Lafortune's earlier plans to have the water piped into the center of the village materialized. In May, the Eskimos began building the line with heavy four-inch pipe provided by the Bureau of Education. "When the system is well established," he wrote on 15 May, "it will be an easy matter to keep the village clean. With the pressure we are going to have, the dumps and garbage will surely fly." By 5 June, the water system was completed and it was quickly discovered that its purging powers surpassed all expectations. "The elevation is about 300 feet. When they left the water flow in the main, they found out that they had harnessed the devil. The dirt flew faster than they wanted. They cannot stop it for fear to burst out the whole system. No wonder, there is at least 1200 pounds of pressure at the end of that pipe."[24]

To ease the women's work in gathering vegetables, Lafortune proposed to plant and cultivate, right in the village, the various vegetables and greens the women went so far to gather. "With cultivation they could be improved. I think that to be a work proper to the Society." The Eskimos would have to be trained to grow gardens, but "they are extremely apt to do any work of that kind. They catch on so quick."[25]

He also made a great improvement in getting meat into the cold storage cave. "So far," he wrote in his "History" in 1932, "the poor women had to pack the meat on their back to the lower storage which is not at all as good as the upper one. They could not possibly climb up to the top one, there being no ladder. Those times are past, thanks be to God. Now there is not only a ladder but a cable and a hoist able to carry the meat from the beach to the upper storage. Both the ladder and the small cable have been furnished by the Church. The large cable across the mouth of the canyon is from the wreckage of the *Gasco.* It has been supplied by John Katungazuk."[26]

He devised a number of projects over the years, which he thought might help the people economically. One of these was a "crab industry," to have begun in 1931 after Hugh Ibbetson had given Lafortune a hundred and twenty glass jars and a pressure cooker. The next year the project was begun even though there was no longer a cooker since it had exploded when Frances Ross was cooking beans in it. The explosion blew off the top of the stove and scattered burning coals over the entire room, which fortunately was empty at the time. But a few old women went out on the ice for crabs and filled the jars in less than three weeks, and processed them in steam for three hours without pressure.

"Now the question is to put the meat on the market," Lafortune wrote. "We want the natives themselves to do that. That will take from us the odium of commercialism."[27] An election was held to see who would market the product, and Olaranna was chosen. Lafortune was confident that the industry would be a good one. "Thousands of jars can be put up. Later on, it might be canned. That would reduce the price. The crab can be fished winter and summer, and the supply will never be exhausted."[28]

The crab was said to be excellent, but Lafortune said no more about it after that. Perhaps the depression of the early 1930s did not allow a market to develop. He had not, however, given up the idea entirely because in 1933 he "put lots of food in jars; different kinds, crab, seal meat, liver, muktuk, tongues, polar bear, hearts. The result is a complete success. I used these preserves to feed the men who were working on my house."[29]

He was also very much interested in using seal oil for various purposes. One of his experiments was to mix seal oil instead of linseed oil with paint. In June 1932, he wrote in the "History" that he painted the church with white enamel, "some vermilion, and lots of seal oil.

Linseed oil makes a paint that cracks and peels off. Will the seal oil have the same draw-back? I expect not. It is so downright sticky that nothing will crack it. In case it succeeds, it might create a market for seal oil.''

A year later he wrote in the margin of that entry: ''The paint was examined and found badly peeling. So the seal oil does not help much on the maltoid.''[30]

At another time he said, ''I am studying now the properties of their seal oil with a view to use it to better advantage for lighting and heating purposes. With the way they use it now, they cannot possibly bake bread over their lamps, in which they can have only one straight flame. A kind of burner will have to be made that will heat up a large surface. It is quite a problem.''[31]

Later on, one of Lafortune's ideas for using seal oil was more successful than most. During the early part of 1934, having almost run out of coal, he began to buy ''all the blubber I can at $1.00 a can to save the coal. It is very little more expensive than the coal and very satisfactory. If I can have plenty of it, the situation will be safe. All I use now every day for the mass and the [catechism] classes. . .are 2 buckets of coal and ½ can of blubber. Sacks and coal dust are used to the best advantage with blubber. I am thinking very seriously another year (if Almighty God gives me one) to use all the blubber I can, even if I have coal enough. That would help along the natives considerably and stop them from losing so much stuff. I could have lots of tanks and fill them in the spring of the year. The flowing oil could be used by means of a pipe and tank, to drip in the stove. The blubber would be put directly on the coals.''[32]

But of all of his activities on the island, what he loved best was teaching his catechism classes. He held, in almost unvarying routine, four classes of catechism every day in the church. ''To the 1st class I teach the prayers and the easiest part of the catechism of Baltimore. To the 2d class the whole catechism. To the 3d class the history of the Bible and the recapitulation of the catechism. To the 4th class I teach the history of the Church with maps of my own make. For the catechism I use the great catechism in pictures of *La Bonne Presse*. It is perfect. When a pupil can give a good account of every one of those pictures, he knows his catechism thoroughly and a good deal of the Bible. For the adults I give two instructions a week. In the same time I rehearse the hymns appropriate to each season.''[33]

From the very beginning of his work with the Eskimos, Lafortune had used large, colored charts illustrating the Bible and the mysteries of the faith, published by *La Maison de la Bonne Presse* in Paris. He praised these charts frequently and recommended their use. "These people," he wrote to one of his young correspondents, "learn by the eyes. . . . For these people our teaching has to be as concretized as possible."[34]

Catechism classes usually ended in early June with ceremony and a celebration. Lafortune would read the results of the classes—attendance, behavior, and the like ("That always makes quite an impression")—and prizes were awarded. Invariably there were not enough prizes to go around, and the final winners had to be determined by lot. "We should have prizes for all whose attendance is without reproach," he commented in the "History."[35]

He occasionally rewarded the classes with parties and with foods that he himself had prepared. In his "History" for 1933 he wrote, "I gave a party to the 2d class of catechism. Last Thursday. . .I gave another party to the larger boys. If I judge by the quantity they ate, they must have found everything first class. Both parties walked away with 21 loaves of bread, 20 lbs. of jam (dried apples and raisins flavored with Mapleine) and about 5 lbs. of bacon (cooked crisp and ground with the meat grinder). All that makes nice sandwiches. (To make those 20 lbs. of jam I used about 5 lbs. of dried apples and 4 lbs. of raisins.)"[36]

His culinary feats not only sweetened catechism parties but other special occasions. Although he was sure that his first Christmas on King Island would never be forgotten (Chapter 8), he also contributed to many more. For the second Christmas, 1931, he devised a "punch" for the celebrations. "Instead of coffee we gave them water in which we put one lemon for the show of it, and vinegar and sugar and ¾ of a bottle of wine unfit to be used for the mass. We prepared about 6 gallons of it and it all went in a jiffy. With extract of lemon and vinegar and brown sugar we could prepare a good punch for a few cents."[37]

In preparation for his third Christmas on the island he made about 45 loaves of bread with raisins. "Olaranna furnished 25 lbs. of flour, Atluk [who had a small private store] 50 lbs. and some raisins and lard. I put up the balance of the raisins."[38]

And on New Year's Day he rang the church bell and "the crowd comes. Contrary to my first plans, instead of making candies, I made a big box of cookies. It is cleaner. Candies are too downright sticky. To help swallow the cookies, I made about 8 gallons of coffee. The whole thing went in a jiffy."[39]

All of these activities reveal Lafortune's "belonging" to the island and living, it seemed, almost uncritically the life of the islanders themselves. He did indeed recognize the importance of the Eskimos' own cultural traditions, which he either accepted entirely or in part, having reached a compromise in certain matters.

There were, however, some aspects of the traditional culture that he felt were irreconcilable with Christianity. One was the role that the *angatkuq* or shaman (medicine man) had played in the native culture, and another was the custom of spouse-exchange (often called "wife exchange").

He loathed the shamans. To Lafortune, they were "imps, most of the time cripples, deformed individuals who had intercourse with his satanic majesty," or unscrupulous charlatans who resorted to fraud and black magic to dupe and cheat their victims.[40] He made it clear to his parishioners that the *angatkuq* was no longer to play a part in the lives of those baptized.

He denounced spouse-exchange absolutely. To Father Julius Jetté, S. J., who was then near the end of twenty-five years of serving the Koyukon Indians on the middle Yukon, and had called on his fellow Jesuits for accounts he could include in a projected "History of the Alaska Mission," he wrote in 1925: "Previous to their becoming Catholics, they [King Islanders] had the nasty practice in certain times of the year to change wives. That abuse does not exist any more. Thank God."[41]

In keeping with the Christian tradition, Lafortune stressed strongly that Sunday was to be kept holy and was to be a day of rest from work. But he was not a rigorist in this matter. A visitor once asked him what he would do if walrus or whales approached the island at the time of Sunday mass. He answered unhesitatingly, "We would postpone the church services until the men and boys had their chance at hunting. Hungry people do not make good church-goers. Well-fed ones do, and anyhow they would then have something to be thankful for."[42]

Lafortune was not opposed to dancing—as were many Protestant ministers—but he was opposed to dancing during Lent, simply because he thought that dancing was not in keeping with the best spirit of that season which called more for penance than for merriment. One year some of the best polar bear hunting occurred during Lent, but the

15

I urged the natives to have their Christmas celebrations in every house first
than in each casino. That will make the children love their parents, their
homes and their island better than if they have the whole fun in the school house
The midnight mass was in the big Church and very well attended.
The 2 other masses were in the Chapel which was crowded each time.
N.B During the cold part of the winter, the communions will be given in
the Chapel till 9.30 and the mass will be at 10 oclock.

26 Two more polar bears, besides lots of seals. Deo Gratias.
Our epidemy is practicaly gone. May God preserve us from another
spell of it!

31. The last day of the Year 1942. Since Christmas the weather i
ideal. There is hardly any coughing left. We have benediction ev
evening. We have many reasons to thank God. Hee has granted lots
special favors in spite of our unworthiness. Wars and rumors of
war are away from us. In our isolation we feel absolutely safe. A few
planes pass, probably on their way to Russia. We have provisions
for 2 Years. The wolf is away from our door. The hunting i
excellent. "Sit nomen Domini benedictum"!
If this book can be of any use, I will bless God for it.

B. Lafortune S.J.

Last page of Lafortune's "History of the Mission of King Island." *(Oregon Province Archives)*

King Islanders respected his injunction against dancing during that time, although doing so meant breaking with the traditional ritual of holding the polar bear dances the required number of days after the kill. Instead, they carried on their festivities during Easter Week.

Lafortune had appreciated the dances from the time of his arrival in Nome, and in 1922 he wrote to Lonneux: "When their dances were not mixed up with superstition, they were very innocent. The men danced together, but never touched one another. In their dances they walked and hopped around. The women, on the contrary, never walked neither touched one another, and, moreover, they would not move their feet. Their dance consisted in very graceful movements of the arms and head and body. The cadence was perfectly kept by the drummers and singers. They have a music of their own. It always struck me that they learned to sing from the winds and the waves."[43]

The King Islanders were widely known as imaginative, skillful dancers, and when in Nome, they danced in the traditional song and dance festivals for both Eskimos and whites. On the island their dancing was done for more than mere amusement: it had important social and political connotations, and before the advent of Christianity some dances were based on their religion.[44]

On King Island the dancing took place in the *kagri* (singular use; *kagrit*, plural), or the men's house, or community house. During Lafortune's years on King Island there were three men's houses: *kaluilit, agulliit*, and *nutaat*, each *kagri* having its own membership and traditions. This kind of institution and building (on King Island it was built partly underground) was in use throughout western Alaska, and served as a community hall and a place for individual activities. There, the men and older boys spent most of their indoor time, working, carving ivory, socializing, and politicking. They also ate and slept there until they married. Women used the hall to sew the boatskins. Ceremonials, festivals, and various athletic events took place there, and since the roofs were almost the only level surfaces in the whole village, they served as village plazas, and as assembly and work and play areas.[45]

Knud Rasmussen, the Danish ethnologist, visited the village during the summer of 1924 when the people were on the mainland. He described two dance houses as "very ancient; their passage-way and walls are covered with grass of such luxuriance that it almost evens out the rock cleft in which they hang like two fantastic bird nests." Entry to the dance house was first made through a tunnel, six meters long,

A King Island woman, Sungnagazuk, and the interior of the *kagri agulliit* where she was living during the winter of 1937-38. *(Photograph by Hubbard. Archives of the University of Santa Clara)*

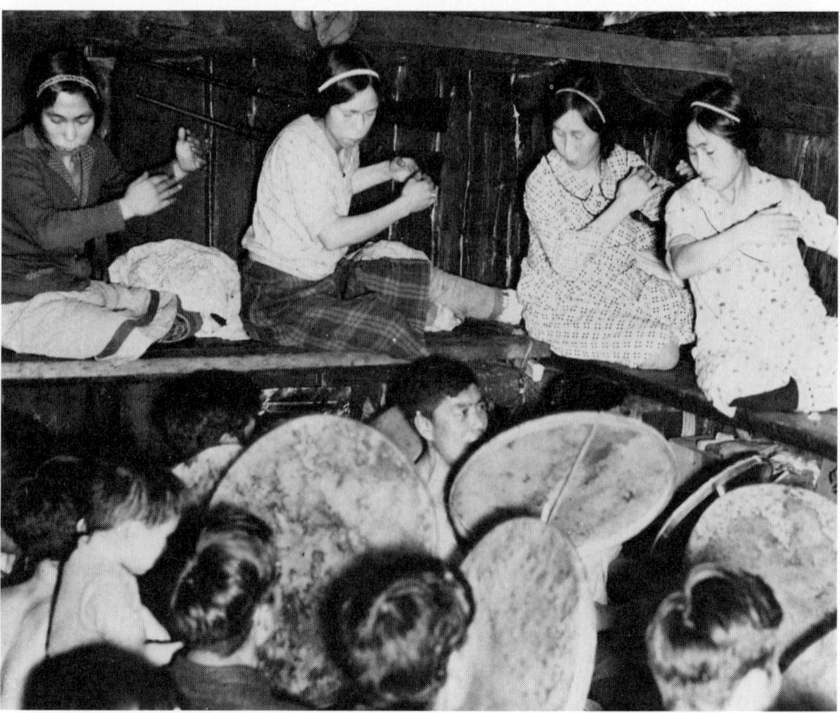

Women's bench dance in the *kagri agulliit*, accompanied by drumming. *(Photograph by Hubbard. Archives of the University of Santa Clara)*

King Island men working in the *kagri agulliit*, 1937-38. *(Photograph by Hubbard. Archives of the University of Santa Clara)*

''built of large stones tightened with sods,'' and then up through a round hole in the floor at the inner end of the tunnel. Inside, the ''festival hall'' was built of thick planks, and on the walls of one house he saw ''about ten tambourines hung along the walls between grotesque and humorous dance masks.''[46]

These men's houses continued to be an important part of village life even after Lafortune founded the mission, and became a good example of the integration of traditional and contemporary ceremonialism. For instance, in November 1943, the *kagri nutaat*, after having been completely renovated, was blessed by Lafortune on the morning of 12 November, and inaugurated with a banquet and dances that evening.[47] Lafortune, however, carried on his activities in his church or in his own quarters throughout his years on King Island.

12 / War Anxieties and Final Delivery

In 1940, Lafortune wrote to Ed. Coyle, "Before long I will need a successor. I cannot live forever. Old age is coming slowly but surely, and old age means proximity of death."[1] He had reason to be reminded of the mortality of man because he was celebrating his golden jubilee as a Jesuit that year, a milestone that he hoped would be ignored. On 11 June, he wrote to his classmate, Joseph Waddel, "I was hoping my fiftieth year in religious life would pass unnoticed. But your charity, in the midst of all your occupations, discovered it and sounded the alarm. . . .Two things console me: (1) the prayers of my best friends, (2) the absence of any commotion. I am going to pass the summer here [King Island], perfectly isolated with my flock."[2]

On 31 July, the feast of Saint Ignatius, founder of the Jesuit Order, Lafortune noted briefly in the "History": "Fifty years ago today I entered the Society. In spite of all my efforts, I could not keep the event unnoticed. Fr. Hubbard had vent of it when in Montreal. He carried the news here and stealthily spread it among the natives. One consoling result of it all was that a large number of natives received holy communion."

The peacefulness of King Island was cherished by Lafortune as a haven for both the King Islanders and himself. There they were protected from disease and other calamities of Nome and the surrounding mainland; and there Lafortune was able to direct their lives the way he wanted amid the grandeur that he found so exhilarating to all of his senses. But when war was declared in Europe in September 1939, he expressed an intimation of what might come to his isolated haven.

"What will happen in Europe and in Canada between now and my return [to Nome] God alone knows. I will know it only next spring."[3]

On 29 August 1940, he wrote in the "History" that he had learned the day before that "conscription was to be a fact in a very short time. It is voted by a large majority; but no referendum. Men aging between 21 & 40 will have to receive 1 year of military training. A war is in the offing. Which one, we don't know."

The first active participation of the King Islanders in war-related activities began on 11 September 1940, when the *Itasca* brought a stack of ugruk skins so that the women could make mukluks (boots) for the army. They were busy sewing until well into the summer of 1941. When the navigation season opened in Bering Strait that year, "a man-of-war bristling with cannons," which came to the island, brought a letter for Lafortune from Sister Marie-Flavius. In answer, he wrote, "Even in this remote corner of the world there is an atmosphere of war. Yesterday a bomber was roaring over our heads. A Japanese ship is snooping around in our environs, and Uncle Sam does not like that." In July, the U.S.S. *Charleston* paid them a visit, and "Captain Andersen. . .walked away with some ivory and paid it back by sending a box of oranges."[4]

Nome was gearing up for war and many ships had to be unloaded throughout the summer. Longshoremen were needed. On the twentieth of May, Lafortune reported: "A wire came from the Lomens through Fr. [Joseph] McHugh. They want 30 men to go and unload the boats, and will send a boat for them on the 25th. They are promised work all summer and to be taken back in the fall. It is very tempting. If they can have 2 days more of hunting, they might go. Otherwise they will be short of oil and dried meat and ivory, things that they cannot buy. I do not know what they will do." On the twenty-second they had "2 days of heavy hunting," and on the twenty-seventh, the *Lucile* arrived and returned to Nome with twenty-five men. On 12 June, the *Lucile* came again for longshoremen. Lafortune noted: "The sea is clear of ice for the moment. 35 went. They were promised work the whole summer and free return in the fall. There will be more longshore work than ever. On account of the preparation for the war, labor is at a premium. The natives could work ivory here and make nearly as good; but in the fall their ivory would be gone, whilst by going to Nome they will have ready money and save their ivory for the winter work."[5]

On the seventh of September, the *Lucile* returned a third time for still more men (although Lafortune does not say whether any of the first groups had returned to the island) "and a bunch of them went." The men returned to the island on 31 October with the distressing news that J. Aresac and Paul Anaolic had been drafted into the army. "If the government takes 2 or 3 boys every summer," he wrote in the "History," "that will be the doom of this place. Only old men cannot possibly live here."

On 8 December, Lafortune, on remote King Island, wrote, "Bad news. Japan declared war to U.S. . . . .Orders came for all the principal towns of Alaska to be ready for an attack at any time. But are they, can they be ready in time? That is the question."

Few Eskimo communities depended on its able-bodied young hunters for survival as much as did King Island, and these men were the very ones who were inducted. On 1 January 1942, Lafortune wrote in the "History": "The year is ushered [in] by dire apprehensions . . . .The war with Japan will probably take away all our able-bodied men. What will become of the others is the poignant question. The military authorities know nothing of the situation here. Both the school teacher and myself will try to remedy the situation. I will write to Father [John B.] Tennelly and to the Bishop. The school teacher, Mr. J. [ohn] Shea, will write to the head of the Bureau of Indian Affairs. With the help of the Sacred Heart we might save the situation."

On 28 May, two boatloads of people left for Cape Prince of Wales "to buy, bargain and trade," and when they returned in June they said that induction procedures were as heartless there as on King Island. "By the reports," wrote Lafortune, "they are pretty ruthless in taking the boys from their old parents. If they do the same thing here, that will be the end of the mission. What could we do without the young strong bodied boys? No hunting, no fuel, no food, no light."[6]

The war was coming closer day by day to this remote outpost. "The government is starting a camp on St. Lawrence Island," he wrote. "That puts us in some danger. The Japs might consider this place as a storage place for the army and bomb us.

"Two days ago [on 3 June] Dutch Harbor was bombed. The freighters will have to be convoyed and plenty too. If the Japs are not too busy in the South they might play us some bad tricks."[7]

Lafortune was also much worried by the news in a Bureau of Indian Affairs bulletin that there would be a scarcity of guns and ammunition because of the war. Without guns, he wrote, "What will our hunters do? Without hunting, it is impossible to live here. We live exclusively from the sea. Food, heat, light, all come from the sea. There is not a single shrub on the island. All the houses are lighted and heated by means of lamps burning the oil from the seal, the oogruk, the walrus. All the food of the Eskimos is impregnated with that oil. Can they return to their old ways of hunting? The present generation doesn't know those ways any more." (Once before, during the depression in 1934, they had little money for ammunition. They solved their hardship by putting only two sharpshooters in each umiak, the other hunters using axes and cutlasses, and then dividing their booty evenly when they got home.)[8]

In June, Lafortune envisioned the worst about the war, and a marginal note, "War in Nome," in the "History" is a preface to his fears. The *Trader* came to barter with the Eskimos and "brought the bad news that the Japs have taken Dutch Harbor, the Pribilof Islands and other islands around there. [This was not the case.] In all probability not a boat will come from Seattle to Nome. Nome is short of provisions and practically deserted. All those who can afford it are going outside by plane. The provisions are rationed. Some Jap. planes flew over Nome to reconnoitre. Some bombers came from Fairbanks to see what was going on there. Probably Nome will be attacked, if not invaded, in a few days."

In June and July 1942, military activity increased in the Bering Strait near King Island. On 27 June, the *Bozo* came "for another batch of longshoremen. A large transport is expected in a few days. In the same time a convoy is going to St. Lawrence Island to fortify the place as fast as possible. That should have been done long time ago. . . .Our radio reports that 300 Jap. planes and 3 large boats are coming to tackle one of our large cities. We have to leave everything in the hands of God. We are well sheltered here."

On 8 July, he reported, "A strange boat paid us a visit. She seems to have no name but only letters and numbers. She comes from the States and is destined for Teller where she will be the greatest part of the summer. They are 12 men aboard. What is her mission? We don't know. Everything is a secret nowadays. But the crew seems to be hungry for ivory and slippers. Is she only a trader?" On the eleventh, "A small transport paid us a visit. Her name is *King*. What was her object we don't know; she fussed around here, either sounding or planting mines. The Captain and one of his officers came to the house . . . .They cleaned the village of all the ivory and slippers that were left, and sent me a few dozens of apples and oranges.''

On 21 July, he wrote, ''The *Trader* comes again bringing back some of our men and to do as much trading as she can. Nome is becoming a regular army camp. Heavy artillery is unloaded. Bombers and ammunitions of all kinds and in huge quantities are also landed. But the stores received nothing so far. All is for the army.''[9]

Before the freeze-up, Lafortune wrote to Crimont, lamenting the effects of the war on the King Islanders: ''It is sad to see a community, no matter how small, go down gradually and come closer and closer to its doom. My consolation is that those who die here die a good death. They are a pretty good crowd. . . .I hope that the boys who are drafted will remain good. Four are gone and two more are threatened. That will leave 20 able-bodied men to procure food, fuel, light, garments for 215 people. . . .That is the way these natives are treated.''[10]

But, as if to mitigate his pessimism, the *Derblay* anchored in front of the village on 24 October with two hundred tons of goods on board, including five hundred dollars' worth of groceries given to the King Island longshoremen by the Lomen Company in appreciation for the quality of their work. ''They are the only ones who know how to stick to their job,'' wrote Lafortune. ''As barge men they are unsurpassed. Not a soldier can rival with them.'' Out of gratitude for all the supplies and their safe landing, a mass of thanksgiving was celebrated on 4 November. ''It was perfectly attended.''

The war years were difficult ones for everyone in Nome, but especially for the Eskimo people. In June 1944, Lafortune was ordered by Bishop Fitzgerald to leave King Island and go to Nome for the summer. ''My mission,'' Lafortune recorded, ''was to keep my people as much as I could from being contaminated by the unspeakable corruption of Nome. . . .Booze and loose soldiers are the curse of Nome. There is an atmosphere of irreligion all over. It is a poisonous atmosphere that renders even our white and Eskimo Catholics partly paralyzed (spiritually).'' In his ''History'' he wrote, ''The natives are just disgusted of Nome. Accidents galore, murders, drunkenness, etc. etc.''[11]

Above all, it was difficult for the young Eskimo women, whom the soldiers often accosted. Lafortune had a ready solution for the soldier who would make a nuisance of himself with the King Island girls. An account of this is given by Edmund A. Anable, S. J., who was in Nome during the war years: "One particular soldier was quite persistent in hanging around one of the King Island girls, to the extent of physically handling her. The men came to Father to ask advice. This is the advice he gave them: 'The next time this man comes to the village [the summer village, a mile east of Nome], grab him, strip him, tie him to a post, and cover his body with old engine oil. Then throw sand on him and release him.' This advice was followed and, although the military had quite an investigation on the matter, the King Island girls were relatively free from molestation after that."[12]

The war deprived the King Islanders of a teacher for 1942-43. In November 1942, Lafortune wrote under "N.B." in the "History": "On account of the war with Japan, we rightly feared that no supply boat was coming. That left me with only 4 barrels of oil for next winter. Then I wrote to the head of the Indian Bureau at Juneau, offering to run the school gratis in case that no supply boat would be coming. In the meantime through the kindness of Fr. McHugh, I procured 10 barrels of oil from Nome. That put me in pretty good shape. In the same time it freed me of my offer to run the school. The supply boat came, but no teacher. The same authorization was given to me. But it is up to me to use it or not. For the sake of the natives I will teach, therefore I had some work done in the chapel to enable the children to write. Next May I might use the school."

He finished the last day of the year 1942 (and the last page of the book in which he had written his "History") with a note of thanksgiving: "We have many reasons to thank God. He has granted lots of special favors in spite of our unworthiness. Wars and rumors of war are away from us. In our isolation we feel absolutely safe. A few planes pass, probably on their way to Russia. We have provisions for 2 years. The wolf is away from our door. The hunting is excellent."[13]

He began the second King Island diary in January 1943. The war during 1943 still seemed far away to him, but he felt that it nevertheless had created a crisis on King Island, one from which it might never recover. In September 1944 he wrote, "A few of our boys are enlisted. They are the following: James Aresac, Paul Anaolic, Joe Kacsac (disabled), Stanislas Apaalic, Frank Yumic, John Suluk (1), John Suluk (2), Tom Pussuc, Simon Sasaanga, Martin Inoctuyuc, Antony Nuresac. Will they ever come back to King Island? It is very doubtful. Some of them have a dislike for this place. There is question of the government giving jobs to the enlisted men after the war. Some of those boys will prefer to fill up some of those jobs than to face the hardships of this island. The outside has too much attraction for them, and the work is so much easier. It will go hard on these people if the young men abandon them. The future is sombre.''[14]

The year before, an accident on the island, unrelated to war, also gave rise to thoughts about the future of King Island: ''Something happened a few days ago ominous enough to give me fears for the future of this place,'' Lafortune wrote to Crimont. ''The village is nestled at the foot of a 900 feet wall of granite full of cracks. So far it was unheard of that any of those rocks ever got loose, but history has changed. A few days ago a boulder got detached and rolled down. It met other rocks, broke in four pieces. One of them punched a hole through one of the walls of a house built by Fr. Hubbard. Had it not been for that house it would have come to my house with more force yet. The three other pieces rolled on the church. They struck with such a force that all the stations of the cross hanging on that wall fell on the floor. One punched a hole through the inner and outer wall; the other broke only the outer wall; the third one tore only the galvanized iron.

''Now if that mountain begins to disintegrate for good, the place will become so dangerous that we will have to quit. Some of those boulders weigh tons. The action of the frost slowly opens the crevices till, finally, with the spring thawing, a crash and a smash up takes place. With your permission I will hang a medal of the Little Flower on the wall that is exposed to danger, and put her in charge of that mountain. That will be one of the biggest jobs she ever tackled.''[15]

His last remarks about the war, written on 22 October 1945, were his thoughts on a world far away from King Island:

''The war stopped for good on the feast of the Assumption [15 August 1945]. The 'Atomic bomb' brought the Japs to their knees. The Germans had surrendered before. A great effort for a durable peace is made by lots of conferences among the conquering nations. Even now . . .there is no real agreement, and Stalin with his puppet government and his puppet Russian Church is the cause of serious unrest. He makes promises today and breaks them tomorrow.

''The great question asked and discussed in the most serious papers is the 'Morality' of the atomic bomb.

''The end of the war is accompanied by lots of troubles. The soldiers have to come back. Will they find work and be satisfied with ordinary wages? If not, there will be strikes and troubles of all kinds. All over the world, communism is making inroads. It shows its head even in the States, and if the working classes are dissatisfied, it will grow more, and become a positive danger. In England the Labor party displaced Churchill and elected Attlee. He is not a communist but the fact that he is elected by the Labor party gives fear."[16]

Lafortune had also begun to write somber thoughts to his friends about his own future. In 1944, when he was 74, he had already written to a niece, "You mention my 40 years spent in Alaska. To me they seem like a dream, so rapidly does life pass. My end is not far off."[17]

In June 1944, the Right Reverend Walter J. Fitzgerald, S. J., came to the Bering Strait, "the first bishop to put his feet on this island." Bishop Fitzgerald stayed ten days, confirmed eleven boys and six girls, but also ordered Lafortune, who had not been off the island since the summer of 1939, to go to Nome for the summer.

This was not at all to Lafortune's liking ("leaving the majority of my people here") but Jesuits have the reputation of being obedient men who obey "at the mere sign of the Superior's wish." Seldom do Jesuit Superiors consider it necessary to issue a command to be carried out in virtue of the vow of obedience. Should one fail to carry out a command of this nature, he is regarded as sinning seriously, at least objectively, against his vow of obedience. Lafortune went to Nome.

By order of Bishop Fitzgerald he had to go to Nome again the following year. This order, coupled with his thoughts about mortality and growing old, must have made him feel even older, since it was an order to go to Nome to get a tooth repaired. Lafortune had never before in his life needed the services of a dentist or a doctor, except to get glasses.[18]

In his correspondence at this time he continued to dwell on death. "How long will I be in King Island," he wrote to one of his correspondents, "is up to my Superiors to decide. But the years begin to tell on me too. Three or four years more will see me on the rocks. We don't bury people in the ground here. We put them on the rocks." And to Augusta Bernard Perry, to whom he had given first communion more than forty years earlier, he wrote, "Before very long. . .we will not have to write letters any more [but] will unhook the phone and speak at any distance [and] will see one another [as we talk]. Of course, I will be dead long before that happens, but it is surely bound to come. . . .Yes, Bishop Crimont is dead and Bishop Fitzgerald is in his place. He is not a strong man and I am afraid he will not last very long. I am 11 years older than him and I can wring his neck.''[19]

Lafortune was less active in Nome in the summer of 1945 than in other years, but his dedication to the lives of the Eskimos was undiminished, and they sought him out at all times. ''Invariably, each day at meal time one or other of the natives would come and by the time he would leave Father's meal would be cold,'' said Anable, pastor of Nome at that time. ''It aggravated me and I determined to stop it. The next time we sat down and I heard footsteps on the stairs, I rose, went out and met the native half way up the stairs. I explained that Father was just sitting down to eat and asked him if he could come back in half an hour. This he agreed to do and I went back to my lunch.

''Father asked if it had been a native, and when I said it was, he rose, ran down the street and brought him back. Needless to say, his lunch was stone cold by the time the native left.

''Then Father came to me, and for the only time [that I recall] he showed himself capable of anger. He levelled his finger in front of my face and informed me that I was never to do that again. He was there for these people twenty-four hours a day and I was not to interfere!''[20]

On 19 October 1945, Lafortune returned to King Island on the *North Star*, and when the King Islanders were ready to go to Nome for their annual trip in June 1946, Lafortune received a letter from Bishop Fitzgerald informing him that he could either stay on the island or go to Nome. Lafortune chose to spend the summer on the island, along with fifteen Eskimos, mostly old people. ''It would be cruel to leave those old folks here without the consolations of religion,'' he wrote.[21] He spent most of that summer in a more leisurely way than any other since his arrival in Alaska, painting his house, the church, and the chapel, and making ''a kind of parterre'' in front of the statue of Christ the King.

In his last letter to his niece, Sister Marie-Flavius, he wrote that he had remained for the summer on King Island with ''the old, who have not too much longer to live. It is the same story everywhere. The earth is an exile, a valley of tears, and by their sins men vie with one another to make it even worse.'' He informed her that his health was ''perfect, but I cannot keep myself from getting older.''[22]

During the winter of 1946 and early 1947, the letters written by Lafortune, who had never had to visit a doctor, continued to dwell on the difficulties of growing old. He repeatedly said that his health was

Nome in 1948, a year after Lafortune's death, showing the old Holy Cross Hospital (middle right). *(Photograph by William A. Shepherd. Dorothy Jean Ray collection)*

good, but he had to admit that he was not as light on his feet as he once had been; that climbing the rocks—the only way to travel on the island—was becoming more difficult. ''Climbing up and down kills me,'' he wrote.[23]

For two years he had hoped to be assigned an assistant (to be his successor) on the island, and on 19 June 1947, he wrote to Fitzgerald that he earnestly hoped Father George E. Carroll, S. J., would come that summer because it would be difficult for him to be there alone: ''A great change came over me this last winter [it is thought that he had a stroke]. I have lost at least the half of my strength. I am not sick, but I am weak. My steps are faltering, easy exhausted. . . .I cannot account for that change except for my age. It is my duty to tell you those things, though I hate to give you that worry. With another Father with me I would be ready to tackle one or two more winters. I would hate to die without the priest.''[24]

On 21 June 1947, just before he left King Island for Nome (his glasses needed to be changed), he wrote to Louis L. Renner, S. J.: ''Your very welcome letter of Nov. 1946 came two days ago. The reason for the delay is that there is no mail schedule whatever to this place. . . .A few days ago a tug came for longshoremen and brought us some mail.

''When we put our feet on this island we step out of the world. We have no recourse whatever. More than anywhere else we feel in the hands of God's Providence.

''I don't hope to see you in the mission. I have not long to live; I will be 79 in a few months. Kindly pray God to grant me a happy death.''

Though his letters contain a clear premonition of death, they also reveal that he was planning to return to King Island in the fall of 1947. But around 14 July, Father Lafortune collapsed at the altar of St. Joseph's Church in Nome, during mass, apparently from a slight stroke. He was taken to the hospital in Nome where he remained until 29 July, when he was sent to St. Joseph's hospital, run by the Sisters of Providence, in Fairbanks. There, he declined steadily, his eyesight failed, and others had to write for him. He could no longer say mass, which he had heretofore done virtually every day of his priestly life. All he could do was attend and serve the daily masses celebrated in the hospital chapel by the hospital chaplain, John W. Laux, S. J. He suffered several strokes, and a month before his death his mind wandered, his memory failed him, and his conversations rambled.[25]

On 14 October, on King Island, Thomas Cunningham, who had replaced Lafortune, wrote in the King Island diary that Lafortune had "the right to be sick for the first time in his life,"[26]—and for the last time, for in the evening of the twenty-second, Lafortune had a heart attack after supper; ten minutes later he died, with the chaplain and all the Sisters present.

In 1909, he had written to his niece that he expected to remain at his western post all of his life, and that "I will not leave this country until I have buried the last of my Eskimos; or it is very probable that the Eskimos will bury me before they all disappear." Ironically, not one Eskimo, of all that he had served for forty-four years (with the possible exception of "Blind Joe" Terigluk) was present at his death or at his funeral.[27]

And he was not buried on the rocks of King Island but in the little Catholic plot of the Fairbanks cemetery.

13 / The Little Father of the Eskimos, an Historic Figure

On 25 June 1939, the seventy-year-old Lafortune wrote to the Jesuit author, Théophile Hudon, "Console yourself. You will never have to write my biography. When death has once caught up with me, I will very quickly be forgotten."[1] But he was not quickly forgotten. Even his given name, Bellarmine, lives on among the King Island Eskimos, and as recently as June 1975, I was told that James E. Poole, S. J., the pastor of the Nome parish, had difficulty persuading the King Island drummers to perform in the new liturgical ceremonies because they did not think that Father Lafortune would have approved. To this day, Lafortune's word is still law for many of the older Catholic Eskimos in and around Nome.

Less than two weeks after Lafortune was buried, Thomas Cunningham wrote in the King Island diary, "Baptized baby of Alvana today. The parents wished the name of Bellarmin. Father Lafortune's first namesake."[2] If the parents were upholding the traditional Eskimo belief that the spirit of the namesake lives on in the child, there is more than a touch of irony in the fact that they named their baby Bellarmine, for Lafortune had spent the better part of his missionary life trying to eradicate every trace of "superstition" from the beliefs of the Eskimos, an endeavor which, according to his fellow missionaries, he pursued with unparalleled success.

Although the naming appears to be a great tribute to Lafortune personally, it might, nevertheless, be construed as a sign of his ultimate failure as a missionary if the custom is regarded as a "superstitious" holdover from pre-Christian days. To the Eskimo people, however, the term "superstition" is meaningless, and they have little difficulty harmonizing traditional beliefs with the relatively new Christian teaching. Yet, Lafortune himself probably did not consider this a serious infraction of Christian teachings, for he had permitted it to survive throughout his decades among the Eskimos.

There was no doubt in Lafortune's mind that he had eradicated all "superstition" from the culture of the King Islanders. Even by Christmas 1929, as has been reported, he wrote, "To think that less than 30 years ago those people had their medicine men and their superstitious dances and practices and to see them now kneeling devoutly before the crib and praying most earnestly caused us a great consolation, and we have not the least doubt that Our Lord looked down on the simple faith of these people with the greatest complacency."[3] Except for the custom of spouse-exchange, the role of the medicine men, and a few unspecified "superstitious" practices, Lafortune found little to criticize in the age-old Eskimo culture, and ardently wished that it had been left—except for being Christianized—as it was before the coming of the white man.

The Eskimos remember Lafortune affectionately as "the little Father" who brought them "the Christianity." The whites remember him as a pioneer missionary and historic figure above the average. Jesuits who served with him in Nome have described him as "a great missioner" and "a little giant."[4] What was it in Lafortune's character that enabled him to earn a lasting place in the minds and hearts of Alaskans?

Above all, he was physically tough and level-headed, a combination that permitted him not only to weather numerous blizzards and hazardous traveling conditions without mishap, but to persevere and succeed in his apostolate to the Eskimos, especially when almost insurmountable obstacles—immorality, disease, and drunkenness—were put in his way by unscrupulous whites, particularly the whalers, the whiskey peddlers, the soldiers, and the "irreligious miner." Lafortune did not condemn all the whites, but only the "scum, the impure, the greedy, the impious, the sensual element of our race. . . .There was material for a magnificent nation in those people [the Eskimos]. What a pity that it came in contact with the most perverse element of the white race."[5] Except for the whalers, Lafortune said that this "most perverse element" was concentrated in and around Nome.

While Nome was still little more than a mining camp, it was described by one of its first priests, John B. Carroll, as a place where "gold abounded, and wickedness did still more abound."[6] Throughout Lafortune's years on the Seward Peninsula, Nome seemed to change so little that he was never inclined to modify this severe judgment—except that gold no longer abounded. From his earliest to his very last years in Nome, Lafortune felt that there were no words harsh enough to describe the town and the influence that its worst citizens had on the Eskimos. Given this situation, it is no wonder that over two dozen priests came to Nome and left during the first half of the twentieth century. But Lafortune stayed on.

Lafortune's impassioned statements about the adverse influence of Nome and the whites on the Eskimos reveal a great deal about the psychological makeup of the man himself. His hopes that the people might yet "thrive under the influence of the virtue of the Church" and find salvation in religion and hygiene may strike us (the heirs of religious skepticism and uncertainties of every kind) as unduly sanguine and rather naive. Yet, the Lafortune who expressed these beliefs was at that time not a starry-eyed young missionary new to Alaska but a veteran of almost two decades among the Eskimos. Despite his views, he never yielded to despondency or despair. Instead, his plans for helping the Eskimos remained undiminished and his efforts on their behalf unflagging in the face of what he thought were almost insurmountable odds. His zeal was fired not only by the conviction that he was doing God's work, but by his unshakable faith in the innate goodness of the Eskimo people and in their ultimate potentiality for being saved.

Yet, he wrote from a narrow ethnic viewpoint, as did many missionaries (both Protestant and Catholic) at that time, and was so intimately associated with the people in a provincial area that he was unable to be completely compassionate toward the people he thought were bringing trouble to the Eskimos. For example, he seemed to be unable to recognize that medical care was saving many lives at the very time he made some of his most scathing remarks about the heritage the white man had brought to the Seward Peninsula.

In carrying out his assignment of taking "charge of the Eskimos," Lafortune was very much helped by his special gift of seeing with unusual clarity what needed to be done. By the end of his third year in Alaska he had already outlined all of the major projects that were to occupy him for the rest of his missionary life: the Eskimo workshop-chapel, the building of a schooner, and the establishing of missions at Marys Igloo, Little Diomede, and King Island; and by 1908 he had evolved a plan for an orphanage. Eventually, all of Lafortune's major projects, with the exception of moving the Nome Eskimos to Cape Woolley, were successfully carried out.

Lafortune was a patient man. One might think that a person like Lafortune, who had tremendous energy (he was "always in a hurry"), a great sense of order, and well-formulated goals would be given to outbursts of impatience. This seems not to have been the case. John A. Concannon, who knew him well, wrote, "Though a man of strong character and quick perception. . .Father Lafortune was a man of great patience and remarkable self-control. He had made it a principle never to be impatient or brusque with his charges."[7] Yet, patience did not come easily to him. To Martin Lonneux he wrote, "Their way of raising their children baffles me. Unlimited is the patience of the mother, whilst the child is a little tyrant. Time and again I felt like lambasting the youngsters. But I controlled myself because I know that the natives hate nervousness. It is very seldom that they lose their temper."[8]

Perhaps nothing so tested Lafortune's patience as saying the Sunday mass for the Eskimos. Segundo Llorente described one he attended: "The Sunday Mass I witnessed was quite a sight. The whole King Island crowd was there. Mothers had their babies in their arms, nursed them publicly; children roamed around between the pews; the babies cried or screamed; the mothers struggled vainly to soothe them while Fr. Lafortune at the altar gesticulated and at the top of his voice did all he could to convey to his vociferous audience the message of the gospel in the Eskimo language, which he mastered. He preached a very long sermon. 'Poor Father,' I said to myself, 'he has been doing this kind of preaching from way, way back.' "[9]

As one reads through Lafortune's many letters, diary entries, and manuscripts, one is struck by their uniform tone, reflecting the extraordinary overall stability of his character. Nothing indicates that he ever changed his basic views or attitudes, and one senses a powerful drive and tension at the bottom of a genuine harmony and equilibrium of personality.

There is little in the documents or testimony of witnesses to indicate that Lafortune ever had doubts about himself or about his work.

Rather, the contrary is true. His clear understanding of himself and his role as a missionary made him a man of direct action and often blunt words. Llorente wrote of him, "He expressed himself fearlessly with absolutely no ambiguity."[10] At times his strong expression seemed merciless. When Joseph Terigluk (Chapter 12) asked about his wife, Lafortune wrote to him, "You ask me how your wife is. . . . Your wife is dead, and she died just as she lived. I told you that God would punish her. She lived bad, she died bad, and she was buried like a dog. And if you live bad, you will die bad, and you will be also buried like a dog."[11]

In July 1936, a special investigation committee on Indian affairs, consisting of four U.S. senators, came to Nome to investigate the condition of the natives. The committee was told that Lafortune knew the Eskimos well. When asked, under oath, what he thought about the native situation, he focused on the serious and widespread problem of alcohol abuse. We have his answer to the committee on this subject in a letter to his niece. "Among other things," Lafortune wrote, "I told them that the only way was to punish the Eskimos, that their prisons were a farce, an invitation, an encouragement to drink and the ruin of the Eskimos. 'What measures should be taken?' I was asked. Here is what I told them: 'For the first offense throw the drunkard into a dark room for two days, and give him absolutely nothing to eat or drink. After two days, let him go with the warning that for the second offense he will have to spend five days in prison under the same conditions, for the third offense, eight days.' You should have seen the expressions on the faces of those senators!"[12] Though his words to Terigluk and the committee were harsh, his intent was admonitory rather than vindictive. They were not meant to hurt, but to have a "salutary effect." Lafortune often regarded sickness or accidents as God's way of giving some errant member of his flock "a lesson" or of "opening his eyes" for his spiritual good. At the time of Nome's destructive fire in 1934, Lafortune wrote, "Nome had a little touch of hell. Will that open the eyes of the crowd? Let us hope."[13]

Nor did Lafortune hesitate to express his forthright opinions about fellow priests with the same frontier frankness. Having dedicated his life to the evangelization and welfare of the Eskimos, and being by nature more inclined toward the practical than the theoretical, he had no patience whatever with the priest-archeologist. In July 1937, Raymond W. Murray passed through Nome on his way to Saint

Lawrence Island. On the thirty-first, Lafortune wrote in the Nome diary, "A few days previous a certain Father Murray, a scientist(?) from Notre Dame University, passes here on his way to St. Lawrence Island with the view of finding in the dumps of the Eskimos a trace of some ancient civilization. Apparently even the Catholic universities are getting pretty shallow. The Father will be over there for 2 or 3 weeks with another scientist that has as much religion as a malemute and two women. He will say no mass but he will dig in the dumps and the dirt accumulated for perhaps centuries to find vestiges of some ancient civilization!"

Lafortune's disdain for Murray's scientific pursuits is all the more striking in view of the fact that during his youth he himself had made such a name as a teacher of science that he was sent to Paris to study advanced mathematics. But it is not out of character. Lafortune's conservative religious background, his narrow understanding of his apostolate to the Eskimos, and his activist nature did not allow the scientist in him to develop. This was unfortunate, for he was a careful observer of Eskimo life and left in his writings a significant amount of information and raw data of value to scientists.

But Lafortune did have eyes and ears for the esthetic. Although he devoted little creative imagination to his churches or to the formal cultivation of the arts, he was always concerned about having clean, freshly painted, adequately furnished churches and chapels, and well-trained organists and choirs. The altars were generally decorated for feast days, usually with paper flowers. He took joy and pride in the artistic creations of his Eskimo carvers.[14] Nor did the beauties of nature escape him. In one of his many eulogies of King Island he wrote: "That island is a true paradise. If Virgil had seen it, he would have made poetry by the yard. It challenges any artist, and any poet. It is just wild, virgin nature, untouched, unspoiled, lofty, full of light and life. The immensity of the sea, the ruggedness of its crags, the gorgeous panorama displaying the coast of Siberia, the islands of the straits, the saw-tooth ranges, Cape Prince of Wales, and above your head swarms of birds of all kinds, are enough to give repose to wrecked nerves."[15]

Above all, however, it was the beauty of the soul that Lafortune esteemed, and he concentrated his efforts on the salvation of souls and the conditions that made this salvation possible. Ethical and moral values—not scientific or aesthetic ones—were his primary concern.

To Lafortune, morality was virtually synonymous with purity and chastity. He condemned absolutely anything that was impure, unchaste, or immoral. For example, in April 1933, Lafortune baptized an illegitimate child, giving it the name Benedict, and wrote in the "History," "I hope St. Benedict will take it up to heaven as soon as possible." His hope was realized a month later: "Almighty God, in his infinite mercy, called to its early reward the illegitimate child. . . .I profited of the occasion to give a last ride to the question mark. That is an object lesson for all. I hope that the Sacred Heart. . .will protect this place against any further disgrace."[16] According to Lafortune's standards of morality, death was preferable to illegitimate life.

Regarding his own vow of chastity, the limited evidence on the subject indicates that Lafortune observed it faithfully and beyond the shadow of a doubt. But in this matter he was not as scrupulous as were some of the Jesuit missionaries, who, to avoid gossip and scandal, never visited a home if the man of the house was away. According to the King Islanders, Lafortune made an effort to visit some of the homes every day, whether the man of the house was present or not, and he made special efforts to visit regularly the elderly and the sick. When he was in Nome, according to Segundo Llorente, a priest who served with him, "Everyday he visited the natives on the beach to 'see and be seen.' Those natives that wanted to see him did it freely at any time."[17]

As for his vow of obedience, the available evidence indicates that Lafortune always acted in a manner in keeping with his vow. His letters to his Superiors reveal a great deal of initiative and creative planning, but at the same time, also a spirit of deference and submission. Even when his plans were suddenly changed or thwarted "by order of Superiors," he did not yield to the temptation to give up or take matters into his own hands, for he saw in the decisions of his Superiors a manifestation of God's will. To this he could resign himself. His native drive, checked and guided by his Superiors within the framework of his vow of obedience, gave to his apostolic life a tone of tension, but made it, at the same time, a fruitful one.

The *Constitutions of the Society of Jesus*, commenting on the manner of life befitting the Jesuit, state that "the manner is ordinary," and that Jesuits are to live "as becomes poor men." Lafortune interpreted this formula narrowly and lived his vow of poverty more strictly than most of the Jesuits in Alaska at that time. When Edmund Anable visited his residence on King Island shortly after Lafortune left it for the last time, he found "a room twelve feet long, eight feet wide, with a very small table, two old kitchen chairs, a two-burner kerosene stove set on two small boxes, and a shelf nailed on one wall, holding five books! At one end of the room was a double-decker bunk, four and a half feet long. . . ."[18] "Conveniences?" Lafortune wrote in 1941, "I have none and I don't care for any." Michael O'Malley, who was with Lafortune in 1912-13, wrote, "His ideal, and sometimes his practice, was to live as did the Eskimos; to eat frozen fish, sleep on the ground, eat their food, etc. He remarked that nature suggested to them, in need, the thing to do."[19]

While Lafortune asked little for himself, he was conscientious when it came to paying debts of any kind. Concannon said of him, "For their assistance he always paid [the Eskimos]. It was a principle with him never to be a debtor to them in any way. On the other hand, he was always ready to help them and consistently refused even a small gift."[20] It is known, however, that he routinely received food from the natives. On King Island he shared in successful hunts like anybody else on the island. Often he gave in exchange some staples such as sugar or crackers, "to show how glad he was to get the native food. . . .He liked Eskimo foods just like an Eskimo."[21]

Among his correspondents Lafortune had some generous benefactors who regularly sent him gift packages containing food and clothes, among other things. Anable said that Lafortune always gave these away. They went to the needy or as prizes to deserving catechism pupils or to the winners of Fourth of July competitions. Bred to poverty as one of many children born to poor farm parents, vowed to poverty as a Jesuit, and self-disciplined to poverty in the course of his years in Alaska, he habitually and unhesitatingly gave freely what he had freely received. After having dedicated his very life to the service of others, he found the passing on of gifts to others the natural thing to do. According to Concannon, Lafortune was "generous beyond measure," and Anable saw in his life "a living example of poverty."[22]

Yet, for all his personal abstemiousness and austerity, Lafortune was anything but a severe, forbidding, melancholy human being. Many persons remarked about his great sense of humor and his love of singing. Carrie Tate, who was stationed on King Island from 1943 to 1945 as a schoolteacher, called him "a chuckling little old gentleman [who] seems to derive an immense pleasure from life."[23] Michael O'Malley, one of the succession of priests at Nome, wrote that he was always kind with the Eskimos, "indulgent in helping them, patient in listening to them, but resolute in advice or warning. He could be heard laughing with them any time of day, and even when wrapt in sleep at night he was sometimes heard to laugh, an echo of the day."[24] And though not a smoker himself, Lafortune could "enjoy the sight of one who, after a hard working day, puffs with the greatest of satisfaction at his old pipe . . . .In our long, dark, dreary winters, I think a good smoke to be beneficial."[25] Llorente, who lived with Lafortune in 1939, wrote of him, "My impression of him was that he was at the same time stern and mild; stern with himself and with principles he thought untouchable; mild with people in the ordinary daily dealings."[26]

None of Lafortune's efforts to protect the Eskimos from outside influence ever really succeeded. Only in the case of the King Islanders did he see his policy of salvation by isolation become effective to any degree, and then it was nature rather than his own efforts that isolated the natives. During his last years among them, he only partially succeeded in keeping them on the island during the summer because there were always some who made the trip to Nome. Even on the island the isolation that he dreamed of was not complete, for there was always present the influence of the "godless school." Throughout his years in Alaska, Lafortune consistently opposed all schools, except, of course, Catholic schools, and his "History" contains many remarks that reflect his overt anti-school bias.

Lafortune's abiding opposition to schools was a result of his conviction that the schools tended to make whites out of the Eskimos instead of preparing the natives to cope better in their own way of life by teaching them practical skills and hygiene. He wrote his summary statement on the subject of schools in his "History": "It is the universal opinion among all those who come up here and observe that the schools are a downright nuisance. Aboard the *North Star* were 2 doctors, Dr. George from Barrow and Dr. Cordell from Mountain Village. Moreover there was an excellent Catholic nurse, Miss Sheridan. With one voice they condemned the schools as doing more harm than good to the natives. The people of the *Northland* had the same ideas. But the people of Washington don't want to listen to that. The only things important for the welfare of the natives is 1st religion, 2nd a small hospital in every center of some importance, to segregate the sick and thereby overcome the consumption, 3rd just enough machinery to enable them to repair their motors etc. Let them be in their element and live the life of the Eskimos.''[27]

There is no indication that Lafortune, for all his opposition to schools, was able to effectively impede the schooling of the Eskimos. His anti-school attitude may have rubbed off on Eskimo school children by making them less eager to learn, but he never convinced their parents that a school was undesirable. The attitude of the Eskimos was quite the opposite to that of Lafortune, especially that of the King Islanders who regarded a school as an essential part of life.

The isolation that made King Island so attractive to Lafortune made it less so to its native inhabitants, and while Lafortune was still on the island, making every effort to keep the people there—even during the summer—some were already beginning to spend the whole year in Nome. According to Llorente, ''The belief then was that with the passing of Fr. Lafortune, King Island would soon be abandoned. He admitted that every summer it was harder for him to bring them back to the island. When the time came to board the umiaks and return, there was a 'round up' of islanders all over Nome. Some Eskimos managed to hide so well that they were not discovered, so the fleet had to sail for the island without them. It was the handwriting on the wall.''[28]

During the decade following Lafortune's death, the King Island community remained more or less intact on the island, but by 1950 the inevitable move to the mainland and resettlement at the east end of Nome, in King Island Village, had already begun. Accordingly, throughout the 1950s the population on the island fluctuated noticeably: 1950, 141; 1953, 130; 1955, 99; 1956, 76; 1957, 101; 1958, 115; 1959, 62.[29] This variation presented the Bureau of Indian Affairs annually with the question of whether or not to provide a teacher for the island. The school was closed during the school year 1956-57, and permanently after 1958-59. The Bureau gave the following reasons for closing the school: the declining number of school children, the difficulty of finding teachers for a station that had been described in 1935 by the Commissioner of Indian Affairs as a place of ''extreme isolation and undesirable features,'' and ''the rock slide hazard.''[30]

The school was without a teacher during the years 1942-43, 1945-46, 1947-48, and 1956-57, and of the fifteen teachers who taught on King Island during the thirty years of the school's operation, nine stayed only one year.[31] Falling rocks did pose a threat, and according to one engineering-geological study, ''rock falls capable of doing serious damage in the village can be expected two or three times per century if no corrective measures are taken.''[32]

By the time the school was closed, the King Islanders had come to look upon it as an indispensable part of life on the island and accepted none of the three reasons offered by the Bureau as valid for closing the school. To the present day they are somewhat bitter about the Bureau's action. The permanent closing of the school made the complete abandonment of the island only a matter of time.

In October 1945, Lafortune wrote in the King Island diary, ''Others go to the *kaitco* [cold storage cave] and bring 1st class meat. That is what holds those people here.'' This natural, year-round deepfreeze, in which the surplus meat of successful hunts could be preserved against lean days sure to come, always tipped the balance in favor of staying whenever the question of abandoning the island was raised. In the days when famine was often no farther away than a few walrus or seals, the meat in the cave meant the difference between eating and starving. By the middle of the twentieth century, however, modern distribution and preservation of nonnative foods stripped the cave of much of its former significance. It was no longer a cogent reason for staying on the island.

Probably more than anything else, the lack of adequate medical care contributed to the eventual desertion of King Island. For eight months of the year the only medical care available was provided by the missionary or the schoolteacher. This was a source of constant concern, especially to childbearing women, and offered the principal incentive for the gradual migration to Nome.[33]

Another incentive was the attractiveness of living on the mainland where there were job opportunities and a less difficult, demanding life than the island offered. This was especially appealing to the young men, particularly those who had served in the armed forces during the war. They were disinclined to return to the hard life and isolation of their native island, and it was on these young people that the future of the community depended most. King Island was not just a place, it was a wholly different way of life.

The year after the school was closed, only sixty-two persons wintered on the island, a reduction of fifty-three persons from the year before. This prompted the resident missionary of ten years, George E. Carroll, to close the mission in April 1960. This further contributed to the exodus from the island, and the last small band remained on the island during the winter of 1965-66. Since then the island has been uninhabited except for a few weeks each summer when several boatloads of people return to hunt, gather eggs and greens, and simply to visit their former home, to which the older ones in particular are still fondly attached.

It is very unlikely that the King Islanders will ever return again to their island on a permanent basis. The whole village would have to be rebuilt, and many of the skills necessary for a subsistence economy are already lost, especially among the younger persons. But most important of all, the group spirit needed to give the islanders "tribal" cohesion and identity is no longer present. Today the King Islanders are scattered; some live in Seattle, a few in Fairbanks, a fair number in Anchorage. The majority, however, still live in Nome, now in new houses built with funds from the Bureau of Indian Affairs, after the violent storm of 11 November 1974 destroyed King Island Village. The new houses provide an additional incentive for staying in Nome.[34]

Before the new houses were built, the King Islanders again seriously considered establishing a new village at Cape Woolley. For decades, Cape Woolley, on the mainland fifty miles from King Island, had been regarded as an attractive site for a new settlement. From there they would still have easy access to the winter hunting grounds and to the island for the summer "birding" and egg and greens gathering. It would also enable them at any time of the year to go to Nome for essentials or in case of emergency, yet be far enough away from the adverse aspects of Nome. Nome, the older ones feel, is still a threat to their native culture. The younger ones are not retaining the language or certain traditional Eskimo ways. (The King Islanders never considered Christianity a threat to their basic Eskimo culture.) Today the major threat to the native culture is the real problem of alcoholism and its effects on its victims. The "booze" against which Lafortune so often and so forcefully spoke out is still flowing freely and steadily, taking its toll among the Bering Strait Eskimos, the King Islanders included.

By the time of Lafortune's death, there were well-established Catholic communities at Kotzebue, Teller, and Nome, and on Little Diomede and King islands. Kotzebue has had a resident pastor from 1929 to the present, and Teller has been a station visited by the priests of Nome. The village of Marys Igloo was abandoned a number of years ago, and the Pilgrim Hot Springs mission was closed by Anable on 31 July 1941. The buildings were in bad repair, firewood had become scarce, but above all there were no longer enough orphans to warrant keeping the mission open.[35]

Between 1936 and 1947, "Father Tom" Cunningham spent a total of eight years on Little Diomede, and Father Vsevolod Rochkau was on the island from 1955 to 1958. When there was no priest in residence on the island, it was visited from time to time by priests from King Island, Kotzebue, or Nome. From 1958 to 1978 it was visited several times a year by a priest from Nome.[36] In the summer of 1978, Thomas F. Carlin, S. J., built a new church on Little Diomede and took up permanent residency there. After Lafortune left King Island for the last time in June 1947, Cunningham was its resident pastor from October 1947 to July 1950, and George E. Carroll, from October 1951 until April 1960.

The Nome parish has never been without a priest, and the Church is an active part of religious life in Nome. On 14 July 1971, the Catholic radio station KNOM, built by Poole, went on the air with a signal strong enough to reach Siberia and all of western Alaska. (The people of Hooper Bay are regular listeners.) Its slender 236-foot antenna replaces Jacquet's "white man's star," and is a symbol of hope dedicated "to help people help themselves."[37]

Lafortune's visions of what he wanted "his" Eskimos to be may not have worked out quite the way he had planned, yet he had succeeded in the one area—religion—where it meant the most to him. A great deal of the credit for the growth of the missions to their stature today can be attributed to his steadfast and unifying devotion toward an undeviating goal, the missionizing of the Eskimos.

Notes

Chapter 1

1. Letter, Lafortune to Martin Lonneux, Nome, 12 June 1922. The Lafortune-Lonneux correspondence is found in the Oregon Province Archives of the Society of Jesus, Crosby Library, Spokane, Washington, hereafter cited as OPA.
2. "Nome Diary," pp. 1-2, OPA.
3. Lafortune 1904b, pp. 49-50.
4. The French Bellarmin is hereafter standardized to the English Bellarmine, and the surname, occasionally spelled La Fortune, or simply Fortune, to Lafortune. It was thus that he signed his name. Much of the information concerning Lafortune's early life is taken from Waddel's writings and from the official Jesuit "curriculum vitae" of Lafortune in Archives de la Compagnie de Jésus, Saint-Jérôme, Quebec, hereafter cited ACJSJ.
5. "Curriculum vitae."
6. Letter, Arcade Gingras to Renner, Montreal, 16 July 1975.
7. Letter, Lafortune to Marie Anne Archambault, Poughkeepsie, 24 May 1903, ACJSJ.
8. Oswalt 1963, p. 23; Ray 1975, pp. 205-25.
9. For information concerning the discovery of gold in the Nome area and early Nome, see L.H. Carlson 1946, 1947a, 1947b, and *passim,* Devine 1903 and 1904, Harrison 1905, McLain 1969, Nelson, K. 1958, and "Nome Diary."
10. "Nome Diary," p. 4.
11. Ibid.
12. *The Yukon Catholic,* Vol. 1, No. 7, January, 1902, p. 1; Devine 1905, p. 274; "Nome Diary," p. 16.
13. Acts of the U. S. District Court for the District of Alaska, Second Division, 1901, OPA.
14. Van der Pol's petition of 22 November 1901 to the U. S. District Court, OPA.
15. Cocke 1974, pp. 186, 188.
16. Letter, Frank H. Richards to John G. Stanley, Nome, 19 January 1902, OPA.
17. Letter, Leopold Van Gorp to Frank Richards, Holy Cross, 28 February 1902, OPA.
18. Devine 1903, pp. 68-69.

19. "Nome Diary," p. 39; letter, Lafortune to the Catholic Editing Company, Nome, 5 January 1913, OPA.
20. Harrison 1905, p. 57.
21. *Nome Nugget,* 18 November 1903; Lafortune 1904a.
22. *The Yukon Catholic,* Vol. 1, No. 7, January, 1902, p. 2.
23. "Nome Diary," p. 42.
24. Lafortune's very first holy communicant, Augusta Bernard Perry, the daughter of the well-known arctic sea captain and explorer, Peter Bernard, wrote to Renner about his work in Nome: "I was the first child to receive First Communion. That was Fr. Lafortune's doing. Three of us were prepared. Edith Selina thought she should walk to the altar first!! Fr. Said: 'No favoritism—we will go alphabetically!' So—Augusta Bernard was the first. I think possibly he did that on purpose, as he always referred to me as his helper" (Letter, A. B. Perry to Renner, Conway, N. H., 16 March 1975); letter, ibid., 4 April 1975.
25. Lafortune 1904a.
26. Ibid.
27. Ibid.; letter, Lafortune to *Messager Canadien,* Nome, 20 June 1904, published in *Messager Canadien,* 1904, pp. 449-505.
28. Lafortune 1904a.
29. In an unpaged summary at the beginning of the Nome Diary it is recorded that Van der Pol made the first visit to Council from 6 to 20 March 1902, and Camille went to Teller and Gold Run for the first time between 3 and 12 April. Apparently the first mass was said at Fort Davis on 20 April 1902.

    In this same summary a notation reads: "Council does not prove to be a successful field. There are entanglements. Fr. Devine is deceived by a dreamer, who promises him a church ready-made from the States. He leaves the log church [begun the year before] unfinished, to the dissatisfaction of many of the Catholics."

Chapter 2

1. See Ray 1961, *passim.*
2. Letter, A. B. Perry to Renner, Conway, N. H., 16 March 1975.
3. See Renner 1974.
4. See Carriker 1976.
5. Letter, Joseph Bernard to the rector of Enghien, Nome, 15 August 1907, published in *Lettres de Jersey,* Vol. 27, 1908, pp. 88-94. "The little

Father'' referred to his height, but it also carried overtones of affection (Ross 1958, p. 180).

6. Letter, Lafortune to *Messager Canadien,* Nome, 23 March 1908, published in *Messager Canadien,* 1908, pp. 368-74.
7. Letter, Lafortune to the Catholic Editing Company, Nome, 5 January 1913, OPA.
8. ''Nome Diary,'' pp. 81-82.
9. Concannon, n.d., p. 1.
10. Letter, Lafortune to Lonneux, Nome, 26 December 1924, OPA; letter, Lafortune to Sister Marie-Flavius (Graziella Lafortune), Nome, 16 June 1920, in Waddel 1948b. The Lafortune-Marie-Flavius correspondence is found in this manuscript, and the letters quoted herein have been translated by Renner from this source.
11. Letter, Lafortune to *Messager Canadien,* Nome, 20 June 1904, published in *Messager Canadien,* 1904, pp. 499-505.
12. Letter, Lafortune to Lonneux, Nome, 14 February 1925, OPA.
13. ''Nome Diary,'' p. 84.
14. Letter, Bernard to the rector of Enghien, Nome, 15 August 1907, op. cit.
15. Letter, Lafortune to W. Hingston, Nome, 10 October 1909, ACJSJ.
16. Letter, Lafortune to Julius Jetté, Nome, 9 December 1925, OPA.
17. ''Nome Diary,'' p. 126.
18. Letter, Lafortune to *Messager Canadien,* Nome, 17 February 1909, published in *Messager Canadien,* 1910, pp. 67-70.
19. ''Nome Diary,'' p. 129.
20. Ibid., p. 132.
21. Letter, Lafortune to Edouard Lecompte, Nome, 11 August 1909, ACJSJ.
22. Letter, Lafortune to James A. Rockliff, Nome, 2 August 1913, OPA.
23. ''Nome Diary,'' pp. 153, 159.
24. Ibid., pp. 131, 168b, 168c, 172d.
25. Ibid., p. 172b. Forhan died in California less than two years later.
26. Ibid., p. 17.
27. Ibid., p. 111.
28. Letter, Lafortune to Albert Bellemare, Nome, 22 September 1912, ACJSJ.
29. Letter, Joseph Carrière to James Rockliff, Montreal, 31 May 1913, OPA.

Chapter 3

1. Modern usage spells the village Marys Igloo without an apostrophe.
2. Letter, Lafortune to Joseph Crimont, Nome, 7 December 1906, OPA.
3. Letter, Lafortune to Crimont, Nome, 11 July 1907, OPA.
4. Post [1921]; ''Nome Diary,'' pp. 27, 75, 96; document ''Indenture made 25 April 1907 between B. D. Lloyd and B. Lafortune,'' OPA.
5. Letter, Lafortune to Edward J. Devine, Nome, 6 December 1907, ACJSJ.
6. Letter, Lafortune to Crimont, Nome, 27 March 1908, OPA.
7. ''Nome Diary,'' p. 112; letter, Bernard to the rector of Enghien, Mary's Igloo, 31 May 1909, published in *Lettres de Jersey,* Vol. 28, 1909, pp. 97-111.
8. ''Nome Diary,'' p. 26.
9. Llorente 1969, pp. 13, 32; letter, John B. Sifton to Crimont, Holy Cross, 24 May 1915, OPA; obituary of John B. Sifton, *Woodstock Letters,* Vol. 70, 1941, pp. 432-33; official citizenship paper, issued in St. Louis, Mo., 24 December 1901.
10. Letter, Lafortune to *Messager Canadien,* Nome, 30 May 1916, published in *Messager Canadien,* 1916, pp. 385-87. In the United States National Archives, Record Group 75, in the General Correspondence, 1908-35, there is a file for 1915 titled ''The Bernard-Hunnicutt mess.'' Hunnicutt accused Bernard of taking liberties with his daughter. The charges were never proved.
11. Letter, Lafortune to *Messager Canadien,* Nome, 30 May 1916, published in *Messager Canadien,* 1916, pp. 385-87.
12. Letter, Lafortune to Marie-Flavius, Mary's Igloo, ''towards the autumn of 1915,'' according to Waddel 1948b, p. 42.

Chapter 4

1. ''Nome Diary,'' pp. 129-30.
2. Ibid., pp. 136, 160, 161, 168e.
3. Letter, A. B. Perry to Renner, Conway, N. H., 16 March 1975.
4. From ''Sociability and Customs of the Eskimos,'' by Lafortune. This 14-page manuscript was described by Lafortune as ''some notes about the natives.'' It was sent to Lonneux with a covering letter dated, Nome, 10 September 1922, and will be cited hereafter as Lafortune 1922b.
5. Letter, Lafortune to Crimont, Nome, 7 December 1906, OPA.

6. Madsen 1957, p. 15.
7. Letter, Lafortune to Lecompte, Nome, 11 August 1909, ACJSJ.
8. Letter, Lafortune to Marie-Flavius, Nome, 17 April 1912.
9. Letter, Lafortune to Jetté, Nome, 15 September 1925, OPA.
10. Letter, Lafortune to *Messager Canadien,* Nome, 21 November 1915, published in *Messager Canadien,* 1916, pp. 168-71.
11. Letter, Michael O'Malley to Bernard Hubbard, Spokane, 21 February 1949, OPA.
12. Renner 1974; letter, Stefansson to Lafortune, New York, 22 February 1913, OPA. For information about building the sleds, see "Nome Diary," pp. 5-12, *passim.*
13. On 13 January 1975, Augusta Bernard Perry wrote to Renner from Conway, N. H., "Your footnote to Stefansson's *Friendly Arctic* [Renner 1974] was most interesting to me because credit was given where it belongs. My father, Peter Bernard, was a member of that expedition that left Nome, July 13, 1913—and from which he never returned. He was master of the *Mary Sachs.* When in winter quarters his job was to keep the sleds repaired, as you will note in reading the *Friendly Arctic,* and he wrote, at different times, what an excellent sled the Eskimos had made."

Chapter 5

1. "Nome Diary," pp. 68-69; Post [1921].
2. See Renner 1979.
3. Post [1921]; "Nome Diary," pp. 84-85.
4. "Pilgrim Hot Springs Diary," p. 59. (The pagination of this diary begins with page 59.) Unless otherwise indicated, information about the Hot Springs in this chapter is taken from this diary, pp. 59-77.
5. "Nome Diary," pp. 79, 86, 87; letter, E. D. Evans to Governor Thomas Riggs, Nome, 21 June 1919, University of Alaska Archives; letter, Hubert Post to L. E. O'Keeffe, Nome, 14 May 1931, OPA.
6. "Pilgrim Hot Springs Diary," p. 67.
7. "Nome Diary," p. 87.
8. The winter 1918-19 was an exceptionally cold one (Ray 1975, p. 7); letter, E. D. Evans to Governor Riggs, Nome, 21 June 1919, University of Alaska Archives.
9. Hugh Ibbetson, who helped Lafortune make coffins, recalled events during the influenza epidemic more than fifty years later in a letter to Renner, dated Corona, California, 10 July 1974:

"The local undertaker was one of the first to succumb. When the natives started to die, Fr. Lafortune was the only one to look after the bodies. When he knew of a death, he would hitch up his dogteam, usually after dinner, and bring the body to the church hall, for there was no place else to take them. The temperature being below freezing, there was no problem in this way. I started building coffins out of 1x12 boards, but after a week it became evident that even with Fr.'s help it was impossible to keep up with the deaths . . . Fr. went to U. S. marshal Jordan and got him [to go] to the pool halls and round up help. The marshal persuaded a number of the able-bodied to come to the hall and take over the coffin job, gratis. One night Fr. brought in the body of a man who died with his arms around his heating stove. He was most likely trying to get the last warmth out of the dying fire. The body was frozen. We had no way of thawing it out, so we built a square box for him."

10. "Nome Diary," p. 88.
11. Ibid., pp. 88-89.
12. "Pilgrim Hot Springs Diary," pp. 67-68.
13. Ibid., p. 68.
14. By actual count, over 700 Eskimos are known to have died during the epidemic (letter, Evans to Riggs, Nome, 21 June 1919, University of Alaska Archives).
15. Letter, Ibbetson to Renner, Corona, California, 21 April 1974.
16. On this trip to Nome, Lafortune had Ibbetson with him, and while in Nome he taught him how to bake bread. Ibbetson recalls: "I was doing the cooking at Nome and didn't know how to make bread, so we were buying it from the bakery. Fr. Lafortune didn't think much of this bread, and besides it was expensive. He said it had too many holes in it. He said, 'Hugh, I will show you how to make bread.' And he did. It was some of the best I have ever eaten. It was not too full of holes" (letter, Ibbetson to Renner, Corona, California, 10 July 1974).
17. Ibid.
18. Ibid.
19. Letter, Frederick Ruppert to Franics C. Dillon, Nome, 24 February 1919, OPA.
20. "Pilgrim Hot Springs Diary," pp. 80, 82, 96.

Chapter 6

1. Lafortune 1922a.

2. Letter, Lafortune to "Reverend Father Provincial" [Francis C. Dillon], Nome, 9 June 1922, OPA.
3. "Nome Diary," p. 108.
4. Information from Barbara Kokuluk, personal interview, 1974; letter, Edmund A. Anable to Renner, Fairbanks, Alaska, 25 April 1974.
5. Letter, Lafortune to Crimont, Nome, 9 October 1922, OPA.
6. "Nome Diary," p. 111.
7. "Pilgrim Hot Springs Diary," p. 233.
8. "Nome Diary," pp. 112, 113.
9. Ibid., p. 113.
10. "Pilgrim Hot Springs Diary," p. 250.
11. "Nome Diary," p. 114.
12. "Pilgrim Hot Springs Diary," p. 256; letter, Post to Crimont, Hot Springs, 21 December 1923, OPA.
13. "Old John" was the father of John A. and John E. Kakaruk. He was also referred to as "Old Man Kakaruk" (letter, Jeanne Gabriel to Renner, Nome, 15 March 1976); "Pilgrim Hot Springs Diary," p. 256; letter, Peter Wilhalm to "Dear Brother," Hot Springs, 6 January 1924, printed in *Kahlekat*, No. 9, August 1924. This number of the now defunct little periodical is preserved in the Ursuline Provincialate, Santa Rosa, California.
14. "Pilgrim Hot Springs Diary," p. 258; Renner 1977-78.
15. "Pilgrim Hot Springs Diary," pp. 256, 257.
16. Ibid., p. 256; letter, Post to Crimont, 21 December 1923, OPA; Post 1924.
17. Post 1924; letters, Post to Crimont and Delon, both dated Hot Springs, 21 December 1923, OPA; letter, Lafortune to Lonneux, Nome, 26 December 1923, OPA.
18. Wilhalm 1953; letter, Lafortune to Crimont, Nome, 25 March 1924, OPA; letter, Wilhalm to "Dear Brother," Hot Springs, 6 January 1924. See note 13 above.
19. "Nome Diary," p. 114.
20. All but one of the six dogs were eventually accounted for. Mudd returned to the mission. Mink was found with the body. "One was found in an abandoned roadhouse at 18 miles from the Springs," and "Two others were found 12 or 15 days after on Salmon Lake" (letters, Lafortune to Lonneux, Nome, 26 December 1923, OPA, and Lafortune to Crimont, Nome, 25 March 1924, OPA). See also "Nome Diary," p. 118, and note 18 above.

21. Letter, Sister Mary of the Blessed Sacrament to Crimont, Hot Springs, 19 December 1923, OPA; *Nome Nugget,* 29 December 1923; letter, Lafortune to Lonneux, Nome, 26 December 1923, OPA.
22. Letter, Lafortune to Lonneux, Nome, 10 September 1925, OPA.
23. Letter, Lafortune to Lonneux, Nome, 14 September 1925, OPA.
24. Letter, Lafortune to Marie-Flavius, Nome, 13 March 1926.
25. "Nome Diary," pp. 119, 121-22.
26. Nobile 1961, pp. 86-87.
27. "Nome Diary," p. 123. Amundsen and his party were not invited. No reasons are given for this serious breach in etiquette. Possibly it did not occur to the parochial-minded Catholic community of Nome to invite them; or possibly, Nobile, who was at complete odds with Amundsen at this time, requested or even insisted that the latter be excluded. That Amundsen was not insensitive to this discourtesy is evident from his own comments on the subject. "Naturally, I keenly felt the slight put upon Ellsworth, my comrades, and myself by this public demonstration which ignored us. It was the climax of a series of incidents of the same tenor, and I should be less than candid if I did not record it and express my feeling that the whole situation revealed bad taste and bad manners on the part of the people of Nome" (Amundsen 1927, pp. 210-11).
28. "Nome Diary," p. 124. The revenue cutter *Bear* served for many years in Bering Sea and Arctic Ocean waters.
29. Hrdlička 1944, p. 84.
30. "Nome Diary," p. 124.
31. Concannon, n.d., p. 1.
32. "Nome Diary," p. 131.
33. Letter, Lafortune to Marie-Flavius, Nome, 18 October 1928.
34. Letter, Patrick Savage to Joseph Piet, Nome, 4 November 1928, OPA.
35. Letter, Philip Delon to Piet, Kashunak River, 100 miles from "Nowhere," 30 July 1928, OPA.
36. Michael Saclamana, personal interview, 1974.
37. Letter, Joseph McElmeel to Wlodimir Ledochowski, Nulato, Alaska, 18 November 1938, Archivum Romanum Societatis Iesu, hereafter cited ARSI.
38. Concannon, n.d., p. 3; Renner field notes, 1974; letter, Lonneux to Renner, St. Michael, 19 May 1949; letter, Thomas Cunningham to "Rev. Archivist" [Wilfred P. Schoenberg], King Island, 9 March 1949, OPA.

39. Letter, Lafortune to Piet, Nome, 24 July 1929, OPA.

Chapter 7

1. Lafortune 1929-42 ("History of the Mission of King Island," hereafter cited, "History"), p. 2.
2. Ibid. Hubert Post gave a slightly different version: "A niece of the chief, Elizabeth Nulanak, died at the age of three, and was a marvel of faith. Even at that age she seemed to have the wisdom of riper years, and not long before her death she addressed those present, exhorting them to be faithful to God and the Church. Then she said, 'We will all go to heaven,' and expired. From that day most of the King Islanders began to think more frequently of the saving of their souls" (letter, Post to "My Lord" (Crimont), Nome, 26 October 1917, OPA).
3. Letter, Lafortune to Crimont, Nome, 4 December 1907, OPA.
4. "History," p. 103; Lafortune 1925; letter, Lafortune to Ed. Coyle, King Island, 8 June 1940, OPA.
5. Letter, Lafortune to Lecompte, Nome, 11 August 1909, ACJSJ.
6. Letter, Lafortune to Jetté, Nome, 15 September 1925, OPA.
7. "Nome Diary," p. 42; Post 1916a.
8. Letter, Post to Crimont, Nome, 13 July 1916, OPA; "Nome Diary," p. 42.
9. According to Lafortune's "History," (p. 3), Aresac died in 1912, but this date is incorrect. Post's letter of 26 October 1917 to Crimont (OPA), and the "Nome Diary," p. 45, make it clear that Aresac died on 15 August 1916.
10. Ray 1975, pp. 22-23.
11. Lafortune 1925; Bogojavlensky 1969, pp. 9, 19. "The people of King Island and Little Diomede were called, collectively, *imaangmiut* by mainland people. The King Islanders, as inhabitants of *Ugiuvuk,* were the *Ugiuvangmiut,* or "people of *Ugiuvuk.*" "Literally glossed *[imaangmiut]* means 'people of the open water.' *Imaaq* is 'open water' as found in the winter sea ice. For eight months of the year, from October to July, these islands are isolated from the mainland of the two continents by the ever-moving ice fields that choke the North Bering and Chuckchi *[sic]* Seas. Shifting leads in the ice constantly open and close. These are called *imaaq* and this is the 'open water' that makes the islands inaccessible" (Curtis 1970, p. 105) (Bogojavlensky 1969, p. 8).
12. Much of the information concerning the physical features of King Island has been taken from Hopkins and Chapman 1966.

13. Many persons have described King Island. F. E. Kleinschmidt said in 1910, "A more forsaken, wildly-desolate, oppressingly-isolated isle, wrapped in cold deathliness, cannot be imagined" (Kleinschmidt 1910, p. 279). Post saw it as nothing more than "a huge heap of rocks piled up in Behring Sea" (letter, Post to "My Lord" (Crimont), Nome, 26 October 1917, OPA). Knud Rasmussen, the Danish cultural anthropologist, described it, in 1924, as "the most inhospitable place" he had ever seen, "with steep cliffs on all sides, in calm weather usually swathed in mist, in clear weather windy" (Rasmussen 1952, p. 72). Two years later, the physical anthropologist Hrdlička sailed past the island and viewed it as "an isolated high rocky mass where a colony of Eskimo live in what would seem impossible conditions, but where they get much walrus" (Hrdlička 1944, p. 94); and Frances Ross, who had gone to the island for research in 1931, saw it from the deck of the *Boxer* as "a grim and desolate granite mass" (Ross 1958, p. 17).
14. Letter, Lafortune to Joseph Waddel, King Island, 4 July 1939, ACJSJ.
15. Muir 1917, pp. 119-20.
16. Lafortune 1922b.
17. "Nome Diary," p. 131; *Woodstock Letters,* Vol. 58, 1929, p. 453.
18. Bogojavlensky 1969, p. 19; Ray 1975, pp. 74-75, 122.
19. Colby 1939. p. 385.
20. Letter, Lafortune to Jetté, Nome, 15 September 1925, OPA.
21. Letter, Lafortune to Lonneux, Nome, 5 June 1929, OPA.
22. "Nome Diary," p. 132.
23. Rasmussen 1952, p. 74.
24. Letter, Lafortune to Augusta Perry, Nome, 8 September 1923, OPA.
25. Letters, Lafortune to Crimont, Nome, 20 February and 25 March 1924, OPA.
26. On this general subject, see Ray 1975, Chapter 16.
27. See Lafortune 1925.
28. Letter, Lafortune to Crimont, Nome, 16 April 1926; letter, Lafortune to Lonneux, Nome, 18 April 1926, OPA.
29. Letter, Lafortune to Jetté, Nome, 15 September 1925, OPA.
30. Letter, Lafortune to Lonneux, Nome, 10 September 1925, OPA.
31. Letter, Lafortune to Marie-Flavius, Nome, 6 July 1925.
32. Lafortune 1925.
33. Letter, Lafortune to Marie-Flavius, Nome, 5 July 1926.

Chapter 8

1. Letter, Lafortune to Crimont, Nome, 15 June 1929, OPA.
2. Letter, Lafortune to Piet, King Island, 16 September 1929, OPA.
3. Ibid.
4. Ibid.; letter, Post to "My Lord" (Crimont), Nome, 26 October 1917, OPA. Lafortune wired Nome, by way of the Bureau of Education boat, that they needed lumber. It was sent to King Island on a small company boat, the *Sierra*, by Father Patrick Savage, but the boat tossed and rocked for two days without being able to unload. Finally the captain became worried about the ice and sailed to Seattle with their lumber (letter, Lafortune to *Jesuit Missions,* King Island, no date, published in *Jesuit Missions*, Vol. 4, 1930, p. 239).
5. "Historical Record" and "Description of the Station" filled in by Arthur Nagozruk, Sr., 1930. Department of the Interior, Bureau of Education, Alaska Division, Bureau of Indian Affairs files, Juneau, Alaska.
6. "History," p. 3.
7. Letter, Lafortune to Piet, King Island, 16 September 1929, OPA.
8. "History," p. 87.
9. Letter, Lafortune to Piet, King Island, 16 September 1929, OPA.
10. Letter, Lafortune to *The Western Jesuit*, King Island, no date, published in *The Western Jesuit,* Vol. 5, No. 10, December, 1930, p. 1.
11. Ibid.
12. "History," pp. 11-12; letter, Lafortune to Marie-Flavius, King Island, 27 June 1930.
13. "History," p. 14. The name Olaranna is spelled variously in the sources and is here standardized to this spelling. Lafortune usually spelled this name Aolarana.
14. This and the following information is from Ross 1958, pp. 33-34.
15. See Bogojavlensky 1969, p. 203.
16. "History," p. 14; letter, Lafortune to Marie-Flavius, King Island, 27 June 1930.
17. "History," pp. 15-16.
18. Letter, Lafortune to Crimont, Nome, 15 June 1929, OPA; "Nome Diary," p. 132. See also Glody 1934, *passim.*
19. "History," p. 17.
20. Ibid., p. 18.
21. See Renner 1976.
22. Telegram, George Feltes to Piet, Kotzebue, 17 October 1930, OPA.
23. Ray 1971, p. 19; "History," p. 19.

24. Letter, Lafortune to Crimont, Kotzebue, 10 November 1930, OPA.
25. "Nome Diary," p. 135; "Kotzebue Diary," p. 2.
26. "Kotzebue Diary," p. 1.
27. Concannon, n.d., p. 4.
28. "Kotzebue Diary," p. 3.
29. "Litterae Annuae Domus," Nome, 1922.
30. Letter, Lafortune to Marie-Flavius, Kotzebue, 3 May 1931.
31. "Kotzebue Diary," p. 3.
32. "Nome Diary," p. 141; "History," p. 19; letter, Lafortune to Crimont, King Island, 27 September 1931, OPA.
33. Letter, Lafortune to L.A. Schmid, Nome, 31 August 1931, OPA.
34. Log of the *Northland*, 24 September 1931, Records of the United States Coast Guard, National Archives, Record Group 26; "History," pp. 19, 20; letter, Lafortune to Crimont, King Island, 27 September 1931, OPA.
35. Letter, Lafortune to Crimont, King Island, 27 September 1931, OPA.
36. Ibid.; "History," p. 20.
37. "History," p. 23.
38. As a general rule the bishop confers the sacrament of confirmation. In mission territories, however, the power to confirm is often granted to the pastors of remote stations.

Chapter 9

1. "History," pp. 27-29.
2. Ibid., p. 31.
3. Ibid., pp. 31-32.
4. Ibid., p. 33.
5. Ibid., pp. 31, 33. This is a rather strange notation, because quite a few Wales and Teller Eskimos were employed by the movie makers in various capacities, and the movie, *Eskimo*, was produced by Metro-Goldwyn-Mayer.
6. "History," pp. 36-37.
7. Ibid., p. 37.
8. Ibid., pp. 39-40.
9. Letter, Lafortune to Marie-Flavius, Nome, 25 July 1933; letter, Lafortune to Crimont, King Island, 5 June 1933, OPA.
10. "Nome Diary," p. 159.
11. Ibid., p. 162.
12. Ibid., p. 164. Apparently the discrepancy between his lamenting the fact that King Island was to be without a priest during the winter 1934-35, and

his earlier expressed hope of spending that same winter on Diomede escaped Lafortune. Surely he did not expect somebody else to be on King Island in his place.

13. Letter, Lafortune to Crimont, Nome, 26 March 1935, OPA.
14. Letter, Lafortune to Marie-Flavius, Nome, 25 August 1935.
15. "History," pp. 73-75.
16. Llorente, in "Nome Diary," p. 191.
17. Concannon, in "Nome Diary," pp. 185-87.
18. For information concerning this subject and Lafortune's mind in the matter, see letter, Francis B. Prange to Wlodimir Ledochowski, Akulurak, Alaska, 18 July 1937, ARSI.
19. "Nome Diary," p. 170.
20. Log of the *Duane,* 7 October 1937, Records of the United States Coast Guard, National Archives, Record Group 26.
21. For a biographical sketch of Hubbard, see Spearman 1965; see also Bogojavlensky and Fuller 1973, p. 66.
22. Bogojavlensky 1969, p. 37.
23. "History," p. 86.
24. Ibid., pp. 90-91.
25. Letter, Lafortune to *Jesuit Missions,* King Island, 26 October 1937, published in *Jesuit Missions,* Vol. 12, 1938, p. 18; "History," p. 88.
26. Bogojavlensky and Fuller 1973, p. 66.
27. "History," pp. 98-99.
28. Ibid., p. 95.
29. Ibid., p. 89.
30. Letter, Lafortune to Waddel, King Island, 11 September 1946, ACJSJ.
31. Letter, Lafortune to Ed. Coyle, King Island, 8 June 1940, OPA.
32. Letter, McElmeel to Ledochowski, Nulato, Alaska, 18 November 1938, ARSI.
33. "History," pp. 125-27; letter, Lafortune to Marie-Flavius, King Island, 19 October 1940.
34. Letter, Lafortune to Crimont, Nome, 1 March 1937, OPA.

Chapter 10

1. Rasmussen 1952, p. 75; Bogojavlensky 1969, p. 72.
2. "History," p. 131.
3. Letter, Lafortune to *The Indian Sentinel,* Nome, no date, published in *The Indian Sentinel,* Vol. 14, 1933-34, p. 13.
4. Bogojavlensky 1969, p. 73.

5. "History," p. 47.
6. Letter, Lafortune to Crimont, King Island, 21 May 1941, OPA.
7. "History," pp. 44-45. Concerning the drifter, Bogojavlensky and Fuller have written: "It is certainly true that hunting on foot on the moving sea ice can be extremely dangerous. Especially during the headlong pursuit of polar bears in the stormy months of January and February, men will drift away against their will. Nevertheless, case histories and the complex of beliefs about men who drift away suggests that such accidents have an intimate relation to men confronted with dissolving social ties and a sense of being outside the solidary support of a faction. The complex of ideas involving drifters, suicide, and the solidarity of factions presents a logical coherence" (Bogojavlensky and Fuller 1973, p. 76).
8. Lafortune 1925.
9. "History," p. 63.
10. Ibid., p. 141. In his understandable concern for safety, Lafortune seems to have overlooked the fact that chances of getting game are multiplied when hunters spread out. One might also ask, how short does the distance between two hunters have to be before they are no longer "hunting alone?"
11. Letter, Lafortune to Crimont, King Island, 1 June 1940, OPA; "History," pp. 119-20.
12. See Bogojavlensky 1969, pp. 77-78.
13. Letter, Lafortune to Walter Fitzgerald, King Island, 10 June 1945, OPA.
14. "History," pp. 43, 44, 45-46, 47.
15. Ibid., pp. 119, 121.
16. Ibid., pp. 64-65.
17. Bogojavlensky and Fuller 1973, p. 69. More than thirty polar bears were taken during 1937-38, according to these authors, and separate ceremonies were held for each hunter, but Lafortune does not mention this.
18. For a description of the dishes served at a polar bear dance, see Bogojavlensky and Fuller 1973, p. 70.
19. "History," pp. 41, 60.
20. Ibid., pp. 29-30.
21. Ibid., pp. 52, 71, 72.
22. Letter, Lafortune to Waddel, King Island, 4 July 1939, ACJSJ.
23. "History," pp. 122-23.
24. Ibid., pp. 60, 116.
25. Ibid., pp. 41, 109-10.

Chapter 11

1. Letter, Lafortune to Bellemare, Nome, 25 October 1910, ACJSJ; "Nome Diary," pp. 118, 170c; "History," p. 33.
2. Letter, Lafortune to Marie-Flavius, Nome, 3 October 1909.
3. Letter, Lafortune to the Catholic Editing Company, Nome, 5 January 1913, OPA.
4. Lafortune 1922b. His following views are found in this document and in a letter to Lonneux dated, Nome, 23 August 1922, OPA.
5. Letter, Michael O'Malley to Bernard Hubbard, Spokane, 21 February 1949, OPA.
6. "Nome Diary," p. 171; "History," p. 114.
7. "History," p. 132.
8. Ibid., pp. 35-36.
9. Ibid., p. 114.
10. Letter, Lafortune to Crimont, King Island, 1 June 1940, OPA.
11. Letter, Lafortune to Marie-Flavius, King Island, 1 June 1940.
12. "History," p. 124.
13. Letter, Lafortune to Marie-Flavius, King Island, 23 July 1941.
14. Letter, Lafortune to Crimont, King Island, 21 May 1941, OPA.
15. "History," p. 137.
16. Ibid., p. 45.
17. Lafortune 1922b.
18. Letter, Lafortune to Crimont, King Island, 21 May 1941, OPA.
19. Lafortune 1922b.
20. Letter, Lafortune to "Rev. Father," Nome, 15 February 1929, OPA.
21. Letter, Lafortune to Hubbard, King Island, 24 October 1941, OPA.
22. "History," p. 43. For a discussion of the seriousness of dog-killing among the Bering Strait Eskimos, see Bogojavlensky 1969, p. 111.
23. "History," p. 8.
24. Ibid., pp. 50, 51-52.
25. Letter, Lafortune to Piet, King Island, 16 September 1929, OPA.
26. "History," p. 30.
27. Ibid., p. 26.
28. Ibid.
29. Ibid., p. 75.
30. Ibid., p. 30.
31. Letter, Lafortune to Crimont, King Island, 7 March 1932, OPA.
32. "History," p. 63.
33. Letter, Lafortune to J. Hurley, King Island, 25 June 1939, OPA.

34. Letter, Lafortune to Francis Conklin, King Island, 28 March 1946, OPA; letter, Lafortune to Ed. Coyle, King Island, 8 June 1940, OPA.
35. "History," p. 51.
36. Ibid., p. 52.
37. Ibid., p. 25.
38. Ibid., p. 42.
39. Ibid., p. 44.
40. Letter, Lafortune to Lonneux, Nome, 23 August 1922, OPA.
41. Lafortune 1925.
42. Savage 1942, p. 134. I have not been able to find her source for this authentic-sounding anecdote.
43. Lafortune 1922b.
44. For a treatment of the significance of dancing in the lives of the King Islanders, and for a detailed description of the dances, see Bogojavlensky 1969, pp. 183-86; and Bogojavlensky and Fuller 1973.
45. For a more complete treatment of the *kagri* organization, see Bogojavlensky 1969 and Ross 1958.
46. Rasmussen 1952, p. 76.
47. "King Island Diary," p. 9.

Chapter 12

1. Letter, Lafortune to Ed. Coyle, King Island, 8 June 1940, OPA.
2. Letter, Lafortune to Waddel, King Island, 11 June 1940, ACJSJ.
3. Letter to Marie-Flavius, Nome, 4 September 1939.
4. "History," p. 137.
5. Ibid., pp. 135-36.
6. Ibid., p. 145.
7. Ibid.
8. Letter, Lafortune to Waddel, King Island, 16 June 1942, ACJSJ; letter, Lafortune to *Jesuit Missions,* King Island, no date, published in *Jesuit Missions,* Vol. 8, 1934, p. 243.
9. The above notes are from the "History," pp. 146-48. During World War II, Nome had an army post, an airbase, and an ordnance depot. It was also the relay point for military planes being ferried to Russia under the Lend-Lease Act of 11 March 1941.
10. Letter, Lafortune to Crimont, King Island, 8 October 1942, OPA.
11. "King Island Diary," pp. 13, 14; "History," p. 150.
12. Letter, Anable to Renner, Fairbanks, 25 April 1974.
13. "History," pp. 151, 153.

14. "King Island Diary," pp. 14-15.
15. Letter, Lafortune to Crimont, King Island, 30 June 1943, OPA. Lafortune frequently mentioned this saint in his letters to Crimont, a native of France, with a special devotion to the recently canonized French Carmelite nun of Lisieux, Sainte Thérèse, the "Little Flower," patroness of the Alaska mission.
16. "King Island Diary," pp. 20-21.
17. Letter, Lafortune to Soeur Henri du Crucifix, King Island, 21 June 1944, ACJSJ.
18. "King Island Diary," pp. 12-13, 20; letter, Anable to Renner, Fairbanks, 25 April 1974.
19. Letter, Lafortune to Etta M. Whitlam, King Island, 1 July 1945; letter, Lafortune to A. B. Perry, King Island, 9 August 1945, OPA. Bishop Crimont, 88 years old, died in Juneau on 20 May 1945 after forty-eight years in Alaska. His successor, Bishop Fitzgerald, died in Seattle on 19 July 1947 of high blood pressure.
20. Letter, Anable to Renner, Fairbanks, 25 April 1974.
21. "King Island Diary," p. 30.
22. Letter, Lafortune to Marie-Flavius, King Island, 10 September 1946.
23. Letters, Lafortune to Leo J. Robinson, 30 March 1947, OPA; to Waddel, 31 March 1947, ACJSJ; and to Augusta Bernard Perry, 12 April 1947, OPA.
24. Letter, Lafortune to Fitzgerald, King Island, 19 June 1947, OPA.
25. See "Chronicles of St. Joseph's Hospital, Fairbanks," July 1947; letter, Laux to Renner, Spokane, [1974].
26. "King Island Diary," p. 37.
27. Terigluk became blind when a young man and was thereafter known as "Blind Joe." He worked in the Nome hospital until it closed in 1918, and then went to Fairbanks with three Sisters to work in the kitchen of their hospital there. After suffering a slight stroke in 1941, he became a patient in the hospital. He died on 23 February 1956, and was buried only two miles from Lafortune's grave.

Chapter 13

1. Letter, Lafortune to Théophile Hudon, King Island, 25 June 1939, ACJSJ.
2. "King Island Diary," p. 41.
3. "History," p. 11.
4. Concannon, n.d., p. 5; Waddel 1948b, p. 22.

5. Letter, Lafortune to Lonneux, Nome, 23 August 1922, OPA.
6. Carroll 1904.
7. Concannon, n.d., p. 3.
8. Lafortune 1922b.
9. Letter, Llorente to Renner, Anchorage, 16 April 1975.
10. Ibid.
11. Letter, Lafortune to Terigluk, Nome, 15 January 1914, OPA.
12. Letter, Lafortune to Marie-Flavius, Nome, 2 August 1936.
13. Lafortune 1922b; "History," pp. 59, 63-64; "Nome Diary," p. 163.
14. "History," pp. 18, 69.
15. Letter, Lafortune to *Jesuit Missions,* King Island, no date, published in *Jesuit Missions,* Vol. 13, 1939, p. 245.
16. "History," p. 49.
17. Letter, James Poole to Renner, Nome, 10 February 1977; letter, Llorente to Renner, Anchorage, 16 April 1975.
18. Anable 1948, p. 4.
19. Letter, Lafortune to William A. Beaudette, King Island, no date, published in *Jesuit Missions*, Vol. 15, 1941, pp. 18-19; letter, O'Malley to Hubbard, Spokane, 21 February 1949, OPA.
20. Concannon, n.d., p. 4.
21. Postcard, Poole to Renner, Nome, 18 February 1977.
22. Concannon, n.d., p. 5; letter, Anable to Renner, Fairbanks, 25 April 1974.
23. "King Island Diary: 1943-44," unpublished manuscript in possession of Renner, p. 17, under date 17 October 1943.
24. Letter, O'Malley to Hubbard, Spokane, 21 February 1949, OPA.
25. Letter, Lafortune to *The Indian Sentinel,* Nome, no date, published in *The Indian Sentinel,* Vol. 14, 1933-34, p. 13.
26. Letter, Llorente to Renner, Anchorage, 16 April 1975.
27. "History," p. 103.
28. Letter, Llorente to Renner, Anchorage, 16 April 1975.
29. Bogojavlensky 1969, p. 32; "King Island Diary," pp. 128, 152, 169, 183, 195, 202.
30. Memorandum to "the files," from Kenneth K. Crites, subject, "Termination of King Island School Operation, 27 September 1956"; memorandum to Area Director of Schools from Chairman [R.L. Davlin], Area Safety Committee, subject, "Rock Slide Hazard at King Island, 30 March 1959"; letter, James E. Hawkins to Bernard T. Katexac, Juneau, 31 August 1960 (all three documents in BIA Files, Juneau); letter, John

Collier to Charles Hawkesworth, Washington, 9 August 1935, Federal Archives and Records Center, Seattle.

31. "BIA Teachers Assigned to King Island," BIA Files, Juneau.
32. Hopkins and Chapman 1966, p.6.
33. Bogojavlensky 1969, p. 230.
34. *Fairbanks Daily News-Miner,* 15 December 1975.
35. Personal interview with Edmund Anable, 1976.
36. "Little Diomede Diary"; "Nome Diary," pp. 35, 73; Renner 1975-76.
37. See Renner 1973-74.

Sources Consulted

Note: In this bibliography there are listed three kinds of documents written by local Jesuit priests. The "Historia Domus" (history of the house) is a brief account of the state of the parish or mission, normally written every two or three years by the local Superior and sent to the Father Provincial. The "Litterae Annuae Domus" (annual letters of the house) are annual letters giving an account of the current state of the parish or mission, written by the local Superior and sent to the Father General of the Society of Jesus in Rome. The house diaries consist of daily notations entered in a journal, usually by the local Superior.

The following abbreviations are used: ACJSJ: Archives de la Compagnie de Jésus—Province du Canada-français, Saint-Jérôme, P. Q. (the official French abbreviation is ASJCF); OPA: Oregon Province Archives, Spokane; SPA: Sisters of Providence Archives, Seattle.

The Alaskan Shepherd

1962 A bimonthly newsletter to friends and benefactors published by the Diocese of Fairbanks. Copies in OPA.

Amundsen, Roald

1927 *My Life as an Explorer.* New York: Doubleday, Page and Co.

Anable, Edmund A., S. J.

1948 "Unto the End." *Jesuit Missions* 22:2-4.

Annales de la Propagation de la Foi (Lyon/Paris)

1910-11 A mission magazine published in France. Copies in ACJSJ.

Annales de la Propagation de la Foi pour les Provinces de Québec et de Montréal

1904-13 A mission magazine. Copies in ACJSJ.

Anonymous

1925 *The Land of the Midnight Sun: Alaska.* Spokane.

Anonymous

1952 "The Christ of the Bering Sea." *Catholic Digest* 16 (no. 5):121-27.

Aronson, Joseph D.

1940 *The History of Disease among the Natives of Alaska.* Office of Indian Affairs, Washington, D.C.

Bailey, Alfred M.

1971 *Field Work of a Museum Naturalist, 1919-1922.* Denver Museum of Natural History, Denver, Colorado.

Bernard, Joseph, S.J.

1911 "Mon Voyage de Retour chez les Esquimaux." *Annales de la Propagation de la Foi (Lyon/Paris)*:83:323-44.

Bischoff, Adolph D., S.J.
1934 "King Island." *Jesuit Missions* 8:182-83, 194.
Bogojavlensky, Sergei
1969 "Imaangmiut Eskimo Careers: Skinboats in Bering Strait." Ph.D. dissertation, Harvard University.
Bogojavlensky, Sergei, and Robert W. Fuller
1973 "Polar Bears, Walrus Hides, and Social Solidarity." *The Alaska Journal* 3 (no. 2):66-76.
Boileau, George T., S. J.
1941 "An Eskimo 'Snow White'." *Jesuit Missions* 15:52.
Burch, Ernest S., Jr.
1974 "Eskimo Warfare in Northwest Alaska." *Anthropological Papers of the University of Alaska* 16 (no. 2):1-14.
Burg, Amos
1952 "North Star Cruises Alaska's Wild West." *National Geographic Magazine* 102 (no. 1):57-86.
Burnham, John B.
1929 *Rim of Mystery.* New York: G. P. Putnam's Sons.
The Canadian Messenger of the Sacred Heart
1902-4 A Catholic devotional magazine. Copies in ACJSJ.
Carlson, Gerald F.
1966 *Two on the Rocks.* New York: McKay.
Carlson, Leland H.
1946 "The Discovery of Gold at Nome, Alaska." *The Pacific Historical Review* 15 (no. 3):259-78.
1947a "The First Mining Season at Nome, Alaska—1899." Ibid. 16 (no. 2):163-75.
1947b "Nome: From Mining Camp to Civilized Community." *Pacific Northwest Quarterly* 38:233-42.
Carriker, Robert C.
1976 "Father Joseph Bernard among 'les Esquimaux'." *The Alaska Journal* 6 (no. 3):161-66.
Carroll, John B., S. J.
1904 "History of St. Joseph's Residence, Nome, Alaska Ty., from July, 1901, to July, 1904." Manuscript in OPA.
Chapman, R. M. *See* Hopkins, David M., and R. M. Chapman.
Christensen, A. Laurent
1951 "Besøg på Diomede-øen og i paelebyen på King Island" (Visit to Little Diomede and the Pile Town on King Island). *Grønlandske*

Selskab Aarsskrift, pp. 124-31.

"Chronicles of St. Joseph's Hospital, Fairbanks, Alaska"

1947 Manuscript narratives in SPA.

Cocke, Albert K.

1974 "Dr. Samuel J. Call." *The Alaska Journal* 4 (no. 3):181-88.

Colby, Merle E.

1939 *A Guide to Alaska.* New York: Macmillan.

Concannon, John A., S. J.

1962 "Rev. Frederick Ruppert, S. J., Alaska Martyr of Charity." *The Alaskan Shepherd* (November-December), pp. 4-5.

n.d. "Fr. Bellarmine Lafortune, S. J.: Missionary, Scholar, Hero." Manuscript in OPA.

Considine, John J.

1925 *The Vatican Mission Exposition.* New York: Macmillan.

Cook, James

1784 *A Voyage to the Pacific Ocean,* vol. 2. London: W. and A. Strahan.

Curtis, Edward S.

1970 *The North American Indian,* vol. 20. New York: Johnson Reprint Corporation (originally published in 1930).

Devine, Edward J., S. J.

1903 "Alaskan Letters III-VIII." *The Canadian Messenger of the Sacred Heart,* vol. 13.

1904 "Alaskan Letters IX-X." Ibid., vol. 14.

1905 *Across Widest America.* Montreal: Canadian Messenger.

Eide, Arthur H.

1952 *Drums of Diomede.* Hollywood: House-Warven.

Fortier, Ed

1969 "Incredible Journey," part 1. *Alaska Sportsman* 35 (no. 2):6-9; part 2, 35 (no. 3):14-17, 53.

Fuller, Robert W. *See* Bogojavlensky, Sergei, and Robert W. Fuller

Glody, Robert

1934 *A Shepherd of the Far North.* San Francisco: Harr Wagner.

Greely, Adolphus W.

1909 *Handbook of Alaska.* New York: Charles Scribner's Sons.

Harrington, John J.

1867 "King's Island." *The Esquimaux* 1 (no. 10):1.

Harrison, Edward S.

1905 *Nome and Seward Peninsula.* Seattle: The Metropolitan Press.

Healy, Michael A.

1887 *Report of the Cruise of the Revenue Marine Steamer Corwin in the Arctic Ocean in the Year 1885.* Washington: Government Printing Office.

Heath, John D.

1971 "The King Island Kayak." Manuscript in the National Museum of Man, Ottawa.

Heinrich, Albert C.

1955 "An Outline of the Kinship System of the Bering Straits *[sic]* Eskimos." M.A. thesis, University of Alaska.

Hopkins, David M., ed.

1967 *The Bering Land Bridge.* Stanford, California: Stanford University Press.

Hopkins, David M., and R.M. Chapman

1966 *Technical Letter: King Island-1. Engineering Geological Problems on King Island, Alaska.* U.S Department of the Interior, Geological Survey, Menlo Park, California.

Hrdlička, Aleš

1944 *Alaska Diary, 1926-1931.* Lancaster, Pa.: The Jaques Cattell Press (second printing).

Hutchison, Isobel W.

1934 *North to the Rime-Ringed Sun.* London: Blackie.

Ignatius of Loyola

1964 *Spiritual Exercises.* Translated by A. Mottola. Garden City: Doubleday.

1970 *Constitutions of the Society of Jesus.* Translated by G. E. Ganss. Saint Louis: Institute of Jesuit Sources.

The Indian Sentinel

1917-34 A mission magazine. Copies in OPA.

Jenness, Diamond

1929 "Little Diomede Island, Bering Strait." *The Geographical Review* 19 (no. 1):78-86.

Jesuit Missions

1930-47 A monthly mission magazine. Copies in OPA.

Kahlekat

1924 A little periodical published by the Ursuline Nuns. Copies in the Ursuline Provincialate, Santa Rosa, California.

Kelly, Joseph P., S. J.

1940 "Christianity on the Last Frontier." *Jesuit Missions* 14:284-85, 308.

"King Island Diary"
1943-59 Jesuit house diary, in OPA.
Kleinschmidt, F. E.
1910 "A Trip to the Human Rookeries." *Pacific Monthly* (September), pp. 279-85.
"Kotzebue Diary"
1930-77 Jesuit house diary, in OPA.
Krauss, Michael E.
1974 "Native Peoples and Languages of Alaska." Map showing language spoken in each native village. Alaska Native Language Center, University of Alaska, Fairbanks.
Lafortune, Bellarmine, S.J.
1904a "History of St. Joseph's Church, Nome, Alaska. July 1901-1904." Manuscript in OPA. (This is an "Historia Domus" in English.)
1904b "Les Missions de l'Alaska—Notes de Voyage du R.P. Bellarmin Lafortune, S.J." *Annales de la Propagation de la Foi* (Montreal):82 (February), pp. 44-56.
1922a "Litterae Annuae Domus Sti. Joseph, Nome, Alaska." Manuscript in OPA.
1922b "Sociability and Customs of the Eskimo." Manuscript in OPA.
1925 "Informations Desired." Manuscript, Lafortune to Jetté, received on 30 June 1925. In OPA.
1929-42 "History of the Mission of King Island." Manuscript journal in OPA: copy at St. Joseph's Church, Nome.
1930 "Up Rocky Slopes." *Jesuit Missions* 4:79, 97.
1933 "On Lonely King Island." Ibid. 7:5, 21-22.
1941 "Lost in the Ice Fields." Ibid. 15:240.
Ledit, Joseph H., S. J.
1922 "Los Isleños de King Island." *El Siglo de las Misiones* (a mission magazine published in Spain) 9 (no. 102):168-70.
Lettres de Jersey
1907-13 Letters from missionaries published by the French Jesuits on the island of Jersey. Copies in ACJSJ.
"Little Diomede Diary"
1936-55 Jesuit house diary, in OPA.
Llorente, Segundo, S.J.
1931 "Una Isla Singular." *El Siglo de las Misiones* 18 (no. 210):186-92.
1939a "Una Isla Singular en Alaska." Ibid. 26 (no. 286): 208-13.

1939b “Dos Meses en Nome.” Ibid. (no. 288):292-95.

1969 *Jesuits in Alaska.* Portland, Ore.: Service Office Supply.

McLain, Carrie M.

1969 *Gold-Rush Nome.* Portland, Ore.: Graphic Arts Center.

Madsen, Charles

1957 *Arctic Trader.* New York: Dodd, Mead & Co.

Le Messager Canadien du Sacré-Coeur

1903-16 A Catholic devotional magazine. Copies in ACJSJ.

Muir, John

1917 *The Cruise of the Corwin.* Boston and New York: Houghton Mifflin Co.

Muñoz, Juan

1954 “Cliff Dwellers of the Bering Sea.” *National Geographic Magazine* 105 (no. 1):129-46.

Nelson, Edward W.

1899 *The Eskimo about Bering Strait.* Bureau of American Ethnology, Annual Report, vol. 18, pt. 1. Washington, D.C.

Nelson, Klondy, with Corey Ford

1958 *Daughter of the Gold Rush.* New York: Random House.

Nobile, Umberto

1961 *My Polar Flights.* Translated by Frances Fleetwood. London: Frederick Muller Ltd.

“Nome Diary”

1901-60 Jesuit house diary, in OPA.

Nome Nugget

1901-47 Copies seen at the University of Alaska Rasmuson Library.

Orth, Donald J.

1967 *Dictionary of Alaska Place Names.* Geological Survey, Professional Paper no. 567. Washington, D.C.

Oswalt, Wendell H.

1963 *Mission of Change in Alaska.* The Huntington Library. San Marino, California.

Perry, Richard

1967 *World of the Walrus.* London: Cassell.

Le Petit Journal de la Providence

1905-18 Journal published in French by the Sisters of Providence. Copies in SPA.

Petroff, Ivan

1884 “Report on the Population, Industries and Resources of Alaska.”

In *U.S. Tenth Census,* Department of the Interior, Census Office, Washington, D.C.

"Pilgrim Hot Springs Diary"

1918-26 Jesuit house diary, in OPA.

Post, Hubert A., S. J.

1914 "Historia Domus Sancti Josephi, Nome, Alaska:—a 1° Jul. 1913—ad 1um Jul. 1914." Manuscript in OPA.

1915 "Historia Domus Sancti Josephi, Nome, Alaska:—a 1° Jul. 1914—ad 1um Jul. 1915." Manuscript in OPA.

1916a "Historia Domus Sancti Josephi, Nome, Alaska:—a 1° Jul. 1915—ad 1um Jul. 1916." Manuscript in OPA.

1916b "Litterae Annuae, Nome, Alaska: a Jul. 1913—ad Jul. 1916." In OPA.

1917a "Historia Domus Sancti Josephi, Nome, Alaska:— 1916-1917." In OPA.

1917b "Litterae Annuae Sancti Josephi, Nome, Alaska:—a 1° Julii 1916—ad 1um Julii 1917." In OPA.

[1919a] "Historia Domus Residentiae Dnae Nostrae Lapurdensis, Alaska." In OPA.

[1919b] "Litterae Annuae Residentiae Dnae Nae Lapurdensis, Alaska." In OPA.

[1921] "A Few Facts Concerning the Mission of Our Lady of Lourdes Now Located at the Krusamapa Hot Springs, Nome, Alaska." One-page manuscript in OPA.

1924 "Litterae Annuae Domus et Scholae D. N. Lapurdensis (Pilgrim Springs, Alaska). A die lma Julii, 1923 ad diem 30 Junii 1924." In OPA.

Rasmussen, Knud

1952 *The Western Alaska Eskimo.* Posthumous notes edited by Erik Holtved and H. Ostermann. Report of the Fifth Thule Expedition 1921-24, vol. 10, no. 3. Copenhagen: Gyldendalske Boghandel, Nordisk Forlag.

Ray, Dorothy Jean

1961 *Artists of the Tundra and the Sea.* Seattle and London: University of Washington Press.

1964 "Nineteenth Century Settlement and Subsistence Patterns in Bering Strait." *Arctic Anthropology* 2 (no. 2):61-94

1971 "Eskimo Place-Names in Bering Strait and Vicinity." *Names* 19 (no. 1):1-33.

1975 *The Eskimos of Bering Strait, 1650-1898.* Seattle and London: University of Washington Press.

Renner, Louis L., S. J.

1973-74 "KNOM Helps to Make Men Free." *Sign* 53 (no. 4):11-15.

1974 "A Footnote to Stefansson's *The Friendly Arctic.*" *The Alaska Journal* 4 (no. 4):203-4.

1975a "The Eskimos Return to King Island." *Catholic Digest* 39 (no. 5):46-55.

1975b "Julius Jetté: Distinguished Scholar in Alaska." *The Alaska Journal* 5 (no. 4):239-47.

1975c "Return to King Island." *Alaska* 41 (no. 7):6-8.

1975-76 "Catechizing the Vikings of Bering Strait." *Eskimo* 32 (no. 10, New Series):5-20.

1976 "The Beginnings of Missionary Aviation in the Arctic: The 'Marquette Missionary'." *Eskimo* 33 (no. 11, New Series):8-19.

1977-78 "Fr. Frederick Ruppert, S. J.: Martyr of Charity." *Eskimo* 34 (no. 14, New Series):11-22.

1979 "Farming at Holy Cross Mission." *The Alaska Journal* 9 (no. 1):32-37.

Ross, Frances Anna

1958 "The Eskimo Community-House." M. A. thesis, Stanford University.

Roueché, Berton

1966 "First Boat to King Island." *The New Yorker* 42 (no. 35):98-139.

Rychetnik, Joe

1964 "King Island." *Alaska Sportsman* 30 (no. 3):22-24, 34.

Savage, Alma H.

1942 *Dogsled Apostles.* New York: Sheed & Ward.

Spearman, Arthur D., S. J.

1965 "Bernard R. Hubbard, S. J." *Woodstock Letters* (Fall), pp. 466-73.

Stefansson, Vilhjalmur

1921 *The Friendly Arctic.* New York: Macmillan.

Tate, Carrie

1943-44 "King Island Diary." Manuscript in possession of Renner.

Trenchard, John C.

1939 "The Cliff Dwellers of King Island." *Pacific Horizons* (March), pp. 55-62.

Waddel, Joseph, S. J.

1948a "L'apôtre des rochers," part 1. *Le Messager Canadien* (February), pp. 95-99; part 2, (April), pp. 218-21.

1948b ''Vie du Père Bellarmin Lafortune, S. J.: aux glaces polaires durant quarante-quatre ans.'' Manuscript in ACJSJ. (Consists mostly of Lafortune's letters to his niece, Sister Marie-Flavius, and to Waddel.)

Wead, Frank W.

1938 *Gales, Ice and Men.* London: Methuen.

The Western Jesuit

1930-38 A monthly bulletin published by the California Province of the Society of Jesus. Copies in OPA.

Wilhalm, Peter P., S. J.

1953 ''Bro. Wilhalm's Account of Father Ruppert's Death.'' Manuscript in OPA.

Woodstock Letters

1901-49 Published letters from missionaries. (Those from Italian missionaries were translated by the editors of *W. L.*.) Copies in OPA.

The Yukon Catholic

1902 A short-lived newspaper published in Dawson, Y. T., and ''devoted to the interests of the Catholic Church in the North.'' Copy in OPA.

Appendix

A listing of the Priests, Brothers, and Sisters who served in the Seward Peninsula area.

ARVINAK

1929-30 Peter Baltussen

COUNCIL CITY

1903-04 Edward Devine

KING ISLAND

1929-30 Bellarmine Lafortune

1930-31 No priest on King Island.

1931-34 Lafortune

1934-35 No priest on King Island.

1935-36 Lafortune

1936-37 No priest on King Island.

1937-38 Lafortune, Bernard Hubbard

1938-47 Lafortune

1947-50 Thomas Cunningham

1950-51 No priest on King Island.

1951-60 George Carroll

KOTZEBUE

1929-30 William F. Walsh (diocesan priest)

1930-31 Lafortune

1931-32 Baltussen, Hubert Post

1932-33 John Concannon

1933-38 Francis Ménager

1938-41 Segundo Llorente

1941-46 Paul O'Connor

1946-52 George Carroll

1952-54 T. Cunningham

1954-59 William McIntyre

1959-67 Pasquale Spoletini

1967-75 Michael Kaniecki

1975- John Gurr

LITTLE DIOMEDE ISLAND

1936-39 T. Cunningham spent the winters on the island.

1939-40 No priest wintered on the island.

1940-42 T. Cunningham spent the winters on the island.

1942-43 T. Cunningham visited the island from time to time.

1943-44 T. Cunningham spent the winter on the island.

1945 No priest visited the island.

1946-49 T. Cunningham visited the island from time to time.
1950 No priest visited the island.
1951 G. Carroll visited the island in the spring.
1952 No priest visited the island.
1953-54 No priest wintered on the island, but T. Cunningham visited it for several months each spring.
1955-58 Vsevolod Rochkau (eastern rite, non-Jesuit) wintered on the island.
1958-78 Priests from the Nome parish visited the island at more or less regular intervals.
1978 Thomas Carlin

MARYS IGLOO

1908-09 Joseph Bernard
1909-10 No priest at Marys Igloo.
1910-11 Bernard, Bro. Alexi Dugas
1911-15 Bernard
1915-16 Lafortune (almost full time)
1916-18 Lafortune (part time)

NOME—A (Jesuits)

Aug., 1899 Jean Baptiste René
Sep., 1899 Joseph Tréca
Feb., 1900 Tréca
1901 (July-Nov.) Aloysius Jacquet
1901-02 John Van der Pol, Camille Rogatien
1902-03 Joseph Cataldo, Edward Devine, Bro. Bartholomew Chiaudano
1903-05 Van der Pol, Lafortune, Chiaudano
1905-06 Van der Pol, Lafortune, John B. Carroll, Chiaudano
1906-08 Lafortune, Carroll, Bernard, Bro. Felix Montaldo
1908-12 Lafortune, John Forhan, Bro. Alphonsus Lemire
1912-13 Lafortune, Forhan, Michael O'Malley, Lemire
1913-14 Lafortune, Forhan, Bro. Alfred Murphy
1914-15 Lafortune, Hubert Post, Murphy
1915-16 Post, Tréca, Bro. John Twohig
1916-17 Lafortune, Post, Tréca, Bro. Audomare Demers
1917-18 Lafortune, Post, Tréca, Chiaudano
1918-21 Lafortune, Frederick Ruppert
1921-22 Lafortune
1922-23 Lafortune, Ruppert
1923-25 Lafortune

1925-26 Lafortune, Post
1926-27 Lafortune, John Concannon
1927-29 Lafortune, Patrick Savage
1929-30 Savage
1930-31 Post
1931-32 Post, Edward Budde
1932-33 Budde, Francis Ménager
1933-34 Gabriel Ménager, Baltussen (March-July, 1934)
1934-35 Lafortune
1935-36 T. Cunningham
1936-37 Lafortune
1937-38 Concannon
1938 (Oct., Nov., Dec.) No priest in Nome.
1939-40 Joseph McElmeel, Segundo Llorente, Lafortune
1940-41 Joseph McHugh
1941-43 McHugh, T. Cunningham
1943-46 Edmund Anable
1946-47 Anable, T. Cunningham
1947-50 Cornelius Murphy
1950-51 Murphy, T. Cunningham
1951-56 Murphy
1956-60 Lawrence Nevue
1960-63 Nevue, G. Carroll
1963-64 Nevue
1964-65 Llorente
1965-66 Paul Mueller
1966-69 James E. Poole
1969-75 Poole, Harold Greif
1975- Poole, Greif, Bro. Albert Heinrich, FIC (Brothers of Christian Instruction), Bro. Normand Berger, FIC

NOME—B (Sisters of Providence who served in Nome, the years they served, and in what capacity)

Alype, 1907-09, nurse
Anselme, 1902-05, nurse, surgeon
Barnabé, 1903-07, nurse
Bélanger, 1903-11, various duties
Benoît, 1902-07, cook
Bujold, 1907-18, nurse
Célina Henri, 1908-17, cook

Dunstan, 1905-06, teacher
Florida, 1903-14, nurse
Florine, 1906-18, teacher
Lambert, 1902-03, nurse
Laurentin, 1917-18, nurse
Louis-Henri, 1908-11, nurse, cook, various duties
Louis de Valence, 1906-16, nurse, Superior 1915-16
Marie-Amalberge, 1909-17, nurse
Marie-Conrad, 1902-05, Superior
Mary-Edithe, 1911-18, teacher
Marie-Grégoire, 1905-15, Superior 1915-16
Marie-Irmine, 1906-14, nurse
Marie-Napoleon, 1902-03, secretary
Marie-Noemi, 1914-16, nurse, x-ray technician
Marie-Odile, 1904-12, teacher
Marius, 3 September-3 November 1915, nurse
Michel des Anges, 1904-05, teacher
Monaldi, 1905-10, Superior, cook
Robert, 1917-18, Superior, cook
Rodrique, 19 June-2 October 1902, assistant
Romuald, 1915-18, nurse
Tessier, 1907-08, cook, choir director
Paula Cosko, 1969-72, catechist

NOME and LITTLE DIOMEDE—C (Little Sisters of Jesus who served in Nome and on Little Diomede)

Alice Ann, about one and a half years in Nome and on Little Diomede, 1969-77
Ann Cecile, about five years in Nome and on Little Diomede, 1960-77
Annemiek, three years in Nome and on Little Diomede, 1967-73
Clara Nobuko, about four years in Nome and on Little Diomede, 1972-76
Damiene, two and a half years in Nome, 1958-60
Georgette, six months in Nome, 1952
Joel, four months on Little Diomede, 1974
Josephe Alice, about twelve years in Nome and on Little Diomede, 1959-77
Nicole, five years in Nome and on Little Diomede, 1961-67
Odette, four and a half years in Nome and on Little Diomede, 1956-64
Solange May, twelve years in Nome and on Little Diomede, 1953-77

Therese Johanna, two years in Nome, 1970-73

Yvonne May, nine years in Nome and on Little Diomede, 1952-65

NOTE: Little Sisters went to Little Diomede for the first time in 1954.

PILGRIM HOT SPRINGS—A (Jesuits)

1918-19 Bellarmine Lafortune

1919-21 Lafortune, Hubert Post, Bros. John Hansen, Peter Wilhalm

1921-25 Post, Hansen, Wilhalm

1925-26 John Lucchesi, Hansen, Wilhalm

1926-30 Post, Hansen, Wilhalm

1930-31 Peter Baltussen, Hansen, Wilhalm

1931-32 John Concannon, Aloysius G. Willebrand, Hansen, Wilhalm

1932-33 Baltussen, Willebrand, Hansen, Wilhalm

1933-34 Baltussen, Hansen, Wilhalm

1934-35 Gabriel Ménager, Hansen, Wilhalm

1935-38 Edward Cunningham, Hansen, Wilhalm

1938-41 E. Cunningham, Wilhalm, Bro. Carl Wickart

1941 Edmund Anable (who closed the mission 31 July 1941), Wilhalm, Wickart

PILGRIM HOT SPRINGS—B (Ursuline Sisters, names and number of years served at the mission)

Thecla Battiston 22

Vivina Severyns 14

Irene Arvin 10

Holy Name (Elise Besse) 12

Rose Whalen 9

Marie des Anges (Dahmann) 8

Mary Louise Ronnebaum 7

Elizabeth Marie Charvet 5

Theresa of St. Joseph (Rosenberg) 6

Clement Marie Schmieder 4

Aloysius (Madeleine Wagner) 4

Berchmans (Eva Bertrand) 3

Catherine Finegan 3

Mary of the Blessed Sacrament (Hargedon) 3

Athanasius (Stevens) 3

Elizabeth Brosmith 2

Lucy Daly 2

Laurentine Kanallakan 2

Antoinette Johnson 1

Index

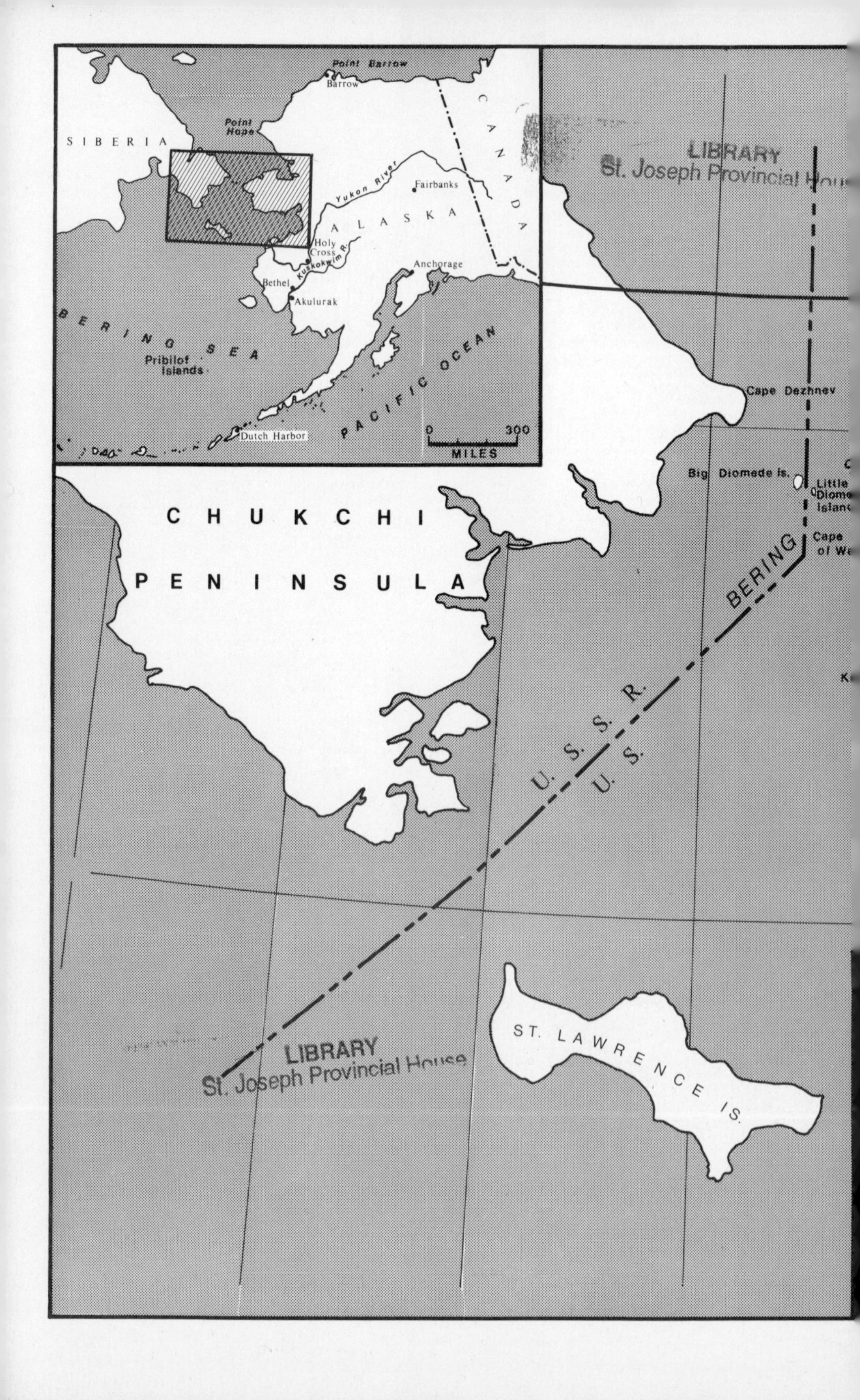
Point Barrow
Barrow
Point Hope
SIBERIA
CANADA
Yukon River
Fairbanks
ALASKA
Holy Cross
Kuskokwim R.
Anchorage
Bethel
Akulurak
BERING SEA
Pribilof Islands
PACIFIC OCEAN
Dutch Harbor
0
300
MILES
Cape Dezhnev
Big Diomede Is.
Little Diomede Island
Cape of Wa
CHUKCHI PENINSULA
BERING
U.S.S.R.
U.S.
ST. LAWRENCE IS.